Windows® 7

VISUAL™
Quick Tips

Visual®

by Paul McFedries

WILEY
Wiley Publishing, Inc.

Windows® 7 Visual™ Quick Tips

Published by
Wiley Publishing, Inc.
10475 Crosspoint Boulevard
Indianapolis, IN 46256
www.wiley.com

Published simultaneously in Canada

Copyright © 2009 by Wiley Publishing, Inc., Indianapolis, Indiana

Library of Congress Control Number: 2009934558

ISBN: 978-0-470-52117-5

Manufactured in the United States of America

10 9 8 7 6 5 4 3 2 1

Trademark Acknowledgments

Contact Us

For general information on our other products and services or to obtain technical support, please contact our Customer Care Department within the U.S. at 877-762-2974, outside the U.S. at 317-572-3993, or fax 317-572-4002.

For technical support please visit www.wiley.com/techsupport.

WILEY

Wiley Publishing, Inc.

Sales

Contact Wiley
at (877) 762-2974 or
fax (317) 572-4002.

Praise for Visual Books

"I have to praise you and your company on the fine products you turn out. I have twelve Visual books in my house. They were instrumental in helping me pass a difficult computer course. Thank you for creating books that are easy to follow. Keep turning out those quality books."

Gordon Justin (Brielle, NJ)

"What fantastic teaching books you have produced! Congratulations to you and your staff. You deserve the Nobel Prize in Education. Thanks for helping me understand computers."

Bruno Tonon (Melbourne, Australia)

"A Picture Is Worth A Thousand Words! If your learning method is by observing or hands-on training, this is the book for you!"

Lorri Pegan-Durastante (Wickliffe, OH)

"Over time, I have bought a number of your 'Read Less - Learn More' books. For me, they are THE way to learn anything easily. I learn easiest using your method of teaching."

José A. Mazón (Cuba, NY)

"You've got a fan for life!! Thanks so much!!"

Kevin P. Quinn (Oakland, CA)

"I have several books from the Visual series and have always found them to be valuable resources."

Stephen P. Miller (Ballston Spa, NY)

"I have several of your Visual books and they are the best I have ever used."

Stanley Clark (Crawfordville, FL)

"Like a lot of other people, I understand things best when I see them visually. Your books really make learning easy and life more fun."

John T. Frey (Cadillac, MI)

"I have quite a few of your Visual books and have been very pleased with all of them. I love the way the lessons are presented!"

Mary Jane Newman (Yorba Linda, CA)

"Thank you, thank you, thank you...for making it so easy for me to break into this high-tech world."

Gay O'Donnell (Calgary, Alberta, Canada)

"I write to extend my thanks and appreciation for your books. They are clear, easy to follow, and straight to the point. Keep up the good work! I bought several of your books and they are just right! No regrets! I will always buy your books because they are the best."

Seward Kollie (Dakar, Senegal)

"I would like to take this time to thank you and your company for producing great and easy-to-learn products. I bought two of your books from a local bookstore, and it was the best investment I've ever made! Thank you for thinking of us ordinary people."

Jeff Eastman (West Des Moines, IA)

"Compliments to the chef!! Your books are extraordinary! Or, simply put, extra-ordinary, meaning way above the rest! THANKYOU THANKYOU THANKYOU! I buy them for friends, family, and colleagues."

Christine J. Manfrin (Castle Rock, CO)

CREDITS

Executive Editor
Jody Lefevere

Sr. Project Editor
Sarah Hellert

Technical Editor
Vince Averello

Copy Editor
Scott Tullis

Editorial Director
Robyn Siesky

Editorial Manager
Cricket Krengel

Business Manager
Amy Knies

Sr. Marketing Manager
Sandy Smith

Vice President and Executive Group Publisher
Richard Swadley

Vice President and Executive Publisher
Barry Pruett

Project Coordinator
Katie Crocker

Graphics and Production Specialists
Ana Carrillo
Carrie A. Cesavice
Joyce Haughey
Andrea Hornberger
Jennifer Mayberry

Quality Control Technician
John Greenough

Proofreader
Mildred Rosenzweig

Indexer
Broccoli Information Mgt.

Screen Artists
Ana Carrillo
Jill A. Proll

About the Author

Paul McFedries is a full-time technical writer. Paul has been authoring computer books since 1991, and he has more than 60 books to his credit. Paul's books have sold more than three million copies worldwide. These books include the Wiley titles *Teach Yourself VISUALLY Windows 7, Switching to a Mac Portable Genius, iPhone 3G Portable Genius, Teach Yourself VISUALLY Office 2008 for Mac*, and *Internet Simplified*. Paul is also the proprietor of Word Spy (www.wordspy.com and twitter.com/wordspy), a Web site that tracks new words and phrases as they enter the language. Paul invites you to drop by his personal Web site at www.mcfedries.com, or to follow him on Twitter at twitter.com/paulmcf.

Author's Acknowledgements

It goes without saying that writers focus on text, and I certainly enjoyed focusing on the text that you'll read in this book. However, this book is more than just the usual collection of words and phrases. A quick thumb-through of the pages will show you that this book is also chock full of images, from sharp screen shots to fun and informative illustrations. Those colorful images sure make for a beautiful book, and that beauty comes from a lot of hard work by Wiley's immensely talented group of designers and layout artists. They are all listed in the Credits section on the previous page, and I thank them for creating another gem. Of course, what you read in this book must also be accurate, logically presented, and free of errors. Ensuring all of this was an excellent group of editors that included project editor Sarah Hellert, copy editor Scott Tullis, and technical editor Vince Averello. Thanks to all of you for your exceptional competence and hard work. Thanks, as well, to acquisitions editor Jody Lefevere for asking me to write this book.

HOW TO USE THIS BOOK

Windows 7 Visual Quick Tips includes tasks that reveal cool secrets, teach timesaving tricks, and explain great tips guaranteed to make you more productive with Windows. The easy-to-use layout lets you work through all the tasks from beginning to end or jump in at random.

Who is this book for?

If you want to know the basics about Windows, or if you want to learn shortcuts, tricks, and tips that let you work smarter and faster, this book is for you. And because you learn more easily when someone *shows* you how, this is the book for you.

Conventions Used In This Book

❶ Introduction
The introduction is designed to get you up to speed on the topic at hand.

❷ Steps
This book uses step-by-step instructions to guide you easily through each task. Numbered callouts on every screen shot show you exactly how to perform each task, step by step.

❸ Tips
Practical tips provide insights to save you time and trouble, caution you about hazards to avoid, and reveal how to do things with Windows that you never thought possible!

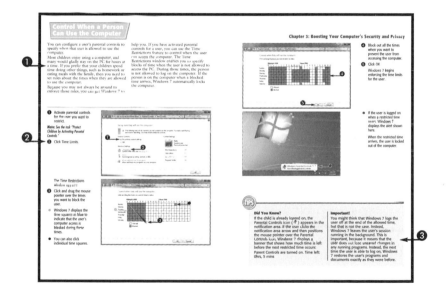

Table of Contents

 Optimizing the Start Menu and Taskbar

 Configuring Windows 7 to Suit the Way You Work

chapter 3 **Boosting Your Computer's Security and Privacy**

Table of Contents

 chapter **4** **Getting More Out of Files and Folders**

chapter **5** **Enriching Your Windows 7 Media Experience**

Maximizing Windows 7 Performance

 Tapping Into the Power of Internet Explorer

Table of Contents

chapter 10 Maximizing Windows 7 Networking

chapter 11 Getting More Out of Your Notebook PC

Chapter

1

Optimizing the Start Menu and Taskbar

Most of what you do in Windows 7 involves the Start menu and taskbar in some way. Whether you are launching an application, starting a Windows 7 utility, opening a recently-used document, dealing with a notification area message, or just checking the current time, you use the Start menu or taskbar to accomplish these tasks.

Because you make use of the Start menu and taskbar so often, it makes sense to optimize these tools to make these more efficient, which will save you time in the long run, and that is what this chapter is all about.

This chapter focuses on the practical aspects of customizing Windows 7 by showing you a number of techniques, most of which are designed to save you time and make Windows 7 more efficient. You begin with several techniques that make your Start menu much easier to deal with, including adding icons permanently, removing unneeded icons, and putting the Run command on the Start menu.

Other techniques in this chapter include displaying clocks for other time zones, adding program icons to the new Windows 7 taskbar, and customizing the icons in the notification area.

Quick Tips

Pin an Item to Your Start Menu

You can customize the Windows 7 Start menu to give yourself quick access to the programs that you use most often.

The items on the main Start menu — including Computer, Control Panel, and your user profile folders such as Documents and Pictures — are very handy because they require just two clicks to launch. To start up all your other programs, you must also click All Programs and then negotiate one or more submenus. For those programs you use most often, you can avoid this extra work by *pinning* their icons permanently to the main Start menu.

All pinned program items appear on the left side of the Start menu, above the list of programs you have used most often. This means that once you have pinned a program to your Start menu, you can always launch that program by clicking Start and then clicking the program icon.

① Click Start.

② Click All Programs.

Note: *After you click All Programs, the name changes to Back.*

③ If necessary, open the submenu that contains the program you want to pin to the Start menu. For example, if the program is in the Accessories submenu, click Accessories.

④ Right-click the program icon.

⑤ Click Pin to Start Menu.

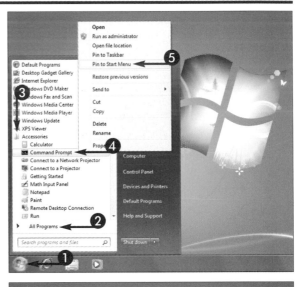

⑥ Click Start.

● Windows 7 adds the program to the main Start menu.

You can also use the same technique to pin any of the often-used program items to the main Start menu.

Chapter 1

Remove an Item from Your Start Menu

You can remove Start menu program items that you no longer use, reducing the clutter and allowing other often-used programs to appear.

The left side of the main Start menu displays a list of shortcuts to the ten programs that you have used most often, so these change as you use your computer. This is useful because it means you can launch one of these programs with just a couple of mouse clicks. However,

you may end up with a program that you used frequently for a while, but now intend to use only infrequently. In that case, it is best to remove that icon from the Start menu to make room for another often-used program.

Similarly, you may have pinned a program to the top of the Start menu, as described in the previous task. If you no longer use a pinned program frequently, you should remove it from the Start menu.

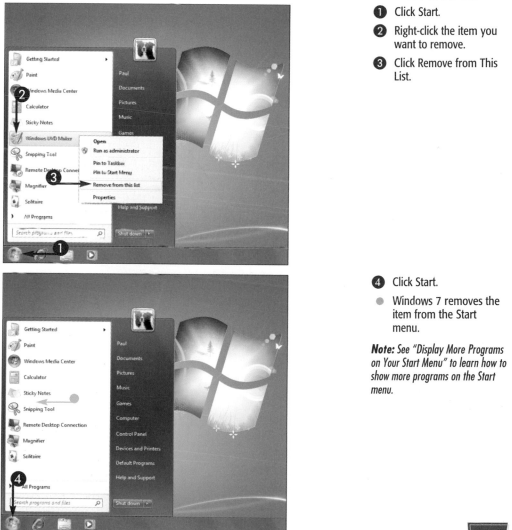

1 Click Start.

2 Right-click the item you want to remove.

3 Click Remove from This List.

4 Click Start.

● Windows 7 removes the item from the Start menu.

Note: See "Display More Programs on Your Start Menu" to learn how to show more programs on the Start menu.

Pin a Program to the Taskbar

You can place your favorite programs a mouse click away by pinning them to the new Windows 7 taskbar.

In this chapter's first task, you learned how to pin a program icon to the Start menu, making that program just two clicks away. If you have a program that you use frequently, you might prefer to have that program just a single click away. You can achieve this by pinning that program to the new Windows 7 taskbar.

As with previous versions of Windows, the Windows 7 taskbar displays an icon for each running program. However, one of the new features with the revamped Windows 7 taskbar is the capability of storing program icons, much like the Quick Launch toolbar in previous versions of Windows. Once you have a shortcut icon for a program pinned to the taskbar, you can then launch that program just by clicking the icon.

You can pin a program to the taskbar either by running the Pin to Taskbar command, or by clicking and dragging a program icon to the taskbar.

PIN A PROGRAM USING A COMMAND

① Click Start.

② Click All Programs.

Note: After you click All Programs, the name changes to Back.

③ If necessary, open the submenu that contains the program you want to pin to the Start menu. For example, if the program is in the Accessories submenu, click Accessories.

④ Right-click the program icon.

⑤ Click Pin to Taskbar.

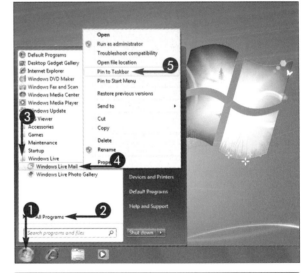

● Windows 7 adds an icon for the program to the taskbar.

You can also use the same technique to pin any of the often-used program items to the taskbar.

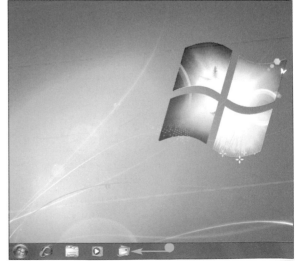

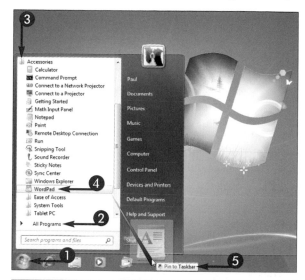

PIN A PROGRAM USING YOUR MOUSE

① Click Start.

② Click All Programs.

Note: *After you click All Programs, the name changes to Back.*

③ If necessary, open the submenu that contains the program you want to pin to the Start menu. For example, if the program is in the Accessories submenu, click Accessories.

④ Click and drag the program icon to any empty section of the taskbar.

⑤ When you see the Pin to Taskbar banner, drop the icon.

● Windows 7 adds an icon for the program to the taskbar.

You can also use the same technique to drag and drop any of the often-used programs to the taskbar.

Note: *To remove a pinned program icon, right-click the icon and then click Unpin This Program from Taskbar.*

TIPS

Taskbar Trick!

As you drop program icons onto the taskbar, Windows 7 displays the icons left to right in the order you added them. If you prefer a different order, click and drag a taskbar icon to the left or right and then drop it in the new position. Note that this technique applies not only to the icons pinned to the taskbar, but also to the icons for any running programs.

Remove It!

If you decide you no longer require a program pinned to the taskbar, you should remove it to reduce taskbar clutter and provide more room for other taskbar icons. To remove a pinned program icon, right-click the icon and then click Unpin This Program from Taskbar.

Pin a Destination to a Taskbar Icon

You can pin a destination such as a folder, document, or Web site to a taskbar icon for easy access.

In the task "Pin a Program to the Taskbar," you learned how to add icons for your favorite programs to the taskbar so that you could launch any of those programs with a single click. However, rather than favorite programs, you might have favorite folders, documents, music tracks, or Web sites that you launch frequently. Windows 7 calls such items *destinations*.

Although you cannot pin destinations directly to the taskbar, you can pin them to the jump list associated with a taskbar icon. This means that you can launch a destination by right-clicking its program's taskbar bar icon and then clicking the destination in the jump list. This is almost always going to be much quicker than running the program and opening the destination using the program's commands.

You can pin a destination to a taskbar icon either by running the Pin to This List command, or by clicking and dragging a destination to the taskbar icon.

PIN A DESTINATION USING A COMMAND

① Right-click the taskbar icon of the program associated with the destination.

② Right-click the destination icon.

Note: *If you do not see the destination in the jump list, you must use the mouse method described on the next page.*

③ Click Pin to This List.

● You can also click the Pin to This List icon (📌).

● Windows 7 adds an icon for the destination to the Pinned section of the program's jump list.

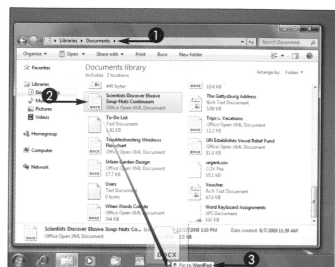

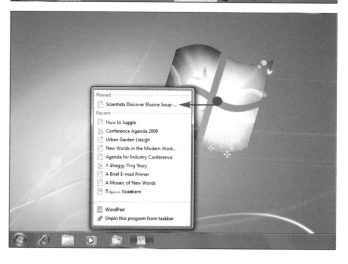

PIN A DESTINATION USING YOUR MOUSE

1 Open the folder that contains the item you want to pin.

2 Click and drag the icon to any empty section of the taskbar.

3 When you see the Pin to *Program* banner (where *Program* is the name of the application associated with the destination), drop the icon.

● Windows 7 adds an icon for the destination to the Pinned section of the program's jump list.

TIPS

Taskbar Trick!

If the program associated with the destination does not already have a taskbar icon, you do not need to pin the program to the taskbar separately. Instead, follow steps 1 to 3 on this page to drop the destination on an empty section of the taskbar. Windows 7 adds a new icon for the program to the taskbar and pins the destination to the program's jump list.

Remove It!

If you no longer require a destination pinned to its program's taskbar icon, remove it to reduce clutter in the jump list and provide more room for other destinations. To remove a pinned destination, right-click the icon and then click Unpin from This List ( ). You can also click the Unpin from This List icon that appears to the right of the destination.

Add the Run Command to the Start Menu

If you often use the Run dialog box to open programs, folders, and Web sites, you can make the dialog box much easier to launch by adding the Run command to the main Start menu.

The Run command opens the Run dialog box, which enables you to open many different types of files by typing the file's address. The Run command enables you to launch programs, folders, documents, Web sites, e-mail messages, Command Prompt commands, and more.

The Run dialog box is a very handy tool, but if you use it frequently, you will be disappointed to find out that Windows 7 buries the Run command in the Accessories menu (select Start, All Programs, Accessories, Run). This is very inconvenient and very time-consuming. However, you can fix this problem by customizing Windows 7 to display the Run command on the main Start menu. This enables you to open the Run dialog box with just a couple of mouse clicks.

1 Right-click Start.

2 Click Properties.

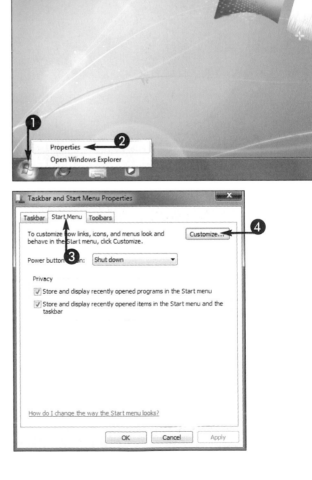

The Taskbar and Start Menu Properties dialog box appears.

3 Click the Start Menu tab.

4 Click Customize.

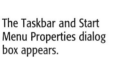

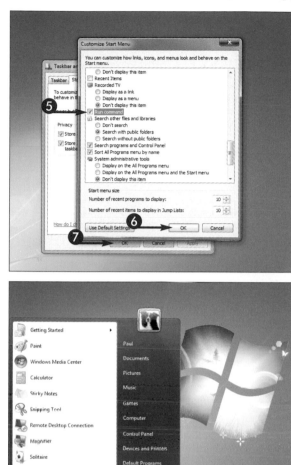

The Customize Start Menu dialog box appears.

⑤ Click the Run Command check box (☐ changes to ☑).

⑥ Click OK.

⑦ Click OK.

⑧ Click Start.

● Windows 7 displays the Run command on the Start menu.

Customize It!

If your Windows 7 Start menu is overcrowded, you might not want to add the Run command. One solution is to remove other Start menu items you do not use by following steps 1 to 4 and then deactivating the check boxes for the items you want to remove. Alternatively, leave Run off the main Start menu and launch the Run dialog box by pressing Windows Logo key+R.

Did You Know?

To start an e-mail message from the Run dialog box, type **mailto:** followed by the e-mail address of the recipient. For example, to start an e-mail message addressed to president@ whitehouse.gov, type **mailto: president@whitehouse.gov** in the Run dialog box and then click OK.

Configure the Start Menu Power Button

You can customize the Start menu's power button to run a different command, such as Restart or Sleep.

The Windows 7 Start menu comes with a power button labeled Shut Down by default. This means that you can shut down your PC by clicking Start and then clicking the power button. However, you may find that you rarely shut down your PC. For example, you might prefer to put your computer into sleep mode instead of shutting it down altogether. Similarly, you may find that you lock your

computer or switch users far more often than you shut down.

Unfortunately, choosing commands such as Sleep, Lock, and Switch User in Windows 7 requires three clicks: click Start, click the arrow beside Shut Down, and then click the command you want to run.

Fortunately, the power button is customizable, meaning that you can replace the Shut Down command with any of the following: Lock, Log Off, Restart, Sleep, or Switch User.

① Right-click Start.

② Click Properties.

The Taskbar and Start Menu Properties dialog box appears.

③ Click the Start Menu tab.

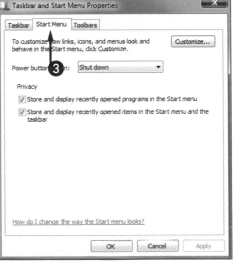

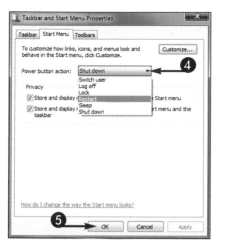

④ Click the Power Button Action list and then click the command you want Windows 7 to run when you click the power button.

⑤ Click OK.

⑥ Click Start.

● Windows 7 displays the new command on the power button.

TIPS

Did You Know?

If you prefer to put your computer into sleep mode instead of turning it off, you can configure Windows 7 to activate sleep mode automatically. Click Start, type **power**, and then click Power Options. Click the Change When the Computer Sleeps link, choose a time in the Put the Computer to Sleep list, and then click Save Changes.

Customize It!

If you restart your computer frequently, you can pin a restart shortcut to the taskbar for one-click restarts. Right-click an empty section of the desktop, click New, and then click Shortcut. In the Create Shortcut Wizard, type **shutdown /r /t 0**, click Next, type a name, and then click Finish. Drag the new shortcut and then drop it on an empty part of the taskbar.

You can make your Windows 7 computer more efficient by displaying a list of your recently used documents on the Start menu.

You make Windows 7 efficient by configuring it to give you easy access to the programs and documents that you use most often. However, sometimes the document you want to open is not necessarily one that you use frequently, but one that you used relatively recently. It does not make sense to pin such a document to the

Start menu or to a program's jump list, but it would still be nice to be able to access that document quickly.

You can achieve this by taking advantage of Windows 7's Recent Items list. This is a list of the 15 documents that you have used most recently. By adding this list to the Start menu, you can launch any of those files with just a few mouse clicks.

① Right-click Start.

② Click Properties.

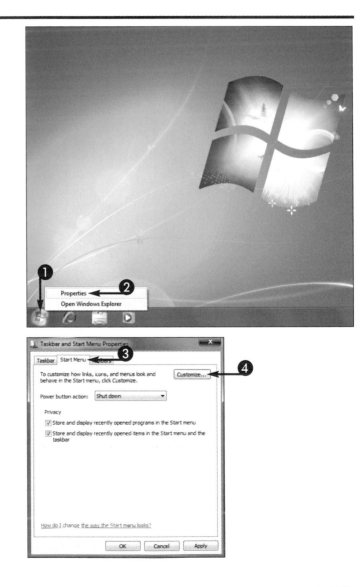

The Taskbar and Start Menu Properties dialog box appears.

③ Click the Start Menu tab.

④ Click Customize.

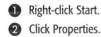

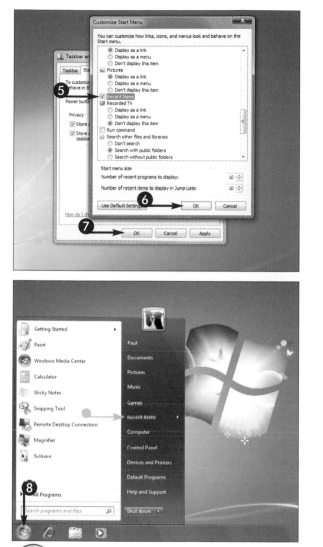

The Customize Start Menu dialog box appears.

5 Click the Recent Items check box (☐ changes to ☑).

6 Click OK.

7 Click OK.

8 Click Start.

● Windows 7 displays the Recent Items menu on the Start menu.

Delete It!

Although it is handy to have a list of recently used files on the Start menu, you might end up with a confidential or private document on that list. If other people have access to your computer, you probably do not want to give them such easy access to a sensitive file. To remove such a file from the Recent Items list, click Start, click Recent Items, right-click the file, and then click Delete.

Did You Know?

You will mostly use the Recent Items list to open documents: click Start, click Recent Items, and then click the file. However, you can also use the Recent Items list to open the folder that contains a document. This is handy if you want to rename the file or look for related files in the same location. Click Start, click Recent Items, right-click the file, and then click Open File Location.

Launch Control Panel Icons Faster by Using a Menu

You can quickly access items in the Control Panel by converting the Start menu's Control Panel item into a menu.

Control Panel is the Windows 7 customization shop, with nearly 60 icons. Using these icons, you can customize and modify features such as accessibility, the display, folders and fonts, the Internet, and user accounts. You can install and uninstall programs and devices, and you can tweak specific devices such as game controllers, the keyboard, the mouse, the modem, printers, scanners, and more.

The longer you use Windows 7, the more you appreciate the Control Panel. The problem, however, is that the default Control Panel window uses a category view that groups the Control Panel icons into categories, such as System and Security, and Appearance and Personalization. That view hampers more experienced users, who must often negotiate several windows to get to the icon they want. Converting the Start menu's Control Panel item into a menu on the Start menu enables you to easily find and choose any Control Panel item.

① Right-click Start.
② Click Properties.

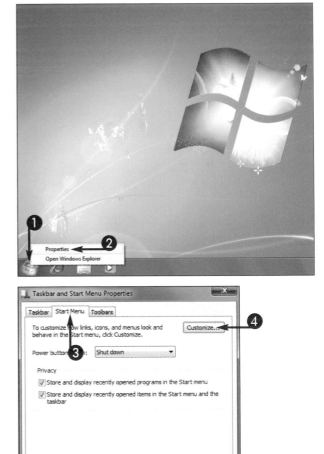

The Taskbar and Start Menu Properties dialog box appears.

③ Click the Start Menu tab.
④ Click Customize.

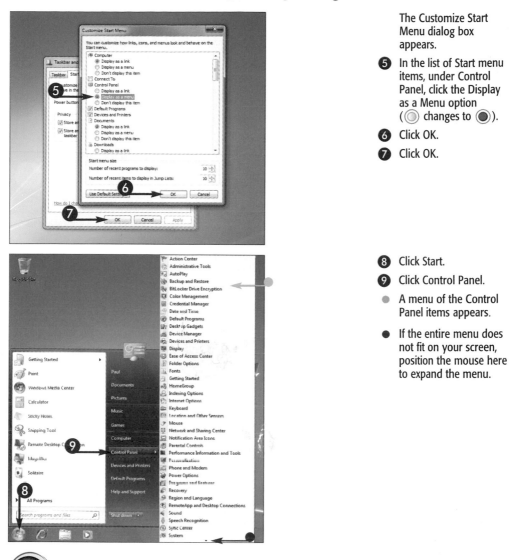

The Customize Start Menu dialog box appears.

5 In the list of Start menu items, under Control Panel, click the Display as a Menu option (⊙ changes to ⊚).

6 Click OK.

7 Click OK.

8 Click Start.

9 Click Control Panel.

● A menu of the Control Panel items appears.

● If the entire menu does not fit on your screen, position the mouse here to expand the menu.

More Options!

There are other Start menu items that you can display as menus. Follow steps 1 to 5 to display the Customize Start Menu dialog box. The following branches have a Display as a Menu option that you can click (⊙ changes to ⊚): Computer, Documents, Games, Music, Personal libraries, Pictures, Recorded TV, and Videos.

More Options!

For easier access to your preferred Web sites, follow steps 1 to 5 to display the Customize Start Menu dialog box. Click the Favorites menu check box (☐ changes to ☑) to display a menu of Internet Explorer favorites. Click OK to return to the Start menu tab, and then click OK.

You can give yourself easy access to some useful and powerful Windows 7 features by adding the administrative tools to the Start menu.

Windows 7 ships with a collection of advanced features called the administrative tools. With these programs and utilities you can schedule tasks, control services, monitor performance, create data sources, implement security policies, and much more.

You normally access these tools by clicking Start, clicking Control Panel, clicking System and Security, and then clicking Administrative Tools. If you find that you use one or more of these tools frequently, you can save time by displaying the administrative tools as a list on the Start menu. This makes each tool just a few mouse clicks away.

 Right-click Start.

② Click Properties.

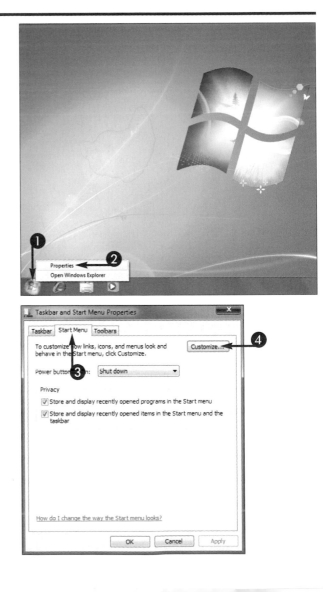

The Taskbar and Start Menu Properties dialog box appears.

 Click the Start Menu tab.

④ Click Customize.

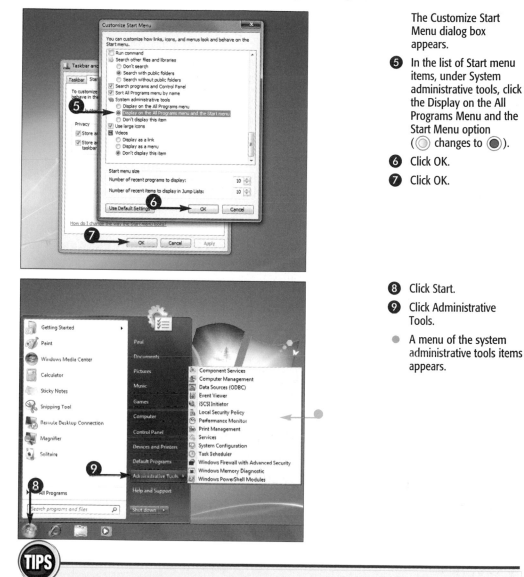

The Customize Start Menu dialog box appears.

⑤ In the list of Start menu items, under System administrative tools, click the Display on the All Programs Menu and the Start Menu option (◯ changes to ◉).

⑥ Click OK.

⑦ Click OK.

⑧ Click Start.

⑨ Click Administrative Tools.

● A menu of the system administrative tools items appears.

TIPS

Try This!

If you find that the right side of the Start menu is getting crowded and hard to navigate, consider displaying the administrative tools only as a submenu of the All Programs menu. To set this up, follow steps 1 to 4 in this task. Under System Administrative tools, click the Display on the All Programs Menu option (◯ changes to ◉).

Customize It!

If you find that your Start menu is getting cluttered, but you prefer to leave the Administrative Tools menu in place, consider removing some Start menu items that you do not use very often. Follow steps 1 to 4 in this task, and then consider deactivating the Default Programs and Help check boxes (◉ changes to ◯).

Display More Programs on Your Start Menu

You can customize the Start menu to display more of the programs you use most often.

The list displaying your most-frequently used programs appears on the left side of the Start menu, above All Programs. As you work with your programs, Windows 7 keeps track of how many times you launch each one. The programs that you have launched most often appear on the Start menu for easy, two-click access. The program you have used most often appears at the top of the list, followed by the

next most-often-used program, and so on. When another program becomes popular, Windows 7 drops the bottom program and adds the new one.

The default Start menu shows the ten most popular programs. If you find that some of your regular programs are constantly getting dropped from the Start menu, you can increase the size of the list to force Windows 7 to display more programs.

 Right-click Start.

 Click Properties.

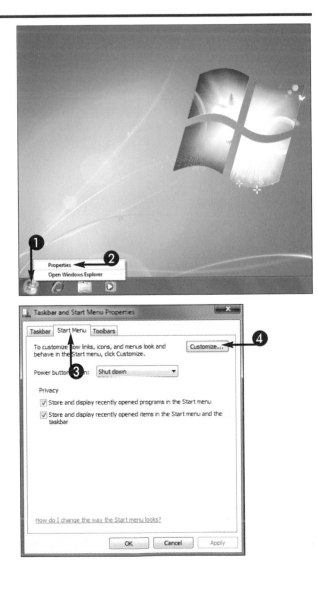

The Taskbar and Start Menu Properties dialog box appears.

❸ Click the Start Menu tab.

❹ Click Customize.

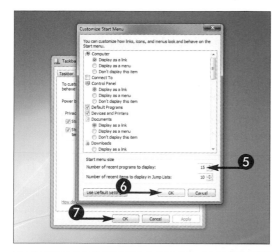

The Customize Start Menu dialog box appears.

⑤ Type the number of programs you want to see.

Note: *The maximum number of programs is 30.*

⑥ Click OK to return to the Taskbar and Start Menu Properties dialog box.

⑦ Click OK.

● Windows 7 adjusts the size of the Start menu's most frequently used program list.

More Options!

The height of the Start menu is restricted by the height of your screen. To display more Start menu items without changing the screen height, follow steps 1 to 4 to open the Customize Start Menu dialog box. In the list, click to deselect the Use Large Icons check box (☑ changes to ☐), and then click OK. Using smaller icons enables more items to appear on the Start menu.

Customize It!

If you want to get even more items on the Start menu, you can change the height of your screen by increasing the screen resolution. Right-click the desktop, click Screen Resolution to open the Screen Resolution window. Click the Resolution dropdown list, click and drag the Resolution slider up to a higher setting, and then click OK.

Display a Clock for Another Time Zone

If you deal with people in another time zone, you can make it easier to find out the current time in that zone by customizing Windows 7 to show a second clock configured for the time zone.

If you have colleagues, friends, or family members who work or live in a different time zone, it is often important to know the correct time in that zone. For example, you would not want to call someone at home at 9 AM your time if that person lives in a time zone three

hours behind you. Similarly, if you know that a business colleague leaves work at 5 PM and that person works in a time zone seven hours ahead of you, then you know that any calls you place to that person must occur before 10 AM your time.

If you need to be sure about the current time in another time zone, you can customize the Windows 7 date and time display to show not only your current time, but also the current time in the other time zone.

---

① Click the time.

② Click Change Date and Time Settings.

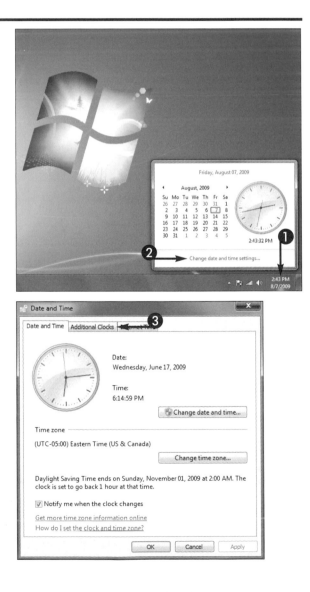

The Date and Time dialog box appears.

③ Click the Additional Clocks tab.

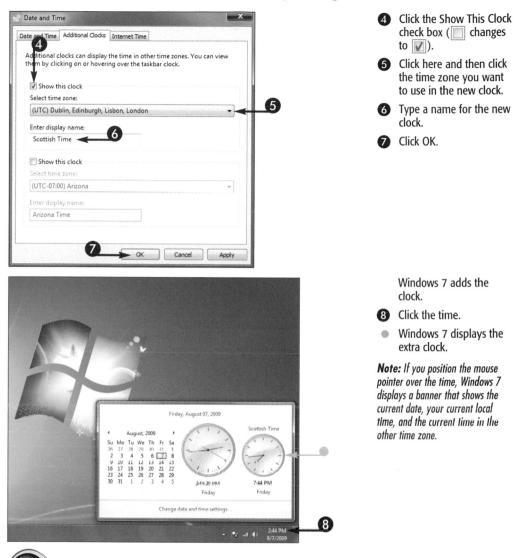

④ Click the Show This Clock check box (☐ changes to ☑).

⑤ Click here and then click the time zone you want to use in the new clock.

⑥ Type a name for the new clock.

⑦ Click OK.

Windows 7 adds the clock.

⑧ Click the time.

● Windows 7 displays the extra clock.

Note: *If you position the mouse pointer over the time, Windows 7 displays a banner that shows the current date, your current local time, and the current time in the other time zone.*

TIPS

Did You Know?

After you customize Windows 7 with the extra clock, you normally click the time in the notification area to see both clocks. However, if you just position the mouse pointer over the time, Windows 7 displays a banner that shows the current date, your current local time, and the current time in the other time zone.

More Options!

If you deal with people in a third time zone, you can customize Windows 7 to display a third clock. Follow steps 1 to 3 to display the Additional Clocks tab. Click the second Show This Clock check box (☐ changes to ☑), click the down arrow (▼) in the list below it to select a time zone, type a name for the third clock, and then click OK.

You can customize the way that Windows 7 displays the icons in the notification area to ensure a particular icon is always visible or to turn off an icon's notifications.

The notification area in the Windows 7 taskbar shows only a few icons: Volume, Network, and Action Center, and notebook PCs also show the Power icon. All other Windows 7 icons and third-party program icons are hidden, and you access them by clicking the Show Hidden Icons arrow to the left of the notification area.

However, Windows 7 does display all notifications generated by the hidden icons, so you never miss important messages.

In certain cases you might want to customize the default arrangement. For example, many notification icons offer quick access to their programs' features when you right-click them. If there is an icon that you right-click frequently, you might want to configure the notification area to show the icon on the taskbar.

① Click the Show Hidden Icons arrow.

② Click Customize.

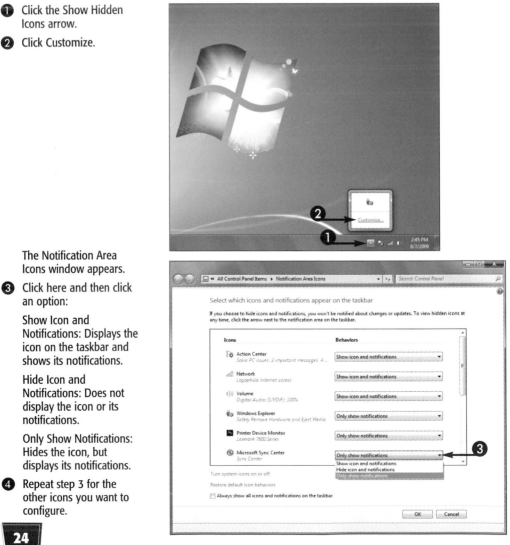

The Notification Area Icons window appears.

③ Click here and then click an option:

Show Icon and Notifications: Displays the icon on the taskbar and shows its notifications.

Hide Icon and Notifications: Does not display the icon or its notifications.

Only Show Notifications: Hides the icon, but displays its notifications.

④ Repeat step 3 for the other icons you want to configure.

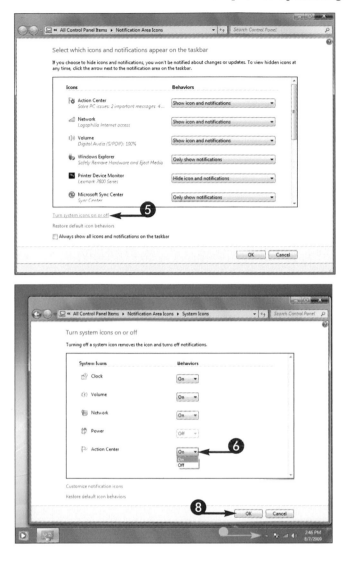

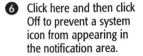

5 Click Turn System Icons On or Off.

6 Click here and then click Off to prevent a system icon from appearing in the notification area.

7 Repeat step 6 for each system icon you want to hide.

8 Click OK to return to the Notification Area Icons window.

9 Click OK (not shown).

Windows 7 puts the new settings into effect.

● Click this arrow to see your hidden icons.

Did You Know?
You can configure the notification area to always show all the icons and their notifications. Follow steps 1 and 2 to open the Notification Area Icons window. Click the Always Show All Icons and Notifications on the Taskbar check box (◎ changes to ◉), and then click OK.

2

Configuring Windows 7 to Suit the Way You Work

Windows 7 is endlessly customizable and offers many features that enable you to modify the look and feel of your system to suit your style and the way you work.

You probably already know how to customize aspects of the Windows 7 screen, such as the colors, fonts, desktop background, and screen resolution. These are useful techniques to know, to be sure, but Windows 7 offers a number of other techniques that put much more emphasis on what is practical. That is, although changing your screen colors might make Windows 7 more interesting, it does not

help you get your work done any faster. However, techniques such as scaling the screen to make the text more readable, changing the screen orientation to portrait, and working with multiple monitors can help you work faster and better.

This chapter focuses not only on aspects of customizing Windows 7 that are designed to save you time, but also those that help you express yourself through your Windows 7 system. For example, in this chapter you learn how to change your user account picture and how to create a custom theme.

Quick Tips

You can customize your Windows 7 user account to use a picture that suits you.

When you install Windows 7, the program asks you to select a picture to go along with your user account. This picture appears at the top of the Start menu as well as in the Welcome screen when you log on to Windows 7. The installation program offers a dozen or so pictures that include a dog, cat, fish, robot, chess set, fireworks, and various nature images. These are fine enough, but perhaps having chosen, say, the fish first time around, you

might decide that it just does not convey who you are.

In that case, you can configure your user account to use one of the other pictures. If none of the predefined Windows 7 images is just right for you, then you can take this technique a step further and choose your own image. You can use any picture you want, as long as it is in one of the four image file types that Windows 7 supports: Bitmap, JPEG, GIF, or PNG.

① Click Start.

② Type **account**.

③ Click Change Your Account Picture.

The Change Your Picture window appears.

● If you want to use one of the predefined images, click the picture you want, click Change Picture, and then skip the rest of these steps.

④ Click Browse for More Pictures.

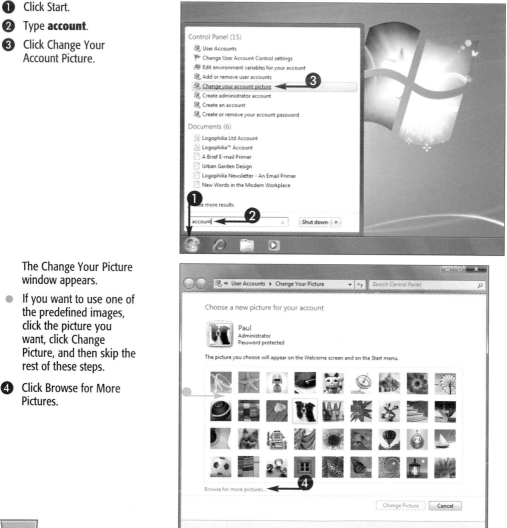

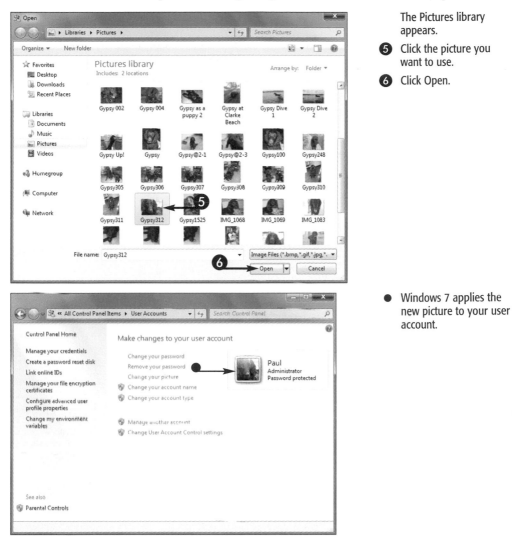

The Pictures library appears.

⑤ Click the picture you want to use.

⑥ Click Open.

● Windows 7 applies the new picture to your user account.

If you are having trouble reading the text on the screen, you can scale the screen to a higher dots per inch setting to make the text more readable.

Running Windows 7 at a high resolution is useful because it means you can fit more items on the screen at once since everything appears smaller. The downside is that, depending on the resolution, some fonts may be too small to read comfortably.

You can solve this problem by increasing the Windows 7 dots per inch (DPI) setting. The default is 96 DPI, which means that Windows

7 uses 96 pixels (dots) for every inch of screen space. (Physical measurements are relative to the screen resolution, so a one-inch line may not actually be one inch long on your screen.)

For example, a line meant to be one inch long is drawn using 96 pixels. However, if you increase the DPI setting, the line appears longer. For example, if you change the DPI to 120, Windows 7 scales the screen to use 120 pixels to create the same line. In other words, if you scale the DPI setting up, everything on the screen appears larger, including the text, which makes it easier to read.

① Right-click the desktop.

② Click Screen Resolution.

The Screen Resolution window appears.

③ Click Make Text and Other Items Larger or Smaller.

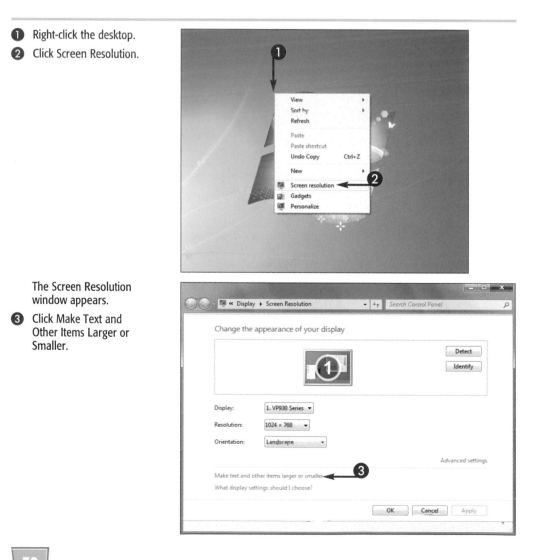

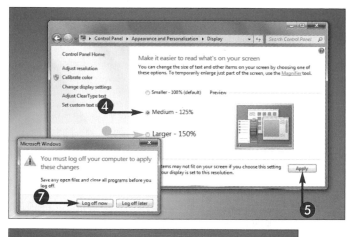

The Display window appears.

④ Click Medium - 125% (◯ changes to ◉).

● If you later find that you still cannot read your screen text easily, follow these steps again and try the Larger - 150% option (◯ changes to ◉).

⑤ Click Apply.

Windows 7 tells you that you must log off for the change to take effect.

⑥ Close any documents and programs you have open.

⑦ Click Log off now.

Windows 7 logs off your account.

When you log back on, Windows 7 puts the new font scaling into effect, as shown here with the Start menu.

 TIPS

More Options!

The Display window has three options: Smaller - 100% (the default scaling), Medium - 125%, and Larger - 150%. However, for some monitors these values do not provide the best balance between readability and how much information fits on the screen. The solution is to specify a custom DPI value by clicking the Set Custom Text Size (DPI) link and typing a percentage value in the text box.

Try This!

Another way you can make your text more readable is to take advantage of Windows 7's ClearType technology, which smoothes fonts to make them sharper and easier to read. To ensure your display is optimized for ClearType, run the ClearType Text Tuner. Click Start, type **cleartype**, and then click ClearType Text Tuner in the search results.

If you have a monitor that can be swiveled to a different orientation, you can configure Windows 7 to match that orientation.

A standard computer monitor comes with an orientation where the screen width is greater than the screen height. For example, on a typical 22-inch LCD monitor, the screen might be 19 inches wide and 12 inches high. (It is called a 22-inch monitor because it is approximately 22 inches on the diagonal.) This is called *landscape* orientation, which is a useful default configuration because you most often require extra width in applications such as

spreadsheets and databases, or you may want to run two programs side by side.

However, plenty of PC applications work better when the screen height is greater than the screen width. For example, a long word-processing document or extended Web page work better in such a configuration, which is known as *portrait* orientation.

Many monitors come with a swivel feature that enables you to turn the screen from landscape to portrait. However, you also need to place Windows in a matching orientation, and this feature is now part of Windows 7.

① Right-click the desktop.

② Click Screen Resolution.

The Screen Resolution window appears.

③ Click the Orientation list to select the orientation you want to use.

④ Click OK.

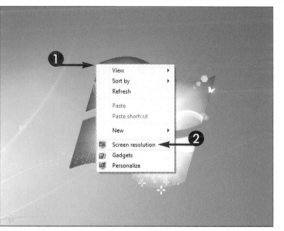

Windows 7 changes the orientation.

 Click Keep Changes.

6 Swivel your monitor into the matching orientation.

TIPS

More Options!

The Portrait option in the Orientation list assumes the top of the desktop will appear on what is the left edge of the monitor when the monitor is in landscape orientation. That is, it assumes you swivel the monitor clockwise 90 degrees to switch from landscape to portrait. If, instead, you swivel the monitor counterclockwise 90 degrees, choose the Portrait (Flipped) option in the Orientation list.

More Options!

If you swivel the monitor 90 degrees to go from landscape to portrait, and then swivel the monitor another 90 degrees in the same direction, you end up back in the landscape orientation. However, if you choose Landscape in the Orientation list, the Windows 7 desktop will appear upside down because you have effectively swiveled your monitor 180 degrees. To get the correct orientation, choose Portrait (Flipped) in the Orientation list.

Configure Windows 7 to Work with Multiple Monitors

You can improve your productivity and efficiency by configuring Windows 7 to extend the desktop across two monitors.

Over the past few years, many studies haves shown that you can greatly improve your productivity by doing one thing: adding a second monitor to your system. This enables you to have whatever program you are currently working with displayed on one monitor, and your reference materials, e-mail program, or some other secondary program on the second monitor. This is more efficient because you no longer have to switch back and forth between the two programs.

To work with two monitors on a single computer, one solution is to install a second video card and attach the second monitor to it. However, many video cards now available come with dual output ports: either one VGA port and one DVI port, or two DVI ports. Choose a card that matches the ports on your monitors.

Once you have installed the new video card and attached the monitors, you then need to configure Windows 7 to extend the desktop across both monitors and choose which monitor is the main display that shows the Windows 7 taskbar and Start menu.

---

① Right-click the desktop.

② Click Screen Resolution.

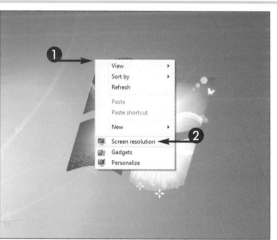

The Screen Resolution window appears.

● Windows 7 displays an icon for each of your monitors.

● To see which icon is associated with each monitor, you can click the Identity button.

③ In the Multiple Displays list, choose Extend These Displays.

④ Click Apply.

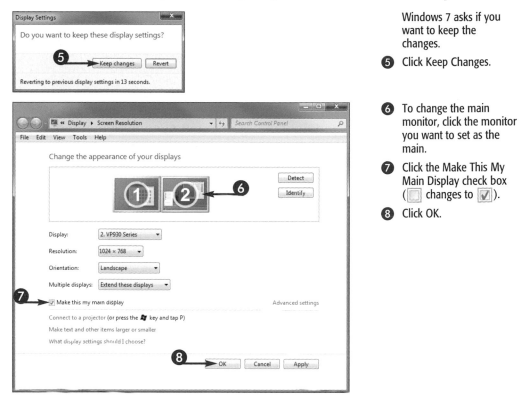

Windows 7 asks if you want to keep the changes.

5 Click Keep Changes.

6 To change the main monitor, click the monitor you want to set as the main.

7 Click the Make This My Main Display check box (☐ changes to ☑).

8 Click OK.

TIP

More Options!
Ideally, you should be able to move your mouse continuously from the left monitor to the right monitor. If you find that the mouse stops at the right edge of your left monitor, then it means you need to exchange the icons of the left and right monitors. To do that, click and drag the left monitor icon to the right of the other monitor icon (or vice versa).

You can put your personal stamp on Windows 7 by creating a custom theme.

In Windows 7, a *theme* is a collection of customization options that you can apply all at once. Each theme includes selections from four customization categories: the Windows 7 desktop background; the Windows 7 color scheme for the Start menu, taskbar, and windows; the sounds associated with Windows 7 events such as error messages and logging in

and out of your user account; and a screen saver.

Windows 7 ships with several predefined themes, and themes are also available online. If none of these predefined themes suits you, you can create your own. You can customize one or more of the four customization categories, and then save your changes to a special theme file.

① Right-click the desktop.

② Click Personalize.

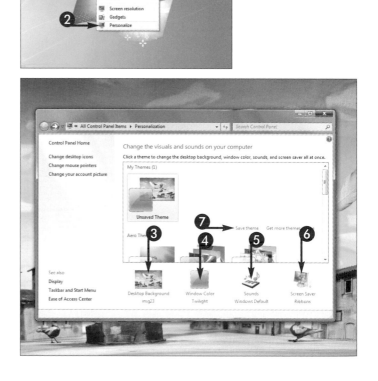

The Personalization window appears.

③ Click Desktop Background to choose a new background.

Note: *For more information on setting the background, see the task "Display a Favorite Photo on the Desktop."*

④ Click Window Color to choose a different color scheme for the Windows 7 Start menu taskbar, and windows.

⑤ Click Sounds to customize sounds.

Note: *See Chapter 5 to learn more about assigning sounds to events.*

⑥ Click Screen Saver to activate a screen saver.

⑦ Click Save Theme.

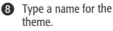

The Save Theme As dialog box appears.

⑧ Type a name for the theme.

⑨ Click Save.

● Your custom theme appears in the My Themes section of the Personalization window.

● The theme name appears here.

Delete It!

If you have a theme you no longer use, you should delete it to reduce clutter in the Personalization window and make your custom themes easier to find and navigate. Follow steps 1 and 2 to open the Personalization window and then click a different theme. Right-click the theme you no longer need, click Delete Theme, and then click Yes when Windows 7 asks you to confirm.

Display a Favorite Photo on the Desktop

You can customize the Windows 7 desktop to display your favorite photo as the desktop background.

If you have a favorite photo that you prefer to use, you can customize the desktop to display that photo. In Windows 7, there are five ways to display a photo on the desktop: Fill, Fit, Stretch, Tile, or Center.

The Fill option zooms in on or out of the photo until it fills the entire desktop. This option usually crops the photo edges.

The Fit option zooms in on or out of the photo until it fits either the width of the desktop or the height, whichever comes first. The rest of the desktop appears black.

The Stretch option expands the photo to fill the entire desktop. This option usually distorts the photo.

The Tile option repeats your photo multiple times to fill the entire desktop.

The Center option displays the photo at its normal size, centered on the desktop.

 Right-click the desktop.

 Click Personalize.

The Personalization window appears.

❸ Click Desktop Background.

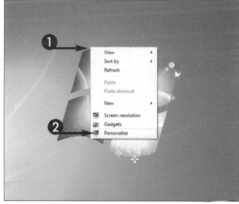

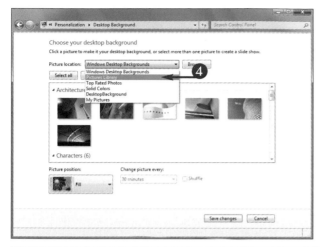

The Desktop Background window appears.

④ In the Picture Location list, click Pictures Library.

⑤ Click the photo you want to show on the desktop.

⑥ Use the Picture Position list to choose how you want the photo displayed on the desktop.

⑦ Click Save Changes.

Windows applies the new desktop background settings.

TIP

More Options!
If you are having a hard time choosing a favorite photo, you can configure Windows 7 to show multiple photos as a kind of desktop-based slide show. Follow steps 1 to 4, and then activate the check box beside each photo you want to use (☐ changes to ☑). Use the Change Picture Every list to select a time interval between photos, and then click Save Changes.

You can give a visitor temporary and secure access to your computer or your network by letting that person log on using the built-in Windows 7 Guest account.

What do you do if you have someone visiting your home and that person wants to, for example, surf the Web or access some media on your computer? You could allow the person to log on using an existing account, but that might not be reasonable because of privacy or security concerns. You could set up a separate user account for that person, but that is probably too much work, particularly for a person on a short visit.

A better solution is to take advantage of the Guest account that comes with Windows 7. The Guest account is given only limited privileges, so anyone logged on under that account cannot access or edit your data, change computer settings, or install programs.

The Guest account is deactivated by default, so to allow your visitor to log on under that account you must first activate it.

① Click Start.

② Click Control Panel.

● The Control Panel window appears.

③ Click Add or Remove User Accounts.

The Manage Accounts window appears.

④ Click Guest.

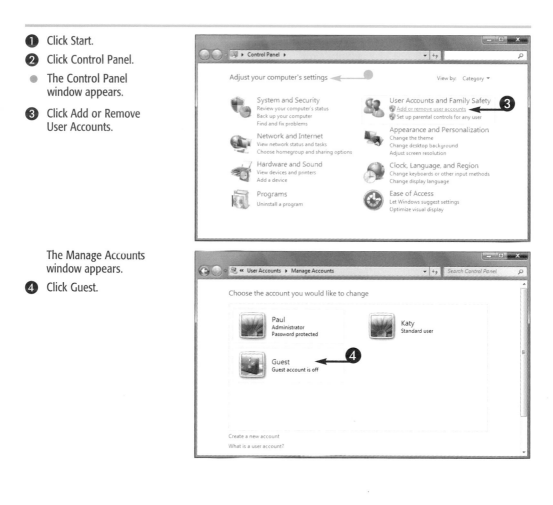

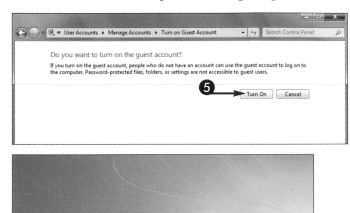

The Turn On Guest Account window appears.

⑤ Click Turn On.

Windows 7 activates the Guest account.

● The next time you start Windows 7, an icon for the Guest account appears in the Welcome window. Click that icon to log on using the Guest account.

Secure It!

If you plan on leaving the Guest account activated for an extended time, you should secure it with a password. Select Start, type **lusrmgr.msc**, and press Enter. In the Local Users and Groups window, click Users, right-click Guest, and then click Set Password. In the Set Password for Guest dialog box, click Proceed, type the new password in the two text boxes, and then click OK.

Reverse It!

When you no longer need to use the Guest account, you should deactivate it again. To turn the Guest account off, follow steps 1 to 4 to open the Change Guest Options window. Click the Turn Off the Guest Account link. Windows 7 immediately deactivates the account.

Synchronize Your System Time

You can keep your system time accurate by synchronizing the time with a server computer on the Internet.

Your computer has an internal clock that keeps track of the current date and time. Windows 7 displays the clock's current time in the taskbar, on the right side of the notification area. You also see the current date, and to view the fill date, position the mouse pointer over the time or date until the date banner appears. For many people, the Windows 7 clock has replaced the traditional wall or desktop clock in the office or den.

Unfortunately, computer clocks are not always very accurate. It is not unusual for the system clock to gain or lose a minute or two a day. Clearly, if you are relying on the Windows 7 clock to know what time it is, you want the clock to be accurate.

Windows 7 can help by enabling you to synchronize the clock with an accurate source. The Internet offers a number of computers called *time servers* that maintain the accurate time. Windows 7 can synchronize with a time server to keep your system clock correct.

---

1 Connect to the Internet.

2 Click the clock.

3 Click Change Date and Time Settings.

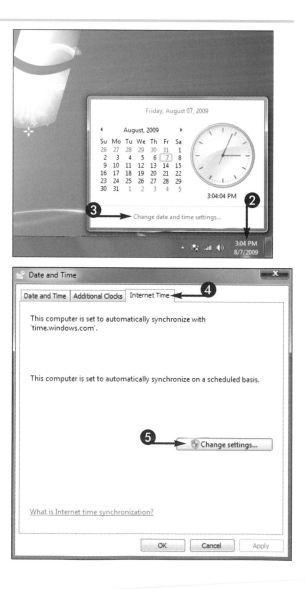

The Date and Time dialog box appears.

4 Click the Internet Time tab.

5 Click Change Settings.

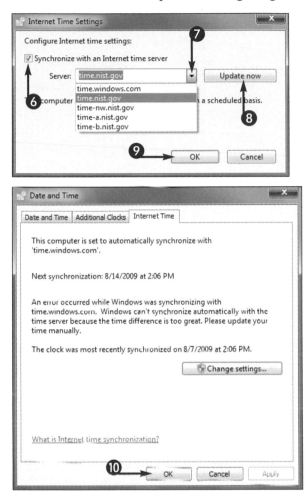

The Internet Time Settings dialog box appears.

⑥ Click Synchronize with an Internet Time Server (☐ changes to ☑).

⑦ Click here and then click the time server you want to use.

⑧ Click Update Now.

Windows 7 synchronizes your system time with the time server.

⑨ Click OK.

⑩ Click OK.

Windows 7 uses the new time server to synchronize your system automatically every 24 hours.

Check It Out!

The default time servers — such as time.windows.com and time.nist.gov — are usually reliable and accurate. You can also type another time server's address in the Server text box. Here are two sites that maintain lists of time server addresses:

http://tf.nist.gov/tf-cgi/servers.cgi

http://ntp.isc.org/bin/view/Servers/NTPPoolServers

Troubleshoot It!

If you are unable to synchronize your system time, first make sure you are connected to the Internet. Also, check that your computer's time and date are not wildly off the current date and time — say, by a day or more. If they are, click the Date & Time tab in the Date and Time Properties dialog box and set a time and date that are close to the current values. Finally, check that your Internet firewall software allows time synchronization.

You can make your computer's startup quieter by turning off the sound that Windows 7 makes each time you turn on or restart your PC.

Windows 7 plays a sound when it starts, and this is often useful because it tells you that the Windows 7 desktop is about to appear, so your computer will soon be ready for use.

However, this sound can be an annoyance if your computer is located in a quiet office, or if you are starting up your home computer early in the morning while other members of your household are still sleeping.

To get rid of this problem, you can configure Windows 7 to bypass the startup sound.

① Click Start.
② Click Control Panel.

The Control Panel window appears.

③ Click Hardware and Sound.

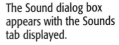

The Hardware and Sound window appears.

④ Click Change System Sounds.

The Sound dialog box appears with the Sounds tab displayed.

⑤ Click Play Windows Startup Sound (✓ changes to ▢).

⑥ Click OK.

The next time you start your computer, Windows 7 does not play the startup sound.

More Options!

Disabling the startup sound makes your PC quieter at startup, but not completely silent. Windows 7 still plays a short sound effect when you log on. To turn off the logon sound, follow steps 1 to 4 to display the Sounds tab. In the Program Events list, click Windows Logon. In the Sounds drop-down list, choose None and then click OK.

More Options!

To turn off the sounds that Windows 7 makes when it exits and logs you off, follow steps 1 to 4 to display the Sounds tab. In the Program Events list, first click Exit Windows and choose None in the Sounds list, then click Windows Logoff and choose None in the Sounds list. Click OK to put the settings into effect.

Reduce System Volume When Making a Phone Call

If you use your computer to place outgoing phone calls or receive incoming phone calls, you can configure Windows 7 to automatically reduce the system volume when you are on a call.

If you use your PC to listen to music or watch TV, you probably turn down the volume when you are about the make a call, or when a call comes in. Unfortunately, your computer might still make error message sounds or other noises while you are on the phone, so many people

turn down or mute the system volume for phone calls.

If you use your PC to place and receive phone calls, you can take advantage of the fact that Windows 7 can recognize this phone activity. Specifically, you can configure Windows 7 to automatically reduce or mute the system volume when it detects that you are either initiating a phone call or are receiving a phone call.

① Click Start.

② Click Control Panel.

The Control Panel window appears.

③ Click Hardware and Sound.

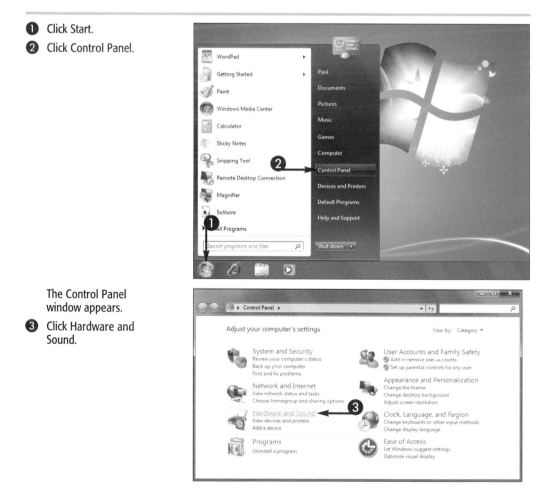

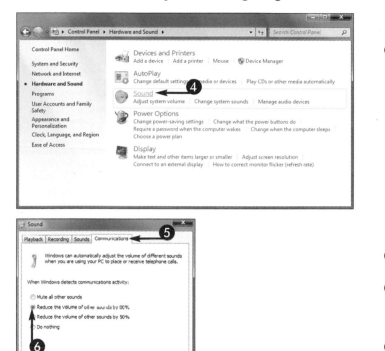

The Hardware and Sound window appears.

④ Click Sound.

The Sound dialog box appears.

⑤ Click the Communications tab.

⑥ Click the audio adjustment option you prefer (◯ changes to ●).

⑦ Click OK.

Windows 7 adjusts the sound volume automatically the next time you place or receive a phone call through your PC.

TIPS

Remove It!

If you prefer to maintain control over your system volume at all times, you can configure Windows 7 to not automatically adjust the system volume when it detects PC-based phone use. Follow steps 1 to 5 to display the Communications tab. Click the Do Nothing option (◯ changes to ●) and then click OK. See the next tip to learn how to control system volume yourself.

Do It Yourself!

If you configured Windows 7 to not automatically adjust the system volume for phone calls, as described in the previous tip, you can control the volume of system sounds manually. Click the Volume icon () in the taskbar's notification area and then click Mixer to open the Volume Mixer. Click and drag the System Sounds slider to set the volume level, or click the Mute System Sounds icon to silence system sounds.

Configure a Device Using Device Stage

You can use Windows 7's new Device Stage feature to configure device settings, as well as run common device tasks.

In previous versions of Windows, interacting with a device usually meant interacting with several different Windows features. For a document scanner, for example, you might use Windows Fax and Scan to run a scan, Device Manager to change the scanner's properties, and perhaps a proprietary program to configure features such as scan profiles.

Windows 7 aims to change all that by offering a single location where you can interact with a device. This location is called Device Stage and, depending on the device, you can use it to run device tasks, configure device properties, set up device features, and more.

Only a limited number of multi-function printers and mobile phones currently support Device Stage, but expect many new devices to be Device Stage–compatible in the near future.

① Turn on and attach the device you want to work with.

② Click Start.

③ Click Devices and Printers.

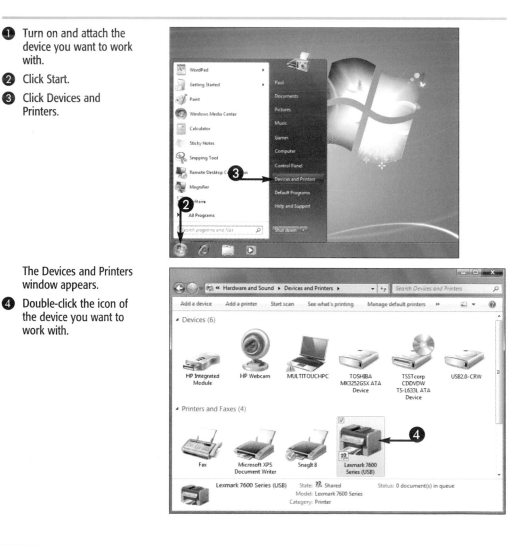

The Devices and Printers window appears.

④ Double-click the icon of the device you want to work with.

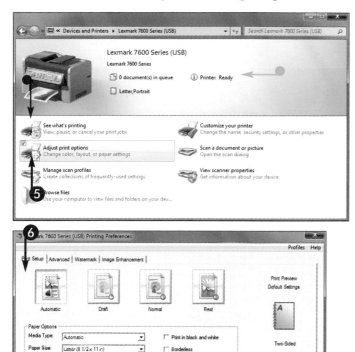

The Device Stage window for the device appears.

Note: *The layout of the Device Stage window varies from device to device.*

- General information about the device, as well as the current status of the device, appears here.

- Tasks associated with the device appear here.

5 Double-click an option to customize your device.

Note: *The name of the option depends on the device. Also, devices such as multi-function printers may have several customization options.*

A dialog box for the device appears.

6 Use the dialog box options to configure the device.

7 Click OK.

TIPS

More Options!

You do not have to open the Device Stage window to work with the tasks and properties of most devices. In the Devices and Printers window, right-click the device icon to see a shortcut menu that offers a wide variety of commands. These commands include standard tasks associated with the device, as well as options for configuring the device.

Remove It!

If a device is not working properly, it appears in the Devices and Printers window with a black exclamation mark inside a yellow triangle (⚠). To attempt to fix the problem, click the device and then click Troubleshoot in the taskbar. If this does not solve the problem and you cannot figure out what is wrong, you can remove the device by right-clicking it and then clicking Remove device.

Boosting Your Computer's Security and Privacy

Many security experts believe that most violations of security and privacy occur not remotely from the Internet, as you might expect, but locally, right at your computer. That is, computer security and privacy are compromised most often by someone simply sitting down at another person's machine while that person is not around. That makes some sense, because having physical access to a computer allows an intruder to install malicious programs, disable security features, and poke around for sensitive data, such as passwords and credit card numbers.

If you are worried about having your security or privacy compromised by someone having direct access to your computer, Windows 7 offers a reassuringly large number of tools and features that you can use to lock up your computer. In this chapter, you learn about most of these tools, many of which are quite simple to implement. Techniques such as activating parental controls, adding a password to your account, putting your screen saver in security mode, and clearing your list of recently used documents and media files are all easy to set up, but provide greatly enhanced security and privacy. You also learn more advanced techniques that take security to the next level, including using advanced file permissions and preventing other people from even starting your computer.

Quick Tips

You can make computing safer for your children by activating the Windows 7 parental controls feature.

Many aspects of computing are not safe for young children. For example, many games have violent or mature content that should not be seen by children younger than a certain age.

You can restrict games and other content by activating the *parental controls* feature. Parental controls also enable you to set time limits on computer use.

Parental controls are also useful for keeping your computer safe from the activities of innocent or inexperienced users. For example, you can prevent children from running certain programs that might be confusing or too difficult to use.

Note that for parental controls to work, you must set up separate user accounts for the children who use your computer. When you create these accounts, make sure you set them up as Standard user accounts.

1 Click Start.

2 Click Control Panel.

The Control Panel window appears.

3 Click Set Up Parental Controls for Any User.

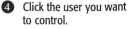

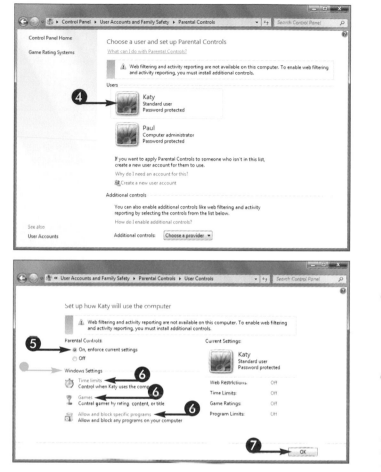

The Parental Controls window appears.

④ Click the user you want to control.

The User Controls window appears.

⑤ Click the On, Enforce Current Settings option (○ changes to ◉).

● The Settings links become available.

⑥ Click the links in the Settings group to configure controls for the user.

Note: See the next three tasks to learn the specifics of configuring these settings.

⑦ Click OK.

Windows 7 enforces parental controls for the user.

TIPS

Important!

If you have not yet created accounts for your children, you can launch the process right from the Parental Controls window. Follow steps 1 to 3, and then click the Create a New User Account link. In the Create New User window, type the user name and then click Create Account. This creates a Standard user with no password. You can click the User Accounts link to add a password to the account.

More Options!

The parental controls that come with Windows 7 do not include Web filtering, which lets you block objectionable material on the Web and configure Windows 7 to not display certain Web sites and content. You can download a Web filter control from a third-party provider, and then select it using the Additional Controls list in the Parental Controls window.

You can configure a user's parental controls to specify when that user is allowed to use the computer.

Most children enjoy using a computer, and many would gladly stay on the PC for hours at a time. If you prefer that your children spend time doing other things, such as homework or eating meals with the family, then you need to set rules about the times when they are allowed to use the computer.

Because you may not always be around to enforce those rules, you can get Windows 7 to help you. If you have activated parental controls for a user, you can use the Time Restrictions feature to control when the user can access the computer. The Time Restrictions window enables you to specify blocks of time when the user is not allowed to access the PC. During those times, the person is not allowed to log on the computer. If the person is on the computer when a blocked time arrives, Windows 7 automatically locks the computer.

① Activate parental controls for the user you want to restrict.

Note: See the task "Protect Children by Activating Parental Controls."

② Click Time Limits.

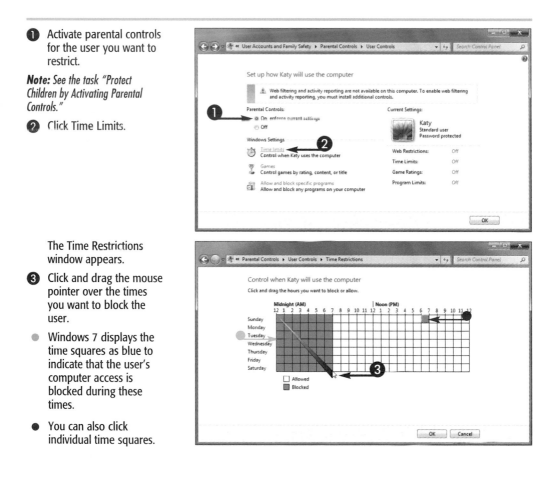

The Time Restrictions window appears.

③ Click and drag the mouse pointer over the times you want to block the user.

● Windows 7 displays the time squares as blue to indicate that the user's computer access is blocked during these times.

● You can also click individual time squares.

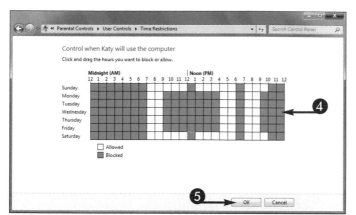

④ Block out all the times when you want to prevent the user from accessing the computer.

⑤ Click OK.

Windows 7 begins enforcing the time limits for the user.

● If the user is logged on when a restricted time nears, Windows 7 displays the alert shown here.

When the restricted time arrives, the user is locked out of the computer.

TIPS

Did You Know?

If the child is already logged on, the Parental Controls icon (🖳) appears in the notification area. If the user clicks the notification area arrow and then positions the mouse pointer over the Parental Controls icon, Windows 7 displays a banner that shows how much time is left before the next restricted time occurs:

Parent Controls are turned on. Time left: 0hrs, 5 mins

Important!

You might think that Windows 7 logs the user off at the end of the allowed time, but that is not the case. Instead, Windows 7 leaves the user's session running in the background. This is important, because it means that the user does not lose unsaved changes in any running programs. Instead, the next time the user is able to log on, Windows 7 restores the user's programs and documents exactly as they were before.

You can configure a user's parental controls to specify the programs that user is allowed to run.

Assuming you have set up your children with Standard user accounts, it is welcome news to know that Windows 7 security is structured in such a way that Standard users cannot do much overall harm to a computer. However, that does not mean you should give your children the run of the PC. There are plenty of executable files on a typical Windows 7 system, and the vast majority of them should be off-limits. However, anything can happen with an overly curious or fumble-fingered child at the keyboard.

To prevent mishaps or confusion caused by starting an improper program, you can configure a child's parental controls so that he or she can start only specific programs.

① Activate parental controls for the user you want to restrict.

Note: *See the task "Protect Children by Activating Parental Controls."*

② Click Allow and Block Specific Programs.

The Application Restrictions window appears.

③ Click *User* Can Only Use the Programs I Allow (where *User* is the name of the user; ⊙ changes to ⊙).

● Windows 7 displays a list of the programs on the computer.

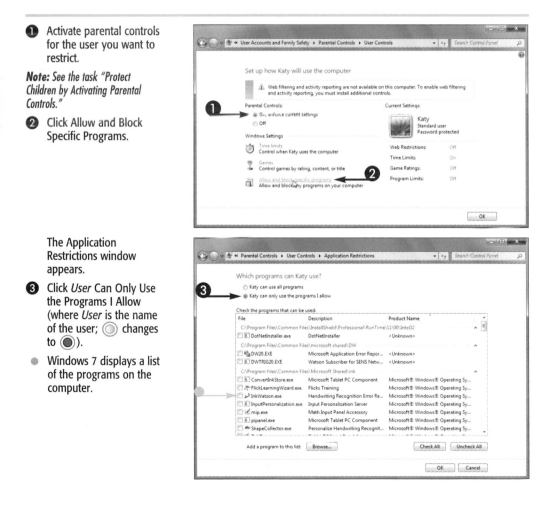

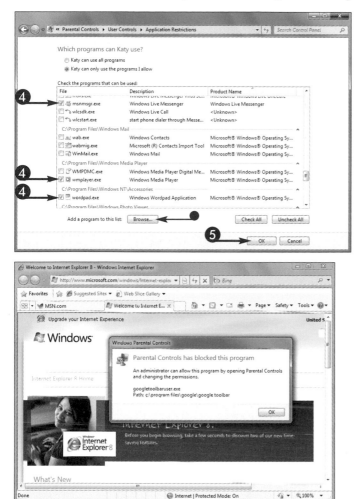

④ Click the check box beside each program that you want the user to run (□ changes to ☑).

● If a program does not appear on the list, you can click Browse and then use the Open dialog box to locate the program.

⑤ Click OK.

If the user attempts to run a program that you did not select, he or she sees the dialog box shown here.

TIPS

Did You Know?

The list of programs in the Application Restrictions window does not include every application on the PC: It bypasses all the games that are installed (including the games that come with Windows 7). To learn how to restrict games, see the next task.

Important!

The list of programs in the Application Restrictions window also does not include programs that Windows 7 has declared essential, such as Windows Explorer and Windows Help and Support. If you click Browse and choose one of these essential programs, you see a dialog box that says "This application is always allowed to run."

You can configure a user's parental controls to specify the types of video games that user is allowed to play.

If you have kids, chances are, they have a computer — either their own or one shared with the rest of the family — and, chances are, they play games on that computer. Playing games is in itself not a problem, and most games benefit a child's problem-solving skills and eye-hand coordination. However, some games contain content unsuitable for younger children, so supervising game play is best.

Unfortunately, it is not always possible to spare the time or the energy to sit beside your child

for every gaming session. It is also true that the older the child, the more likely that a hovering adult will not be appreciated. This means that, for all but the youngest users, your children will have some unsupervised gaming time at the computer.

To avoid worrying about whether your 8-year-old is playing Grand Theft Auto or something equally unsuitable, you can take advantage of the Game Controls feature, which enables you to control gaming using ratings and content descriptors.

① Activate parental controls for the user you want to restrict.

Note: *See the task "Protect Children by Activating Parental Controls."*

② Click Games.

The Game Controls window appears.

③ Click Set Game Ratings.

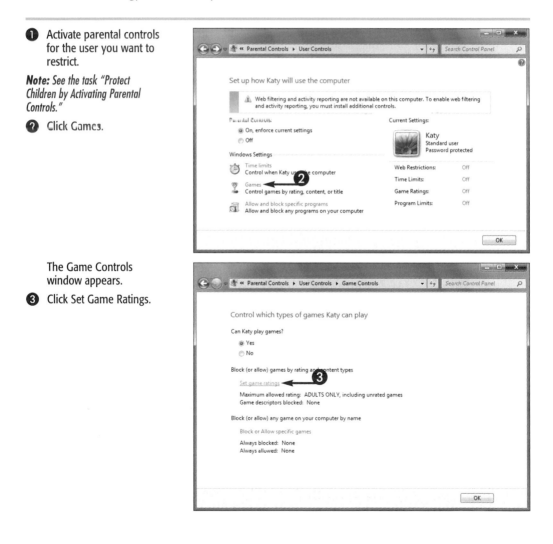

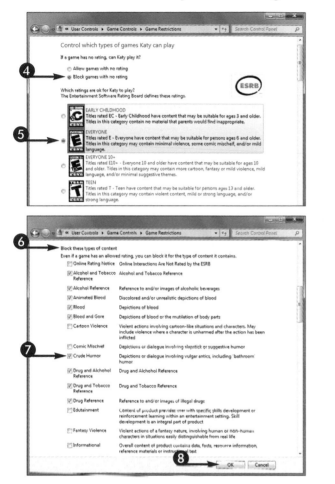

The Game Restrictions window appears.

④ Click Block Games with No Rating (◯ changes to ◉).

⑤ Click the maximum rating that you want to allow your child to play (◯ changes to ◉).

Note: See the tip on this page to learn how to set the game rating system.

⑥ Scroll down to display the Block These Types of Content section.

⑦ Click the check box beside each type of content you do not want the child to see (☐ changes to ☑).

⑧ Click OK.

Windows 7 applies the game restrictions to the user.

Important!

Before setting up the game controls, you should select the game rating system you want to use. In the Parental Controls window, click the Game Rating Systems link to display the Game Rating Systems window. Click the rating system you prefer (◯ changes to ◉). The most commonly used rating system is the one maintained by the Entertainment Software Rating Board (ESRB). Click OK to return to the Parental Controls window.

More Options!

You can also block or allow specific games installed on the computer. In the Game Controls window, click the Block or Allow Specific Games link to open the Game Overrides window. For each game listed, click either Always Allow or Always Block (◯ changes to ◉). To allow or block a game based on its rating, click User Rating Setting (◯ changes to ◉).

If you share files with other network users, you can configure Windows 7 to control which users can access your files and what actions they can perform on those files.

If your computer is part of a network, it is common to give other users access to some of your files by sharing one or more folders with the network. By default, Windows 7 runs the Sharing Wizard when you opt to share a folder. The Sharing Wizard enables you to choose which users can share the folder and how each person shares it: with Read/Write permissions

(the user can make changes) or with Read permissions (the user cannot make changes).

If you want to apply more sophisticated sharing options such as the folder permissions discussed in the task "Protect a File or Folder with Permissions," then you need to switch to Windows 7's advanced sharing features. These features enable you to set permissions for specific users and for groups of users (such as Administrators or Guests), create multiple shares for the same folder, and more.

① Click Start.

② Click Control Panel.

The Control Panel window appears.

③ Click Appearance and Personalization.

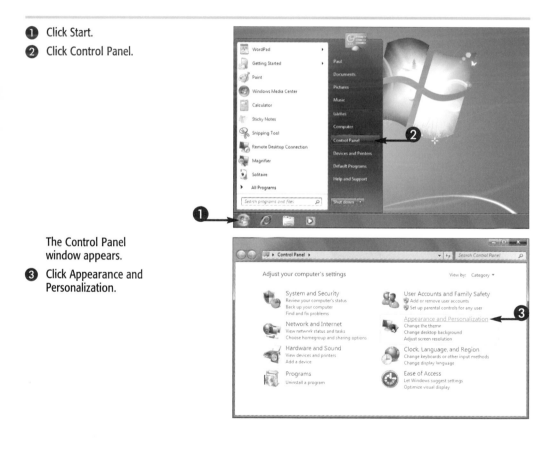

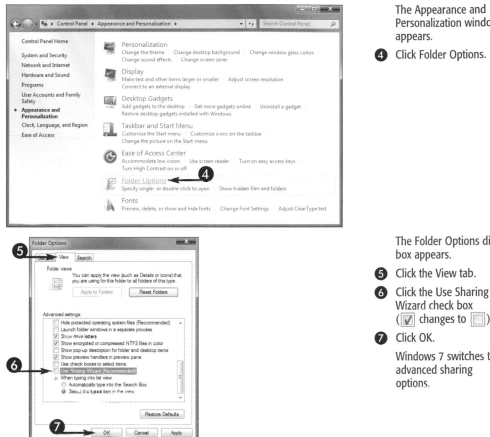

The Appearance and Personalization window appears.

④ Click Folder Options.

The Folder Options dialog box appears.

⑤ Click the View tab.

⑥ Click the Use Sharing Wizard check box (☑ changes to ☐).

⑦ Click OK.

Windows 7 switches to its advanced sharing options.

Did You Know?

If you have a folder window open, a quicker way to get to the Folder Options dialog box is to click Organize, Folder, and Search Options. Alternatively, click Start, type **folder** in the Start menu's Search box, and then click Folder Options in the search results.

Important!

If your computer is part of a workgroup, you can set up an account for each user on every computer in the workgroup. For example, if the user Paul has an account on computer A, you must also set up an account for Paul on computers B, C, and so on. You must assign a password to the account and you must use the same password for the account on all the computers.

Protect a File or Folder with Permissions

Windows 7 offers a sophisticated file security system called permissions. *Permissions* specify exactly what the groups or users can do with the contents of the protected folder. There are six types of permissions.

With **Full Control** permission, users can perform any of the actions listed. Users can also change permissions. With **Modify** permission, users can view the folder contents, open files, edit files, create new files and subfolders, delete files, and run programs. With

Read & Execute permission, users can view the folder contents, open files, and run programs. With **List Folder Contents** permission, users can view the folder contents. With **Read** permission, users can open files, but cannot edit them. Finally, with **Write** permission, users can create new files and subfolders and open and edit existing files.

In each case, you can either allow the permission or deny it.

---

① In a folder window, click the folder or file that you want to protect.

② Click Organize.

③ Click Properties.

Note: *You can also right-click the folder or file and then click Properties.*

The item's Properties dialog box appears.

④ Click the Security tab.

● The Groups or User Names list displays the current groups and users that have permissions for the folder.

Note: *The name in parentheses takes the form* **COMPUTER\ Name**, *where* **COMPUTER** *is the computer's name and* **Name** *is the user or group name.*

⑤ Click Edit.

The Permissions dialog box appears.

⑥ Click Add.

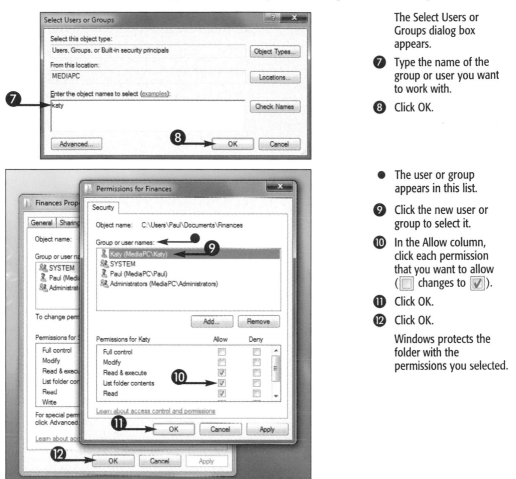

The Select Users or Groups dialog box appears.

⑦ Type the name of the group or user you want to work with.

⑧ Click OK.

● The user or group appears in this list.

⑨ Click the new user or group to select it.

⑩ In the Allow column, click each permission that you want to allow (☐ changes to ☑).

⑪ Click OK.

⑫ Click OK.

Windows protects the folder with the permissions you selected.

TIPS

More Options!

In the Select Users or Groups dialog box, if you are not sure about a user or group name, click Advanced and then Find Now. Windows 7 displays a list of all the available users and groups. Click the name you want in the list and then click OK.

More Options!

You can override a user's group permissions by clicking the corresponding check boxes in the Deny column (☐ changes to ☑). For example, to prevent a member of the Administrators group from viewing the contents of your folder, click the List Folder Contents in the Deny column check box (☐ changes to ☑).

You can configure your Windows 7 user account with a password. Another person cannot log on to your account unless he or she knows the password.

If your user account does not have a password, then your Windows 7 system is not very secure. If you have no other accounts on your system and your account has no password, you are taken directly to the Windows 7 desktop. That may be convenient not only for you, but also for a system snoop who starts your machine while you are not around. With full

access to the system, the snoop can install a virus, a Trojan horse — a program that enables the hacker to control your computer from the Internet — or a program that monitors your keystrokes to grab your passwords. It is also easy for the intruder to root around in your files looking for sensitive information or even to trash your precious data.

The first and most important step towards preventing all of this is to protect your user account with a password.

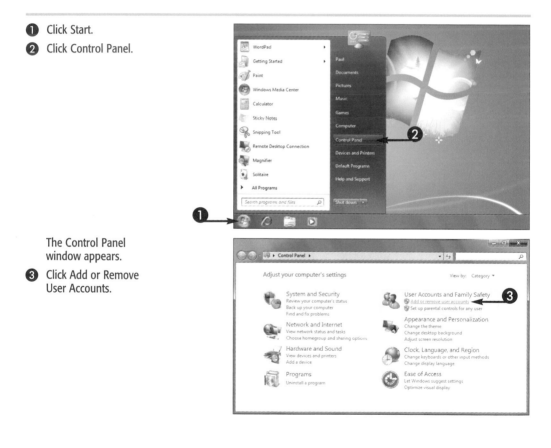

① Click Start.

② Click Control Panel.

The Control Panel window appears.

③ Click Add or Remove User Accounts.

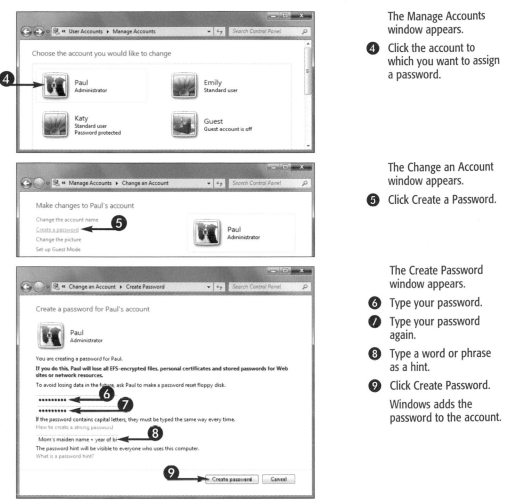

The Manage Accounts window appears.

④ Click the account to which you want to assign a password.

The Change an Account window appears.

⑤ Click Create a Password.

The Create Password window appears.

⑥ Type your password.

⑦ Type your password again.

⑧ Type a word or phrase as a hint.

⑨ Click Create Password.

Windows adds the password to the account.

TIP

Important!

Here are some ideas for creating and protecting a strong password:

- Use a password that is at least eight characters long.
- Because Windows 7 passwords are case-sensitive, mix uppercase and lowercase letters.
- Include at least one number and at least one punctuation mark in your password.
- When you choose a password, select one that nobody can guess, but one that you can remember.
- Do not use obvious passwords such as your name or your birth date.
- Do not write down your password.
- Do not tell your password to anyone.

You can configure Windows 7's user account control (UAC) to suit the way you work.

The basic idea behind the UAC security model is to prevent harmful programs such as viruses and Trojan horses from installing themselves on your PC and changing your system settings. It does this by monitoring your system for four types of events: a program initiating a software install; a program changing system settings; a user changing system settings; and a user running high-level Windows 7 tools such as the Registry Editor.

In Windows Vista, UAC would prompt you for permission to perform any of these events,

which meant most users ended up supplying Windows with administrator credentials quite often. Also, when prompting for credentials Windows Vista would switch to *secure desktop mode*, which meant that you could not do anything else with Windows Vista until you either supplied your credentials or cancelled the operation.

In Windows 7, Microsoft has tweaked UAC to make it configurable so you can tailor the prompts to suit your situation. Microsoft also set up the default configuration of UAC so that it now only rarely prompts you for elevation when you change the settings on your PC.

---

① Click Start.

② Type **user**.

③ Click Change User Account Control Settings.

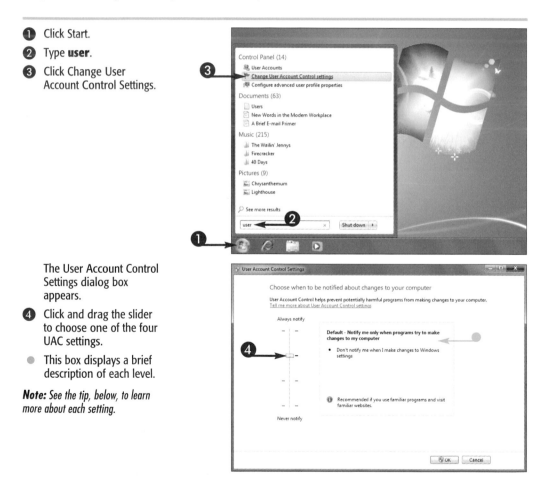

The User Account Control Settings dialog box appears.

④ Click and drag the slider to choose one of the four UAC settings.

● This box displays a brief description of each level.

Note: *See the tip, below, to learn more about each setting.*

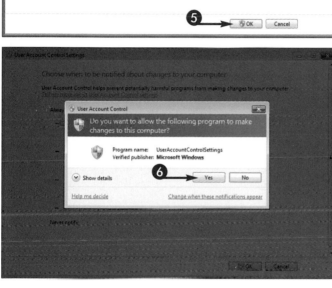

⑤ Click OK.

The User Account Control dialog box appears.

⑥ Click Yes.

Note: If you are not currently using an administrator account, you must provide the password for an administrator account on your system.

Windows 7 applies the new UAC setting.

Note: If you turned off UAC, you must restart your computer to put the new setting into effect.

TIP

Did You Know?
The top level (Always Notify) works much like UAC in Windows Vista because you are prompted for elevation when you change Windows settings and when programs try to change settings and install software. The second highest level is the default setting, and it prompts you for elevation only when programs try to change settings and install software. This level uses secure desktop mode to display the UAC dialog box.

The second lowest level is the same as the Default level — that is, it prompts you for elevations only when programs try to change settings and install software — but this level does not use secure desktop mode when displaying the UAC dialog box. The lowest level (Never Notify) turns off UAC. This level requires a restart to put it into effect.

You can configure Windows 7 to require users to press Ctrl+Alt+Delete before they can log on to your computer. This prevents a malicious program activated at startup from capturing your password.

Protecting your Windows 7 user account with a password (as described earlier in this chapter), though an excellent idea, is not foolproof. Hackers are an endlessly resourceful bunch, and some of the smarter ones figured out a way to defeat the user account password system. The trick is that they install a virus or Trojan horse program — usually via an

infected e-mail message or malicious Web site — that loads itself when you start your computer. This program then displays a *fake* version of the Windows 7 Welcome screen. When you type your user name and password into this dialog box, the program records it and your system security is compromised.

To thwart this clever ruse, Windows 7 enables you to configure your system so that you must press Ctrl+Alt+Delete before you can log on. This key combination ensures that the authentic Welcome screen appears.

① Click Start.

② Click All Programs.

Note: When you click All Programs, the command name changes to Back.

③ Click Accessories.

④ Click Run.

The Run dialog box appears.

⑤ In the Open text box, type **control userpasswords2**.

⑥ Click OK.

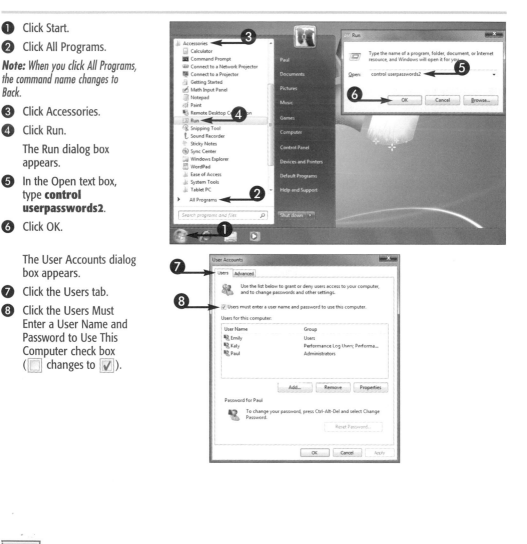

The User Accounts dialog box appears.

⑦ Click the Users tab.

⑧ Click the Users Must Enter a User Name and Password to Use This Computer check box (☐ changes to ☑).

⑨ Click the Advanced tab.

⑩ Click Require Users to Press Ctrl+Alt+Delete check box (☐ changes to ☑).

⑪ Click OK.

Windows now requires each user to press Ctrl+Alt+Delete to log on.

Lock Your Computer to Prevent Others from Using It

You can lock your computer to prevent another person from working with your computer while you are away from your desk.

Security measures such as advanced file permissions and encryption, which are covered in this chapter, rely on the fact that you have entered the appropriate user name and password to log on to your Windows 7 account. In other words, after you log on, you become a "trusted" user.

But what happens when you leave your desk? If you remain logged on to Windows 7, any other person who sits down at your computer can take advantage of your trusted-user status to view and work with secure files. You could prevent this by shutting down your computer every time you leave your desk, but that is not practical. A better solution is to lock your system before leaving your desk. Anyone who tries to use your computer must enter your password to access the Windows 7 desktop.

See also "Automatically Lock Your Computer," next, to learn how to configure Windows 7 to lock your computer after it has been idle for a while.

LOCK YOUR COMPUTER

① Click Start.

② Click the arrow beside the Shut Down button.

③ Click Lock.

The Windows 7 Welcome screen appears.

● The word Locked appears below your user name.

UNLOCK YOUR COMPUTER

① Click inside the Password box.

② Type your password.

③ Click the Go arrow or press Enter.

The Windows 7 desktop appears.

Did You Know?

If you need to leave your desk in a hurry, Windows 7 offers a couple of quick methods for locking your computer. Probably the quickest way to lock your computer is to press the Windows Logo+L keys. Alternatively, press Ctrl+Alt+Delete and then click Lock Computer.

Try This!

If you want a one-click method for locking your computer, right-click the desktop, click New, Shortcut, and then type the following: **rundll32 user32.dll, LockWorkStation**. Click Next, and then click Finish. Drag the shortcut icon and drop it on the taskbar. You can now click the pinned taskbar icon to lock your PC.

You can configure Windows 7 to automatically lock your computer after it has been idle for a specified time.

The previous task described how to lock your computer to prevent an intruder from accessing your desktop while you are away from your PC. The locking technique is easy enough to do, but the hard part is *remembering* to do it. If you are late for a meeting or other appointment, locking up your machine is probably the last thing on your mind as you dash out the door. If you later remember that you forgot to lock your computer, you may spend the next while worrying about your PC.

To avoid the worrying and to reduce the chance that some snoop will access your desktop if you forget to lock it, you can configure Windows 7 to lock automatically after a period of inactivity. Previous versions of Windows required a screen saver to do this, but not Windows 7.

① Click Start.

② Click Control Panel.

The Control Panel window appears.

③ Click Change the Theme.

The Personalization window appears.

Note: *A quicker way to get to the Personalization window is to right-click the desktop and then click Personalize.*

④ Click Screen Saver.

⑤ Click On Resume, Display Logon Screen (☐ changes to ☑).

⑥ Use the Wait spin box to set the number of minutes of idle that must pass before Windows 7 locks your computer.

⑦ Click OK.

Windows 7 now automatically locks your PC when it has been idle for the number of minutes you specified in step 6.

TIP

Check It Out!

Windows 7 is also configured by default to display the logon screen when your computer wakes up from sleep mode. To make sure this setting is activated, click Start, and then click Control Panel to open the Control Panel window. Click Hardware and Sound, and then click Require a Password When the Computer Wakes.

In the System Settings window, examine the options in the Password Protection on Wakeup section. If the Don't Require a Password option is activated, click Change Settings That Are Currently Unavailable to enable the options. (You may need to enter administrator credentials at this point.) Click the Require a Password option (◯ changes to ◉), and then click Save Changes.

You can configure Windows 7 to require a special media to be inserted in your computer before starting up. Without the media, Windows 7 does not allow anyone to log on to the computer.

As a security feature, Windows 7 stores passwords in encrypted form and Windows 7 uses a system key to decrypt the passwords. This system key is normally stored on your computer, and if for some reason the system key were lost, you would not be able to start your computer. For this reason, the system key is also called a startup key.

You can take advantage of this security precaution to make sure that no unauthorized user can start your computer. You do that by having Windows 7 move the startup key to a removable media such as a USB flash drive. If the media is not inserted into the computer at startup, Windows 7 does not allow anyone to log on to the system. In fact, Windows 7 does not even display the Welcome screen, so an unauthorized user cannot even try to guess your password.

You must first configure your removable media to use drive A, so see "Assign a Different Letter to a Disk Drive" in Chapter 4.

① Insert a removable drive, such as a USB flash drive, into your computer, and configure it to use drive A.

② Click Start.

③ Type **command**.

④ Right-click Command Prompt.

⑤ Click Run as Administrator.

Note: *If the User Account Control dialog box appears, click Continue or type an administrator password and click Submit.*

The Command Prompt window appears.

⑥ Type **syskey**.

⑦ Press Enter.

⑧ Click Close to shut down the Command Prompt window.

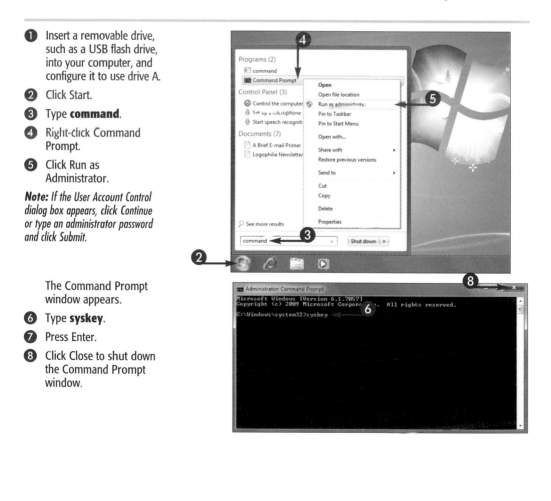

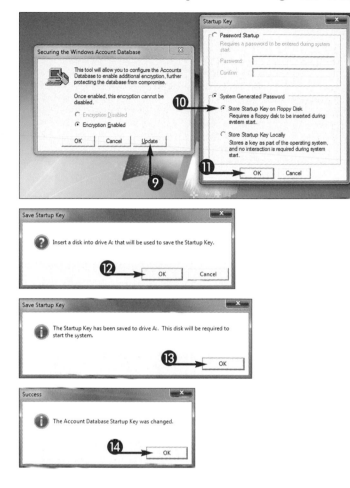

The Securing the Windows Account Database dialog box appears.

⑨ Click Update.

The Startup Key dialog box appears.

⑩ Click the Store Startup Key on Floppy Disk option (◯ changes to ⦿).

⑪ Click OK.

The Save Startup Key dialog box appears.

⑫ Click OK.

Windows 7 saves the startup key to the removable drive and then displays a confirmation dialog box.

⑬ Click OK.

The Success dialog box appears.

⑭ Click OK.

Windows 7 now requires the removable drive that contains the startup key to be inserted each time you log on.

TIPS

Caution!
After saving the startup key to the removable drive, Windows 7 looks for the drive when you start your computer. If Windows 7 does not find the key, the Windows 7 Startup Key Disk dialog box appears. You must insert the drive and then click OK. If you lose or damage the drive, you cannot start Windows 7, so keep the drive in a safe place. Also, be sure to make a backup copy of the drive.

Remove It!
If you decide later on that you no longer want to keep the startup key on a floppy disk, you can revert to storing the key on your computer. Follow steps 1 to 9, click the Store Startup Key Locally option (◯ changes to ⦿), and then click OK. Insert the removable drive that has the startup key, and then click OK.

To enhance your privacy, you can clear the Start menu's Recent Items list and Media Player's list of recently played media files so that other people who use your computer cannot see which documents you have been working on.

The Start menu's Recent Items list is handy because it enables you to quickly open the last 15 documents you have worked on. However, if you know that someone else is going to be using your computer, and you do not have a separate user account set up for that person,

you may not want him or her to see what is on your Recent Items list. To prevent this, you can clear the list.

Windows Media Player maintains a list of files that you have played recently, and it also keeps track of the addresses of Internet media you have recently opened, as well as all the information you have downloaded about the audio CDs and DVDs you played. If someone else is going to use Windows Media Player on your computer, you can maintain your media privacy by clearing all this stored information.

CLEAR THE RECENT ITEMS LIST

① Click Start.

② Right-click Recent Items.

③ Click Clear Recent Items List.

● Windows 7 clears the My Recent Items list.

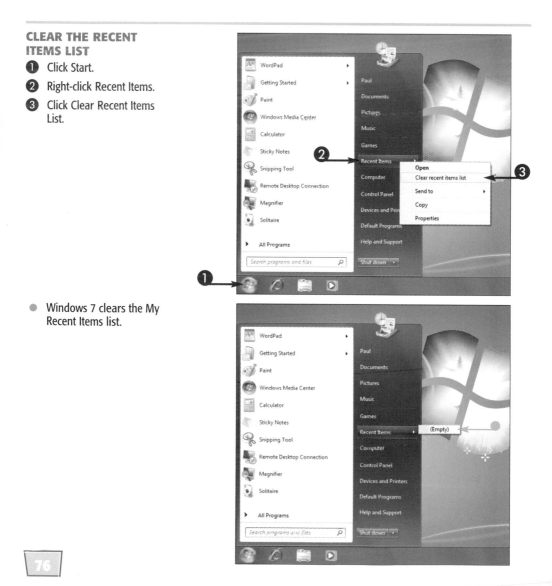

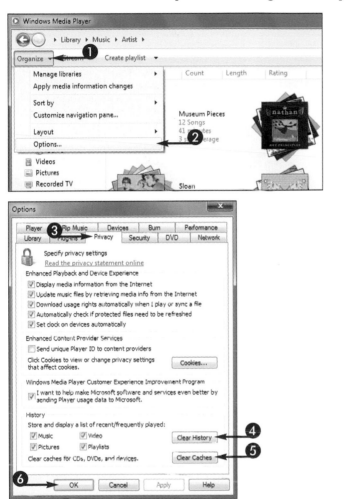

CLEAR RECENT MEDIA

① In Windows Media Player, click Organize.

② Click Options.

The Options dialog box appears.

③ Click the Privacy tab.

④ Click Clear History to clear the list of recently viewed media files and Internet addresses.

⑤ Click Clear Caches to clear the downloaded information about audio CDs and DVDs.

⑥ Click OK.

Windows Media Player no longer lists your recently used media files or Internet addresses.

![TIPS]

More Options!

You can configure Windows 7 to never save recently used documents. Right-click Start, click Properties, and then click the Store and Display Recently Opened Items in the Start Menu and the Taskbar check box (☑ changes to ☐). In the Media Player Privacy tab, click the Music, Video, Pictures, and Playlists check boxes (☑ changes to ☐).

Did You Know?

The easiest way to maintain the privacy of your documents is to create separate user accounts for each person who uses your computer. Click Start, Control Panel, and then click Add or Remove User Accounts. For maximum privacy, make everyone else a Standard user and assign a password to your account, as described earlier in this chapter.

You can prevent damage from some types of malicious programming by activating a feature that stops those programs from running code in protected portions of your computer's memory.

Windows 7 reserves some of your computer's memory as *system memory*, meant for use by Windows itself and by your programs. Windows reserves the rest of the memory for your open documents and other data. When programmers code software, they usually include fixed-size memory locations called *buffers* that hold data. Programs that require

more data grab it from the hard drive and fill up the buffer.

Unfortunately, some poorly programmed software does not include a mechanism that watches for and prevents a *buffer overrun* — when a piece of data larger than the buffer size is loaded into the buffer. The extra data spills over into the system memory, resulting in system crashes. Some hackers use this flaw to deliberately crash or damage systems or even to run malicious code. Windows 7 includes a feature called Data Execution Prevention (DEP) that prevents buffer overruns, and so protects your computer from these attacks.

① Click Start.

② Type **systemproperties advanced**.

③ Click systemproperties advanced in the search results.

Windows 7 opens the System Properties dialog box with the Advanced tab displayed.

④ In the Performance group, click Settings.

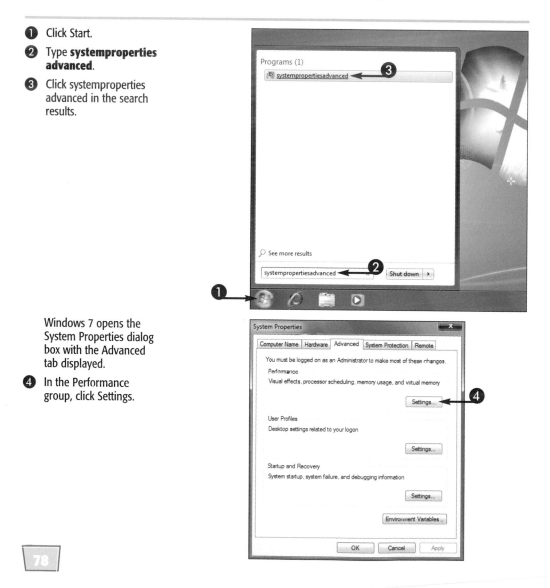

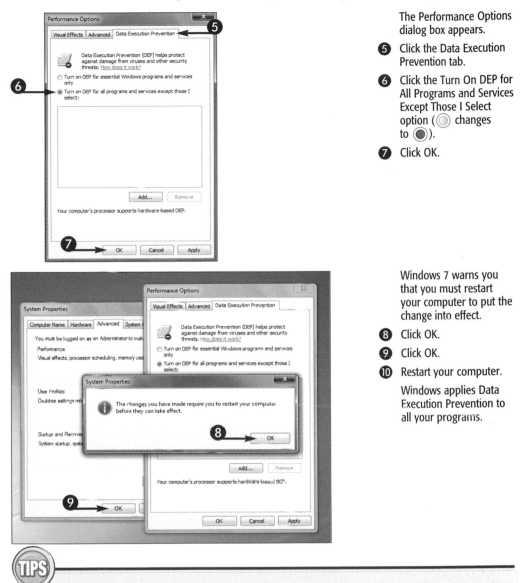

The Performance Options dialog box appears.

⑤ Click the Data Execution Prevention tab.

⑥ Click the Turn On DEP for All Programs and Services Except Those I Select option (◯ changes to ◉).

⑦ Click OK.

Windows 7 warns you that you must restart your computer to put the change into effect.

⑧ Click OK.

⑨ Click OK.

⑩ Restart your computer.

Windows applies Data Execution Prevention to all your programs.

TIPS

Important!

If Windows 7 detects a system memory intrusion, it shuts down the program causing the problem and displays an error message. You should immediately run a virus scan to ensure your computer is not infected. If there is no virus, the troublesome program may not work if DEP is turned on. Contact the software vendor to see if an updated version of the malfunctioning program is available.

More Options!

If you have trouble running a program when DEP is on, and your system is virus-free and no program update is available, you can turn off DEP for that program. Follow steps 1 to 6 and then click Add. Use the Open dialog box to display the program's folder, click the executable file that runs the program, and then click Open.

You can restore your system in the event of a major crash by performing a system image backup using Windows 7's system image backup feature.

Backing up your documents is important because a program crash, power failure, or imprudent deletion could cause one or more documents to be corrupted or lost.

However, PCs can also succumb to more major calamities, such as a virus or a hard drive failure. In such cases, you often lose access to your entire system. If you have just your documents backed up, you can restore them,

but first you must reinstall all your programs and devices, reconfigure Windows 7, apply patches and security fixes, and perform other chores to get your system back to where it was.

A much easier road to recovery is to create a *system image backup*, which is a complete backup of your entire system. If your computer crashes, you can restore it to its previous configuration just by restoring the system image backup. Windows 7 enables you to perform such a backup by using its system image backup feature, which is available only with Windows 7 Business, Enterprise, and Ultimate.

① Click Start.

② Click All Programs.

③ Click Maintenance.

④ Click Backup and Restore.

⑤ In the Backup and Restore window, click Create a System Image.

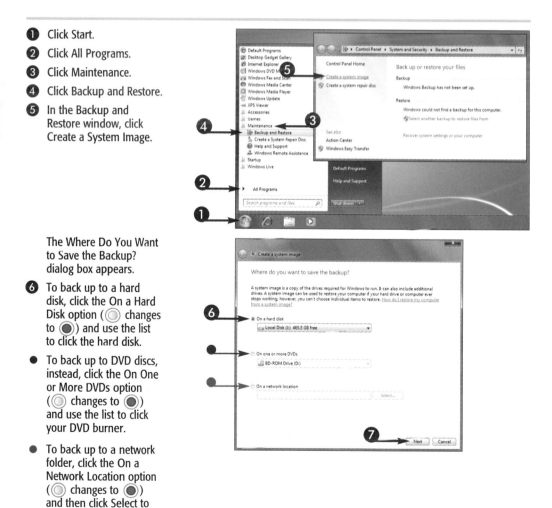

The Where Do You Want to Save the Backup? dialog box appears.

⑥ To back up to a hard disk, click the On a Hard Disk option (○ changes to ⦿) and use the list to click the hard disk.

● To back up to DVD discs, instead, click the On One or More DVDs option (○ changes to ⦿) and use the list to click your DVD burner.

● To back up to a network folder, click the On a Network Location option (○ changes to ⦿) and then click Select to choose the folder.

⑦ Click Next.

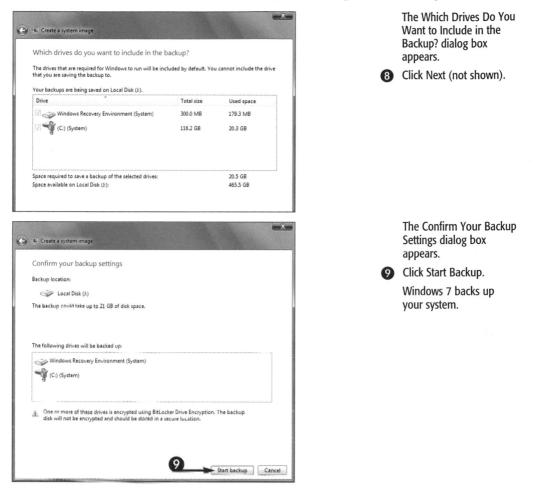

The Which Drives Do You Want to Include in the Backup? dialog box appears.

⑧ Click Next (not shown).

The Confirm Your Backup Settings dialog box appears.

⑨ Click Start Backup.

Windows 7 backs up your system.

Important!

To perform a system image backup to a hard drive, that drive must use the NTFS file system. To convert a drive to NTFS, click Start, All Programs, Accessories, right-click Command Prompt, and click Run as Administrator. Type **convert *d*: /fs:ntfs**, where *d* is the letter of the hard drive you want to convert, and press Enter. If Windows 7 asks to "dismount the volume," press Y and then Enter.

Apply It!

If you need to restore your system, restart your computer and press F8 to display the Advanced Boot Options. In the menu, select the Repair Your Computer option and then click Next. Enter a user name and password for an administrator account on your computer. In the System Recovery Options window, click System Image Recovery.

If you have a program that requires access to the Internet, you can prevent Windows Firewall from blocking it by setting the program up as an exception.

Many programs require access to the Internet. For example, some programs have enhanced versions of their Help systems online at the developer's Web site, and to use this content the program must be able to connect to the Web site. Another common scenario is a program that checks online to see if an update is available and, if so, it downloads and installs that update. Windows Firewall is a security

program that Windows 7 uses to prevent unauthorized access to your computer. It blocks all programs from accessing the Internet, except those set up as exceptions. If you have a program that cannot access the Internet, you can usually solve the problem by configuring that program as an exception to allow it through Windows Firewall.

Note that allowing a program through the firewall makes your computer a bit less secure, so you should perform this task only for programs that require Internet access.

① Click Start.

② Type **firewall**.

③ Click Allow a Program Through Windows Firewall.

The Allowed Programs window appears.

④ Click Change Settings.

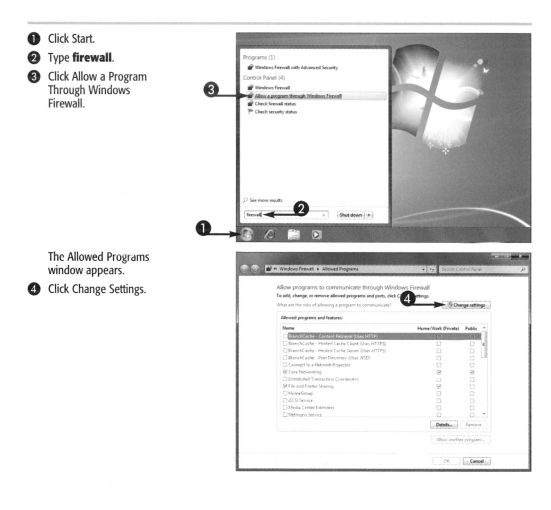

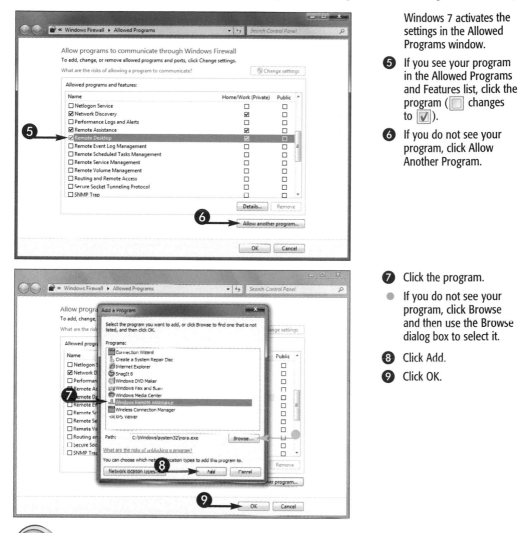

Windows 7 activates the settings in the Allowed Programs window.

⑤ If you see your program in the Allowed Programs and Features list, click the program (☐ changes to ☑).

⑥ If you do not see your program, click Allow Another Program.

⑦ Click the program.

● If you do not see your program, click Browse and then use the Browse dialog box to select it.

⑧ Click Add.

⑨ Click OK.

Reverse It!

After you add a program to the Windows Firewall exceptions list, the program appears in the Allowed Programs window with its check box activated. If the program no longer requires Internet access, you should disable its exception. Follow steps 1 to 4, click the program (☑ changes to ☐), and then click OK.

More Options!

In rare circumstances, a program requires access to the Internet via a specific port. (A *port* is an internal communications channel.) To allow this, follow steps 1 and 2, click Windows Firewall with Advanced Security, click Outbound Rules, and then click New Rule. Click Port, click Next, click TCP or UDP (◯ changes to ◉), type the port number, click Next, click Allow the Connection, click Next, click Next, type a name, and then click Finish.

You can encrypt your most sensitive and confidential files so that no other person can read them. Even if you have set up all the security mechanisms discussed in this chapter, it may still be possible for users to at least view your files. For example, hackers can use utilities to view the contents of your hard drive without logging on to Windows 7. That is not so much of a problem if what you are worried about is other people altering or deleting your files. However, it is a very big problem if your computer has files that contain extremely sensitive or confidential information: personal

financial files, medical histories, corporate salary data, trade secrets, business plans, and journals or diaries.

If you are worried about anyone viewing these or other for-your-eyes-only files, Windows 7 enables you to *encrypt* the file information. Encryption encodes the file so that it is completely unreadable by anyone unless they log on to your Windows 7 account. After you encrypt your files, you work with them exactly as you did before, with no noticeable loss of performance.

① In a folder window, click the folder containing the files that you want to encrypt.

Note: *You can encrypt individual files, but encrypting an entire folder is easier. That way, Windows 7 automatically encrypts new confidential files added to the folder.*

② Click Organize.

③ Click Properties.

The folder's Properties dialog box appears.

④ Click the General tab.

⑤ Click Advanced.

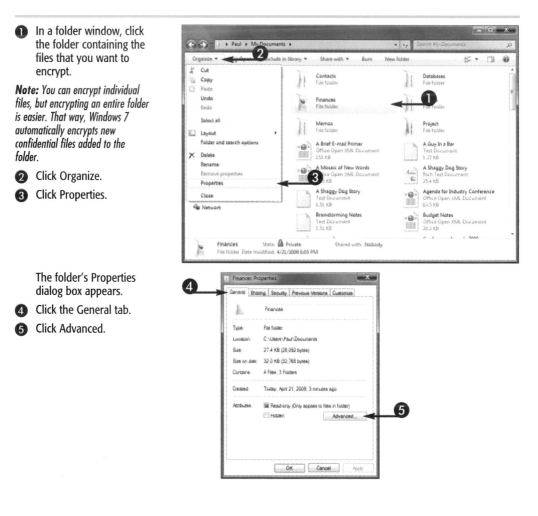

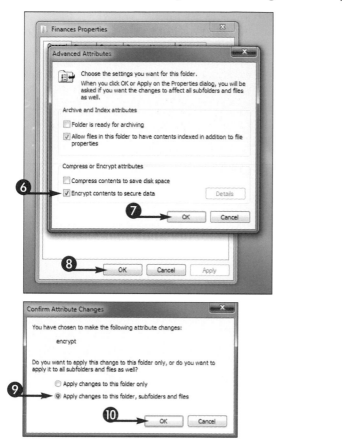

The Advanced Attributes dialog box appears.

6 Click the Encrypt Contents to Secure Data check box (☐ changes to ☑).

7 Click OK.

8 Click OK.

The Confirm Attribute Changes dialog box appears.

9 Click the Apply Changes to This Folder, Subfolders and Files option (◯ changes to ◉).

10 Click OK.

Windows 7 encrypts the folder's contents.

TIPS

Important!

To use file encryption, your hard drive must use NTFS (New Technology File System). To check the current file system, click Start then click Computer. In the Computer window, click the hard drive and then examine the File System information in the Details pane. If you need to convert a drive to NTFS, see the tip in the task "Safeguard Your Computer with a System Image Backup."

More Options!

By default, Windows 7 displays the names of encrypted files and folders in a green font, which helps you to differentiate these items from unencrypted files and folders. If you would rather see encrypted file and folder names in the regular font, click Organize and then click Folder and Search Options. Click the View tab, click the Show Encrypted or Compressed NTFS Files in Color check box (☑ changes to ☐), and then click OK.

Getting More Out of Files and Folders

Although you may use Windows 7 to achieve certain ends — write memos and letters, create presentations, play games, surf the Internet, and so on — you still have to deal with files and folders as part of your day-to-day work or play. Basic tasks such as copying and moving files, creating and renaming folders, and deleting unneeded files and folders are part of the Windows 7 routine.

Your goal should be to make all this file and folder maintenance *less* of a routine so that you have more time during the day to devote to more worthy pursuits. Fortunately, Windows 7 offers a number of

shortcuts and tweaks that can shorten file and folder tasks and make them more efficient. In this chapter you learn a number of these techniques.

For example, you learn how to display file extensions; how to open a file in a program other than the one with which it is associated; how to revert to a previous version of a file; and how to protect a file by making it read-only. You also learn how to customize the Send To menu to make copying files even faster; how to assign a different letter to a disk drive; how to hide drive letters; and how to split a hard drive into two partitions.

Quick Tips

You can make files easier to understand and work with by configuring Windows 7 to display file extensions.

A *file extension* is a code of three (or sometimes four or more) characters that appears at the end of a file name, after the period. For example, in the file name readme. txt, the "txt" part is the file extension. Windows 7 uses file extensions to determine a document's file type. For example, a file with a txt extension is a Text Document type, whereas a file with a bmp extension is a Bitmap Image type. In Windows 7, each file type is

associated with a particular application: Text Document files are associated with Notepad, Bitmap Image files are associated with Windows Photo Viewer, and so on. So file extensions are important because they determine a document's file type and the application that opens the document.

Windows 7 ships with file extensions turned off. This is often a problem because it is difficult to tell what file type a document uses without seeing the extension. Also, with file extensions hidden you cannot change the extension to something else.

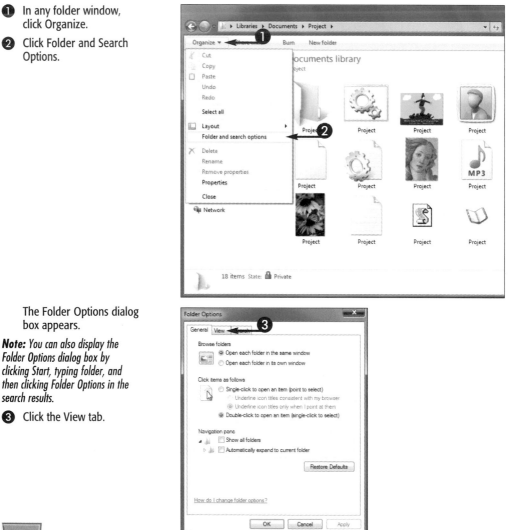

① In any folder window, click Organize.

② Click Folder and Search Options.

The Folder Options dialog box appears.

Note: You can also display the Folder Options dialog box by clicking Start, typing folder, and then clicking Folder Options in the search results.

③ Click the View tab.

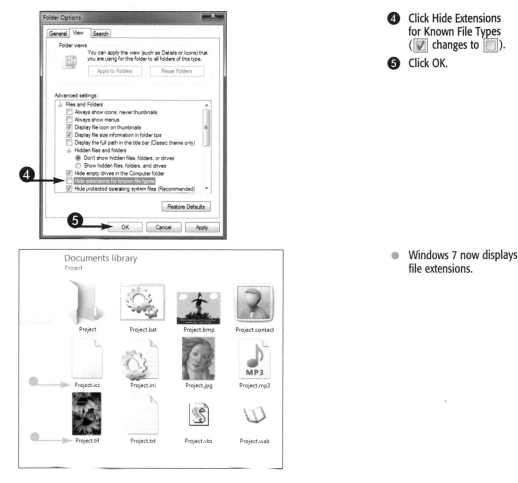

④ Click Hide Extensions for Known File Types (☑ changes to ☐).

⑤ Click OK.

● Windows 7 now displays file extensions.

Did You Know?

Windows 7 ships with file extensions turned off because it does not want novice users imprudently changing extensions and possibly rendering documents unusable. However, changing file extensions has many uses. For example, if you use Notepad to create a Web page, the resulting file uses the txt extension, but most Web page files must use either the htm or html extension, so you must change it.

Apply It!

Once you have configured Windows 7 to display file extensions, you can then edit a file's extension. To do this, use Windows Explorer to navigate to the folder containing the file, click the file, and then press F2. Windows 7 displays a text box around the file name and selects the part of the name to the left of the dot (.). Press the right arrow key to collapse the selection and move the cursor into the extension. Note that Windows 7 will ask you to confirm the extension change.

You can open a file in a different program from the one normally associated with the file. This enables you to use the other program's features to work on the file.

Every document you create has a particular file type. File types are Text Documents, Rich Text Documents, Bitmap Images, JPEG Images, and more. All these types have a default program associated with them. For example, Text Documents are associated with Notepad, and Rich Text Documents are associated with WordPad or Word. Double-clicking a file opens the file in the associated program.

You may have situations where you prefer to open a particular file with a different program. For example, double-clicking a picture file opens in the Windows Photo Viewer. However, you may prefer to open the picture file in Paint or some other image editing program so that you can make changes to the picture.

This task shows you how to open any document in another program.

---

① **Open the folder that contains the file you want to open.**

② **Right-click the file.**

③ **Click Open With.**

Note: *If you see the Open With dialog box, skip to step 5.*

● **If the program you want to use appears here, click the program and skip the remaining steps.**

④ **Click Choose Default Program.**

The Open With dialog box appears.

⑤ **Double-click Other Programs.**

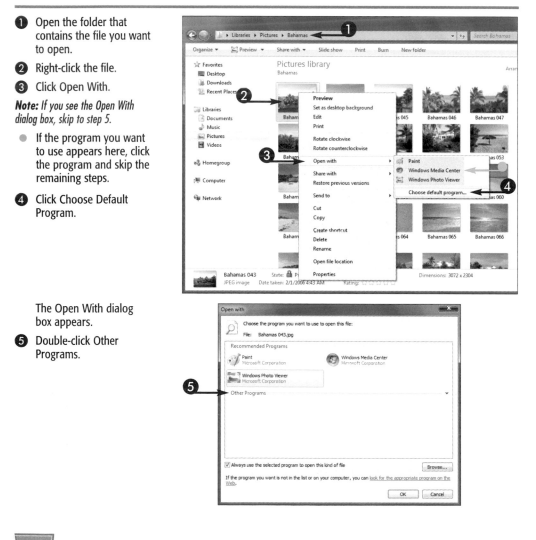

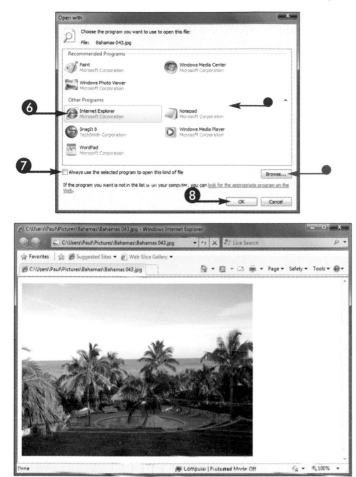

● Windows 7 displays a list of programs you can use to open the file.

⑥ Click the program you want to use to open the file.

● If the program you want to use does not appear in the list, you can click Browse and use the new Open With dialog box to specify the program.

⑦ Click to uncheck the Always Use the Selected Program to Open This Kind of File check box (☑ changes to ☐).

⑧ Click OK.

Windows 7 opens the file in the program you chose.

More Options!

Besides opening the file you selected in the new program, you may prefer to open every other file of the same type — such as Text Document files or Rich Text Format files — in the same program. Follow steps 1 to 6 and then click the Always Use the Selected Program to Open This Kind of File check box (☐ changes to ☑).

Did You Know?

Windows 7 enables you to set the default program for a number of file types at once. Click Start, click Default Programs, and then click Associate a File Type or Protocol with a Program. For each file type, click the file type, click Change Program, and then follow steps 5 to 8.

If you improperly edit, accidentally delete, or corrupt a file through a system crash, in many cases you can restore a previous version of the file.

Each time you start your computer, Windows 7 takes a "snapshot" of its current contents. As you work on your files throughout the day, Windows 7 keeps track of the changes you make to each file. This gives Windows 7 the capability to reverse the changes you have made to a file by reverting to the version of the file that existed when Windows 7 took its

system snapshot. An earlier state of a file is called a *previous version*.

Why would you want to revert to a previous version of a file? One reason is that you might improperly edit the file by deleting or changing important data. In some cases you may be able to restore that data by going back to a previous version of the file. Another reason is that the file might become corrupted if the program or Windows 7 crashes. You can get a working version of the file back by restoring to a previous version.

---

① Open the folder that contains the file you want to restore.

② Right-click the file.

③ Click Restore Previous Versions.

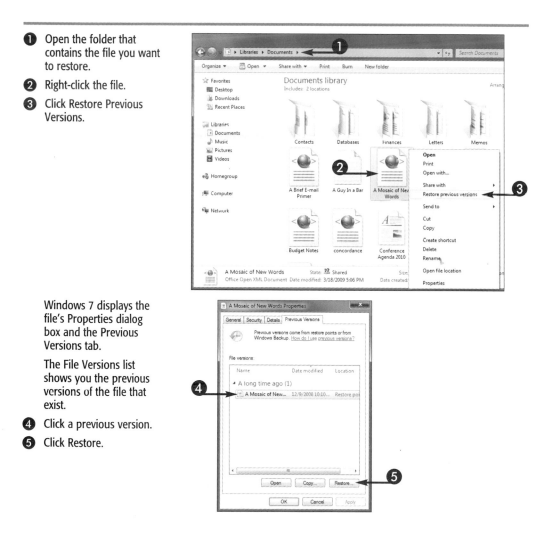

Windows 7 displays the file's Properties dialog box and the Previous Versions tab.

The File Versions list shows you the previous versions of the file that exist.

④ Click a previous version.

⑤ Click Restore.

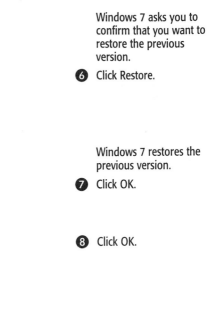

Windows 7 asks you to confirm that you want to restore the previous version.

6 Click Restore.

Windows 7 restores the previous version.

7 Click OK.

8 Click OK.

Did You Know?

Windows 7 also keeps track of previous versions of folders, which is useful if an entire folder becomes corrupted because of a system crash. Right-click the folder and then click Restore Previous Versions.

More Options!

If you are not sure which previous version to restore, click the previous version and then click Open to view the version. If you are still not sure, create a copy: click the previous versions, click Copy, click a folder in which to store the copy, and then click Copy.

Protect a File by Making It Read-Only

You can prevent other people from making changes to an important file by designating the file as read-only.

Much day-to-day work in Windows 7 is required but not terribly important. Most memos, letters, and notes are run-of-the-mill and do not require extra security. Occasionally, however, you may create or work with a file that *is* important. It could be a carefully crafted letter, a memo detailing important company strategy, or a collection of hard-won brainstorming notes. Whatever the content, such a file requires extra protection to ensure that you do not lose your work.

You can set advanced file permissions that can prevent a document from being changed or even deleted (see "Protect a File or Folder with Permissions" in Chapter 3). If your only concern is preventing other people from making changes to a document, a simpler technique you can use is making the document *read-only*. This means that although other people can make changes to a document, they cannot *save* those changes (except to a new file). This task shows you how to make a file read-only.

MAKE A FILE READ-ONLY

1. Open the folder that contains the file you want to work with.

2. Right-click the file.

3. Click Properties.

The file's Properties dialog box appears.

4. Click the General tab.

5. Click the Read-only check box (changes to).

6. Click OK.

The file is now read-only.

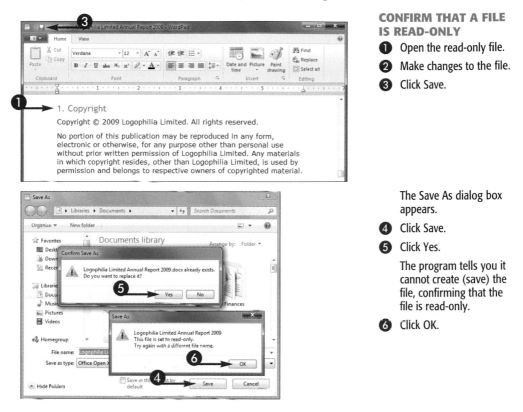

CONFIRM THAT A FILE IS READ-ONLY

1 Open the read-only file.

2 Make changes to the file.

3 Click Save.

The Save As dialog box appears.

4 Click Save.

5 Click Yes.

The program tells you it cannot create (save) the file, confirming that the file is read-only.

6 Click OK.

More Options!

You can hide a file that contains sensitive data to prevent other people from viewing it. Follow steps 1 to 4 on the previous page. Click the Hidden check box (☐ changes to ☑), click OK, and then press F5. The file icon disappears.

More Options!

To see a hidden file, open the folder containing the file, click Start, click Control Panel, click Appearance and Personalization, and then click Folder Options. In the Folder Options dialog box, click the View tab, the Show Hidden Files and Folders option (◯ changes to ◉), and then OK.

Reverse It!

When you want to make changes to the file yourself, you can remove the read-only attribute. Follow steps 1 to 4 on the previous page, click the Read-only check box (☑ changes to ☐), and then click OK.

Save Time by Saving and Reusing a Search

If you have a search that you want to run again in the future, you can save the details of the search. This saves you time because instead of defining the same search from scratch, you can simply reuse the saved version.

You can set up and run a search using the Windows 7 search engine. This is a powerful tool for finding files on your system, but setting up a search — particularly one that uses multiple search filters — can be time-consuming. If there are searches that you plan

on running regularly, it is inefficient to have to set up the same search criteria over and over.

The solution to this problem is to save your search as one of the Windows 7 new search folders. A *search folder* is a collection of files and folders from your system that match a specified set of search criteria. After you set up and run a search, you can save it as a search folder and then reuse it anytime you need it.

SAVE A SEARCH

① In Windows Explorer, set up and run a search.

② Click Save Search.

The Save As dialog box appears.

③ Type a file name for the search folder.

④ Click Save.

Windows 7 saves the search as a search folder.

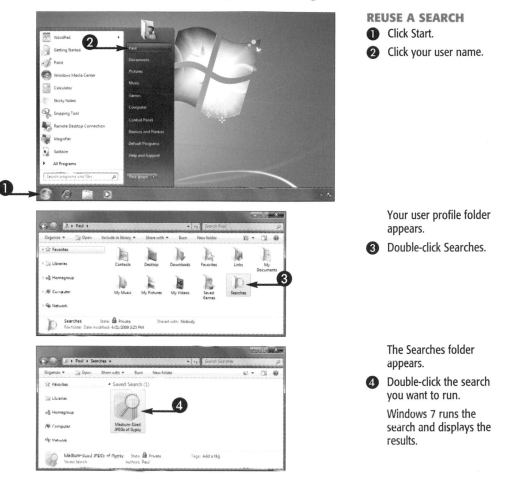

REUSE A SEARCH

① Click Start.

② Click your user name.

Your user profile folder appears.

③ Double-click Searches.

The Searches folder appears.

④ Double-click the search you want to run.

Windows 7 runs the search and displays the results.

TIPS

Did You Know?

To run a search in Windows 7, you have two choices. First, in any folder window type your search criteria into the Search box in the upper right corner of the window. Alternatively, click Start and then type your search criteria into the Start menu's Search box. When the results appear, click the See More Results link.

Remove It!

If you no longer need a saved search, you should delete the search folder to reduce the clutter in the Searches folder. Follow steps 1 to 3 to open the Searches folder, click the search folder you want to remove, and then press Delete. When Windows 7 asks you to confirm, click Yes.

Select Files Using Check Boxes

You can make it easier to select files with some mouse types by turning on a Windows 7 feature that enables you to select files using check boxes.

Windows 7 gives you several methods for selecting multiple files. For example, you can select consecutive files by clicking the first file, pressing and holding the Shift key, and then clicking the last file. Similarly, you can press and hold the Ctrl key and click each file you want to select.

The easiest and therefore the most common method that people use to select multiple, contiguous files is to click and drag the mouse pointer over the files. However, this technique is difficult with certain mouse types, such as the trackball mouse or the trackpad that you see on many notebook computers.

For these mouse types, you can configure Windows 7 to display a check box beside each file, and you can then select any file by activating its check box.

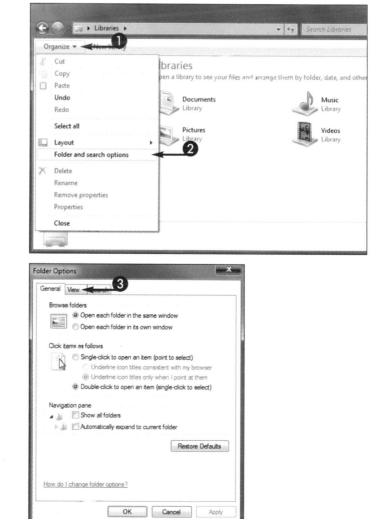

TURN ON CHECK BOX SELECTING

① In any folder window, click Organize.

② Click Folder and Search Options.

The Folder Options dialog box appears.

Note: *You can also display the Folder Options dialog box by clicking Start, typing folder, and then clicking Folder Options in the search results.*

③ Click the View tab.

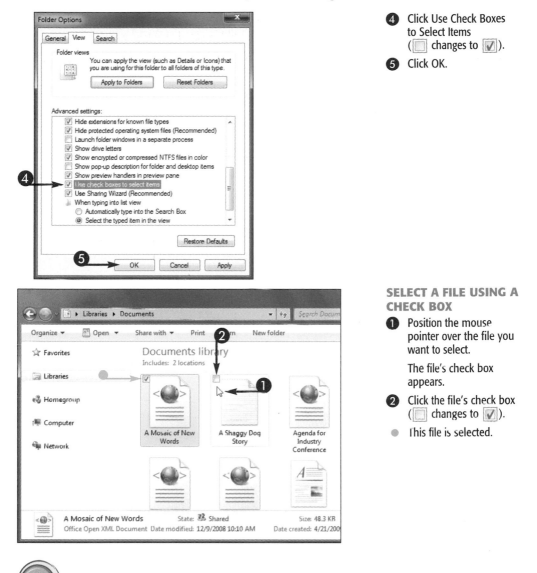

④ Click Use Check Boxes to Select Items (☐ changes to ☑).

⑤ Click OK.

SELECT A FILE USING A CHECK BOX

① Position the mouse pointer over the file you want to select.

The file's check box appears.

② Click the file's check box (☐ changes to ☑).

● This file is selected.

TIPS

Reverse It!

If you select a file by accident, you can fix the problem by clicking the file's check box again to deselect it (☑ changes to ☐). This does not affect any of your other selected files, which is one of the chief advantages of using this method.

Important!

If there is a disadvantage to using this method, it is that you can no longer use the Shift-click technique for selecting multiple, consecutive files. If you have many files to select, consider using the click and drag technique. Otherwise, temporarily turn off check box selecting by following steps 1 to 5.

Add a Folder to the Favorites List

If you have a folder that you use frequently, you can save yourself time and reduce mouse clicks by adding that folder to the Favorites list that appears in the Windows Explorer navigation pane.

Many of the folders you probably use most often are available on the Start menu, including your user profile folder and your Documents, Pictures, and Music libraries.

However, you might have a folder that you use constantly but that takes a while to locate within Windows Explorer. Any folder that you

use frequently should appear on the Windows Explorer jump list, which you display by right-clicking the Windows Explorer icon in the taskbar.

That method should work most of the time, but it might not give you consistent access to the folder. To get easy access to the folder full-time, add the folder to the Favorites list, which appears at the top of the Windows Explorer navigation pane. This gives you one-click access to the folder from any Windows Explorer window.

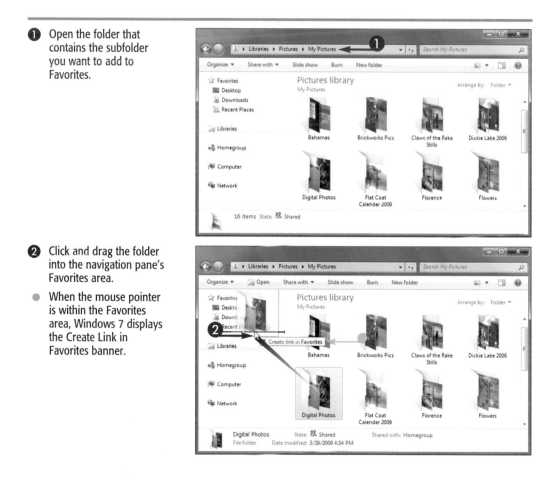

1 Open the folder that contains the subfolder you want to add to Favorites.

2 Click and drag the folder into the navigation pane's Favorites area.

● When the mouse pointer is within the Favorites area, Windows 7 displays the Create Link in Favorites banner.

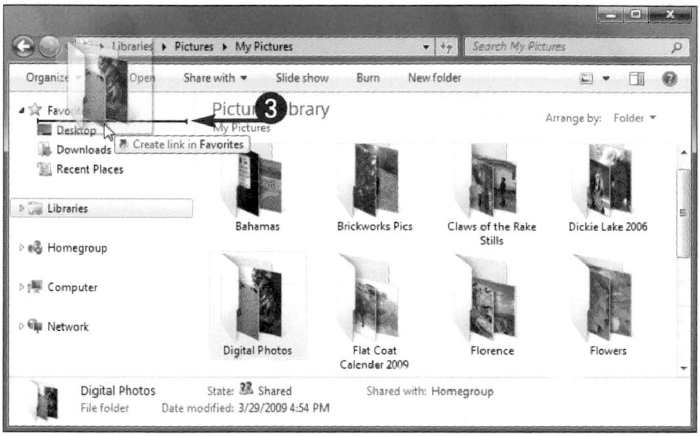

3. Drag the folder up and down within the Favorites area until the bar indicates the place where you want the folder to appear.
4. Release the mouse button to drop the folder on the Favorites area.

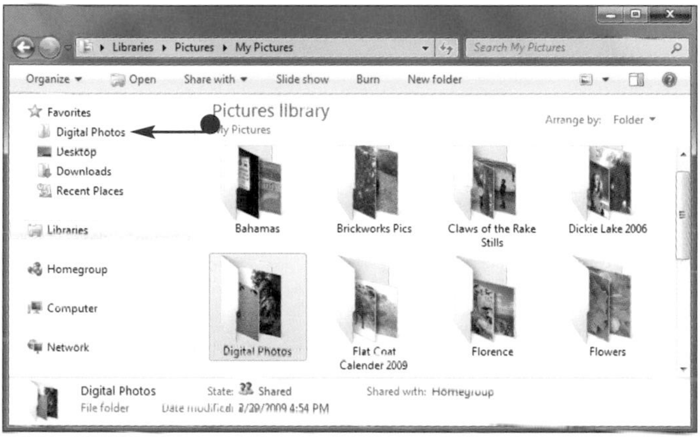

- Windows 7 creates a shortcut for the folder within the Favorites section of the navigation pane.

TIPS

Desktop Tricks!

If you find clicking and dragging folders difficult, there is an easier way to add a folder to the Favorites list. Use Windows Explorer to navigate to and open the folder you want to add. Right-click Favorites in the navigation bar, and then click Add Current Location to Favorites.

Reverse It!

The Favorites list is handy, so you may find you add a number of shortcuts to it over time. If you have any Favorites shortcuts that you no longer use, you should remove them to reduce the clutter in the Favorites list. Right-click the item you want to get rid of and then click Remove.

You can customize the Windows Explorer navigation pane to include all the folders on your system. This can make it easier to navigate folders.

In previous versions of Windows, the left side of the Windows Explorer window displayed the folders pane, which gave you access to all the disk drives and folders on your system. In Windows 7, however, the left side of the Windows Explorer window displays the navigation pane, which shows icons for five

locations on your system: Favorites, Libraries, Homegroup, Computer, and Network. This configuration is fast if the location you want is related to one of these five icons, but some important locations — particularly your main user profile folder — are not easily accessible using the navigation pane.

To work around this problem, you can configure the navigation pane to work like the folders pane.

 Click Windows Explorer.

The Windows Explorer window appears.

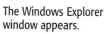 Click Organize.

 Click Folder and Search Options.

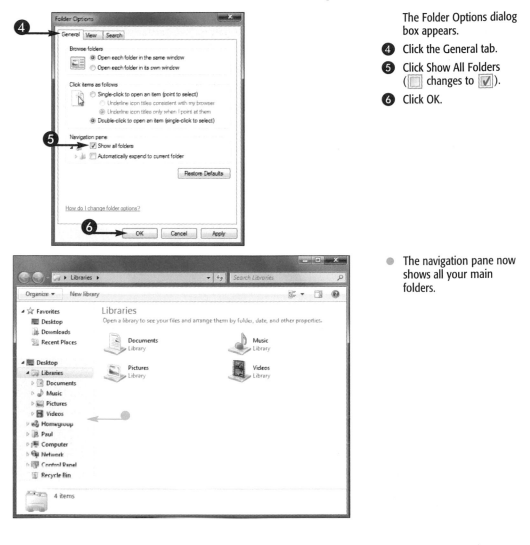

The Folder Options dialog box appears.

④ Click the General tab.

⑤ Click Show All Folders (☐ changes to ☑).

⑥ Click OK.

● The navigation pane now shows all your main folders.

You can enhance the value of the Send To menu, making copying files and folders faster, by customizing the menu with your own destinations.

After you right-click a file or folder, you can then click the Send To command to reveal the Windows 7 Send To menu. This handy menu offers a number of destinations, depending on your computer's configuration: Compressed (zipped) Folder, Desktop (create shortcut), Documents, Fax Recipient, and Mail Recipient. You may also see other removable disk drives, such as a recordable CD drive. When you click

one of these destinations, Windows 7 sends a copy of the selected file or folder to that location. This is much faster than copying the item, finding and opening the destination folder, and then pasting the item.

So making a good thing even better by adding your own destinations to the Send To menu is a great idea. You can add a favorite folder, a folder that you use for backup copies, a folder for a current project, a disk drive, the Recycle Bin, or a network folder. You can even add a printer for quick printing to a specific device.

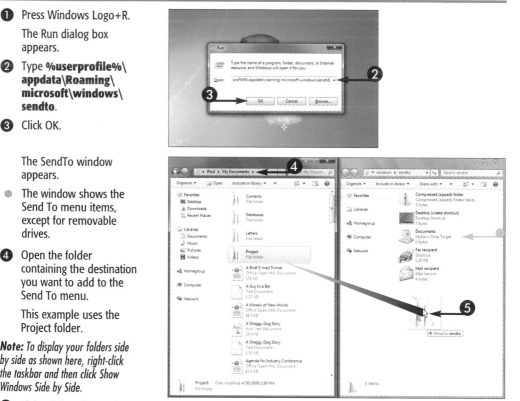

① Press Windows Logo+R.

The Run dialog box appears.

② Type **%userprofile%\ appdata\Roaming\ microsoft\windows\ sendto**.

③ Click OK.

The SendTo window appears.

● The window shows the Send To menu items, except for removable drives.

④ Open the folder containing the destination you want to add to the Send To menu.

This example uses the Project folder.

Note: *To display your folders side by side as shown here, right-click the taskbar and then click Show Windows Side by Side.*

⑤ Right-click and drag the destination item and drop it in the SendTo window.

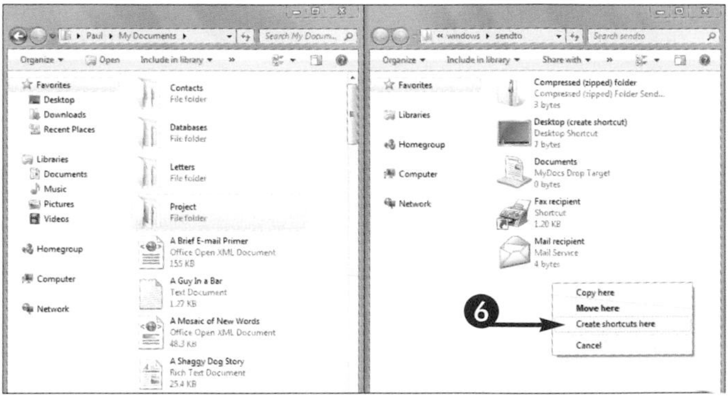

6. Click Create Shortcuts Here from the menu that appears after you drop the item.

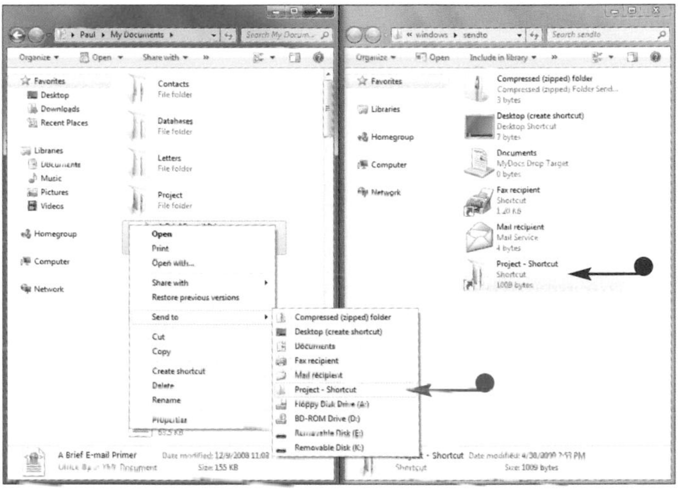

- Windows 7 adds a shortcut for the destination in the SendTo window.
- The destination now appears in the Send To menu. To view it, you can right-click any file or folder, and then click Send To.

TIPS

Customize It!

You can customize the Send To menu with more than just folders. For example, if your system has multiple printers, you can add them to the Send To menu and then easily send a document to any printer. To add a printer to the Send To menu, click Start and then click Printers and Devices. Click and drag the printer to drop it in the SendTo window.

Customize It!

You can also add a program to the Send To menu. When you send a document to the program, the document opens in that program automatically. To add a program to the Send To menu, click Start, click All Programs, and open the menu that contains an icon for the program. Right-click and drag the program icon, drop it in the SendTo window, and then click Create Shortcuts Here.

Make Files Easier to Find by Adding Metadata

You can make your files easier to find by adding custom metadata to each file.

Metadata refers to data — called *properties* — that describes or augments existing data. For example, the name of the person who created a document is a metadata property for that document. Similarly, a digital photo's properties might include the make and model of the camera used to take the image, the exposure time, f-stop setting, and so on.

Although metadata such as the image exposure time and f-stop is determined by the camera,

Windows 7 enables you to add your own metadata to many types of files. For example, you can add the name or names of the file authors; you can add a title and comments about a file; you can give a file a rating of between one and five stars; and you can add one or more *tags*, which are keywords that reflect the content of the file.

Once you have added metadata, you can then use that data to perform powerful searches, as described in Chapter 6.

① Open the folder that contains the file you want to work with.

② Click the file.

● Windows 7 shows some of the file's metadata in the Details pane.

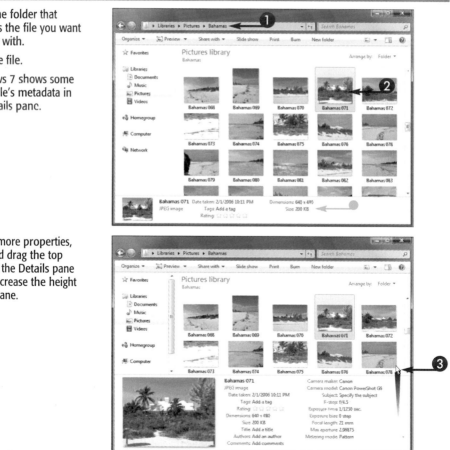

③ To see more properties, click and drag the top edge of the Details pane up to increase the height of the pane.

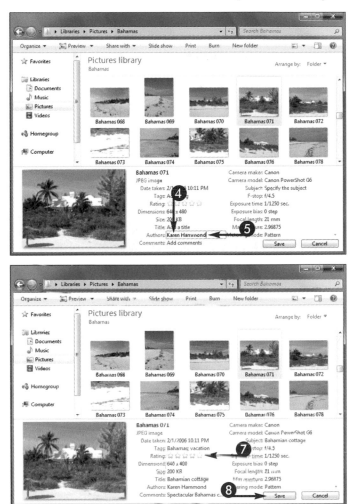

4 Click inside the property you want to edit.

Note: *If you cannot click inside a property, it means that data cannot be edited.*

5 Type the metadata.

6 Repeat steps 4 and 5 to add metadata to other properties as desired.

7 To rate the file, click the star that corresponds to the rating you want to bestow.

8 Click Save.

Windows 7 saves the file's metadata.

TIPS

Try This!

If you have a lot of files to go through, you can reduce the workload by adding metadata to multiple files at once. Select all the files you want to work with. If the files are all of the same type — for example, all images — you can follow steps 3 to 8 to add metadata to all the selected files at once.

More Options!

You can access even more metadata by opening the property sheet associated with a file. Right-click the file and then click Properties to open the property sheet. Click the Details tab to see the complete list of metadata for the file. The Property column shows the name of each property, and you use the controls in the Value column to change each property that can be edited. When you are done, click OK.

Remove Personal Metadata from a File

If you plan on sharing a file with other people, you can remove some or all of the personal metadata you have attached to the file.

The task "Make Files Easier to Find by Adding Metadata" discussed how you can add metadata to a file by modifying one or more file properties, such as the author, title, comments, or tags. Metadata is useful locally for things like searching, but it can also be useful if you share documents with other people because it provides those people with extra information about those documents.

However, it is possible that you could supplement a file with metadata that would be inappropriate for another person to see. For example, you might not want others to know who authored a file, or you might have entered a title or comments that include private or confidential information.

Windows 7 comes with a feature that enables you to create a copy of a file and to remove all the personal metadata from that copy. This enables you to share the clean copy with other people.

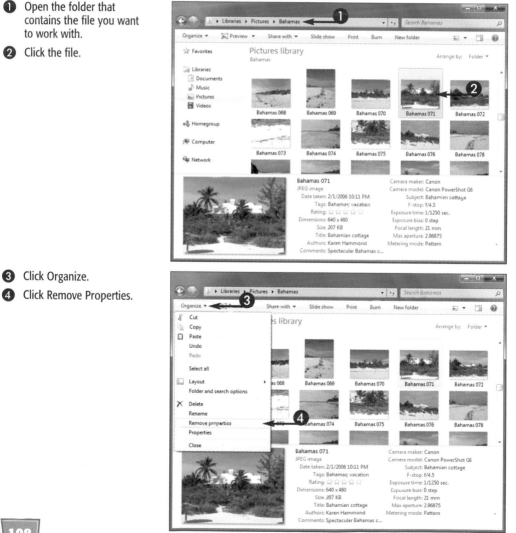

① Open the folder that contains the file you want to work with.

② Click the file.

③ Click Organize.

④ Click Remove Properties.

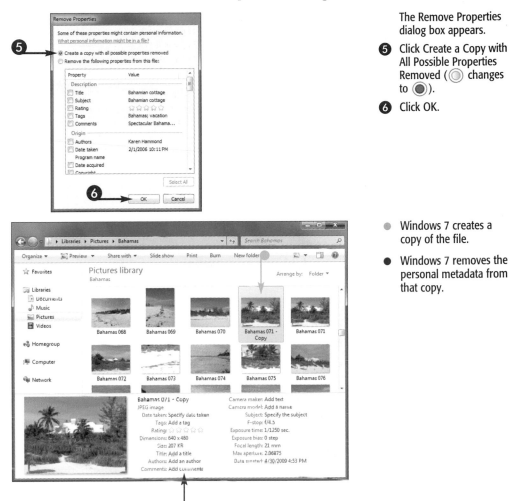

The Remove Properties dialog box appears.

⑤ Click Create a Copy with All Possible Properties Removed (◯ changes to ◉).

⑥ Click OK.

● Windows 7 creates a copy of the file.

● Windows 7 removes the personal metadata from that copy.

More Options!

You can also remove just some of the personal metadata from a file. If you want to leave the original file as is, first create a copy of the file. Follow steps 1 to 4 for the copied file, and then click Remove the Following Properties from This File (◯ changes to ◉). Click the check box beside each property you want to remove (☐ changes to ☑), and then click OK.

Try This!

In many cases you want to remove all but a few of a file's properties before sharing the file. In that case, follow the steps given in the previous tip, but click the Select All button to select every check box. Then click the check box for each property you want to retain (☑ changes to ☐).

You can assign a different drive letter to any hard disk, disk partition, CD or DVD drive, or removable drive attached to your computer.

When you installed Windows 7 on your computer, it surveyed all the disk drives on your system and assigned drive letters to each disk. For example, the drive where Windows is installed is probably drive C, your CD or DVD drive might be drive D, and if you have Flash drive or memory card slots on your PC, they were assigned letters beginning with E.

There may be times when you need or want to change the default drive letters. For example, some programs require a floppy disk drive for certain actions, and it is a rare PC that comes with a floppy drive these days. In most cases you can fool the program into thinking your system has a floppy drive by assigning drive A to a Flash drive or memory card slot.

① Click Start.

② Right-click Computer.

③ Click Manage.

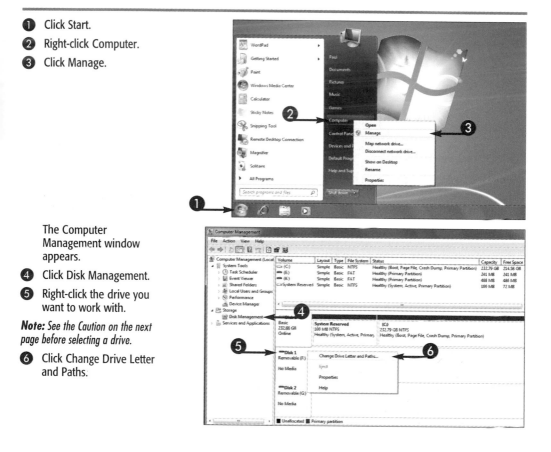

The Computer Management window appears.

④ Click Disk Management.

⑤ Right-click the drive you want to work with.

Note: *See the Caution on the next page before selecting a drive.*

⑥ Click Change Drive Letter and Paths.

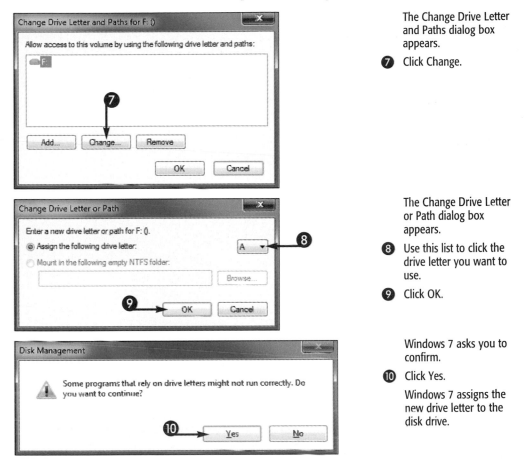

The Change Drive Letter and Paths dialog box appears.

⑦ Click Change.

The Change Drive Letter or Path dialog box appears.

⑧ Use this list to click the drive letter you want to use.

⑨ Click OK.

Windows 7 asks you to confirm.

⑩ Click Yes.

Windows 7 assigns the new drive letter to the disk drive.

Caution!

Do not attempt to assign or change the drive letters associated with drive C and the System Reserved partition. These are crucial for the operation of your PC, and modifying these drives could render your computer unusable.

Did You Know?

If you do not see drive A in the list of possible drive letters, it likely means that Windows 7 mistakenly believes your system has a floppy drive. To disable this "device," click Start, type **device**, and then click Device Manager. Open the Floppy Disk Drive branch, click Floppy Disk Drive, click Action, click Disable, and then click Yes.

You can make the Computer folder neater-looking and less cluttered by configuring Windows 7 to not show the letters associated with each disk drive on your system.

Disk drive letters have been part of computing for decades. The letters were straightforward back when PCs had only a few disk drives, such as A for the floppy drive, C for the hard drive, and D for the CD or DVD drive.

However, in recent years the number of disk drives attached to a computer has grown quickly. Floppy drives are a distant memory,

but hard drives often have multiple partitions, USB Flash drives are commonplace, and many PCs come with multi-slot memory card readers, and all of these drives get their own letter. So it is now common for PCs to assign 10 or 15 drive letters.

Unfortunately, the more drive letters you see in the Computer window, the more cluttered the window appears, and the less meaning each letter has. In many cases, you will probably be better off if you hide the drive letters and assign meaningful names to each drive.

① Click Start.

② Click Computer.

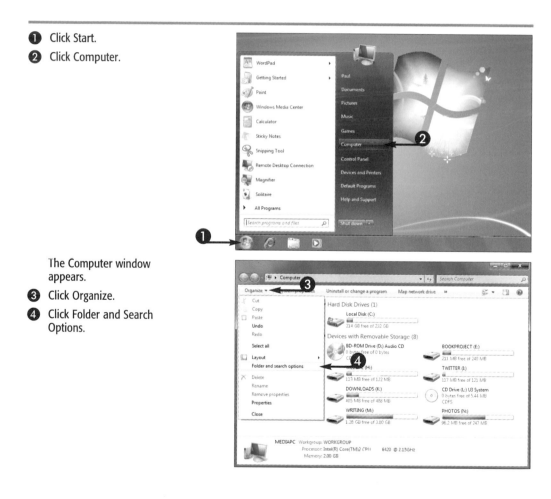

The Computer window appears.

③ Click Organize.

④ Click Folder and Search Options.

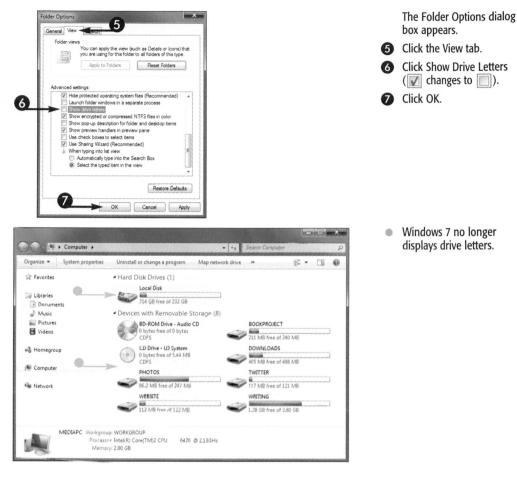

The Folder Options dialog box appears.

⑤ Click the View tab.

⑥ Click Show Drive Letters (☑ changes to ☐).

⑦ Click OK.

● Windows 7 no longer displays drive letters.

Important!
Windows 7 usually provides the same "name" to similar drives. For example, removable drives such as Flash drives and memory cards are usually named Removable Disk. To help differentiate your disks when you hide drive letters, add meaningful names to your drives.

Try This!
To rename a disk drive, open the Computer window, right-click the drive you want to work with, and then click Rename. Windows 7 places a text box around the existing name. Type the new name — you can enter a maximum of ten characters — in the text box, and then press Enter.

Split a Hard Drive into Two Partitions

You can create a separate storage area on your system by splitting your hard drive into two partitions.

In hard drive circles, a *partition* — also called a *volume* — is a subset of a hard drive that you can access and work with as a separate unit. Most hard drives consist of just a single partition that takes up the entire disk, and that partition is almost always drive C. However, it is possible to divide a single hard drive into two partitions and assign a drive letter to each — say, C and D.

Although many partition operations are better left to third-party programs such as Norton PartitionMagic (www.symantec.com) or Partition Manager (www.acronis.com), splitting a partition is something you can do using Windows 7 tools.

In this task, you learn how to divide a hard drive into two partitions. You do that by first shrinking the existing partition and then creating the new partition in the freed-up disk space.

① Click Start.

② Right-click Computer.

③ Click Manage.

The Computer Management window appears.

④ Click Disk Management.

⑤ Right-click the hard drive you want to split.

⑥ Click Shrink Volume.

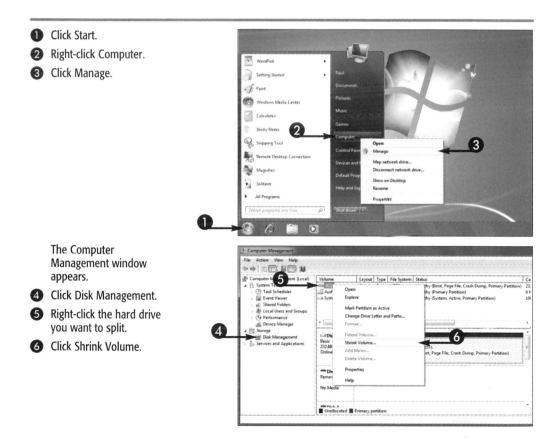

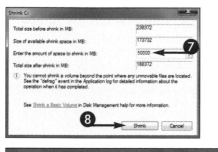

Disk Management displays the Shrink *D*: dialog box (where *D* is the drive letter of the partition).

⑦ Use the Enter the Amount of Space to Shrink in MB text box to type the amount by which you want the partition size reduced.

Note: This will be the approximate size of the new partition that you create a bit later. Also, see the tips, below.

⑧ Click Shrink.

Windows 7 shrinks the partition.

● Windows 7 displays the freed space as Unallocated.

⑨ Right-click the Unallocated space.

⑩ Click New Simple Volume.

---

continued

TIPS

Important!

You cannot enter a shrink size that is larger than the shrink space you have at your disposal, which is given by the Size of Available Shrink Space value. If you are shrinking drive C, the available shrink space will be quite a bit less than the available free space because Windows reserves quite a bit of space on drive C for certain system files that may grow over time.

Did You Know?

How much you shrink the partition depends on how large you want your new partition to be. For example, if you want to use the new partition to store your data, and you currently have 20GB of data, shrink the partition by 30GB to give you some extra room for new files.

Why would you need to split a hard disk into two partitions?

One reason you would do this is to separate your data from Windows. That is, you would create a second partition and then move your data to that partition. This is a good idea because if you ever have to reinstall Windows from scratch, you can wipe drive C: without

having to worry about your data, which remains intact on the other partition.

Another use for a second hard drive partition is to install a second operating system on your computer and dual-boot between Windows 7 and that operating system. In this case, you would create a second partition and then install the other operating system to that partition.

The New Simple Volume Wizard appears.

⑪ Click Next.

The Specify Volume Size Wizard appears.

● Windows 7 displays the maximum partition size here.

⑫ Make sure that the Simple Volume Size in MB text box is set to the maximum value.

⑬ Click Next.

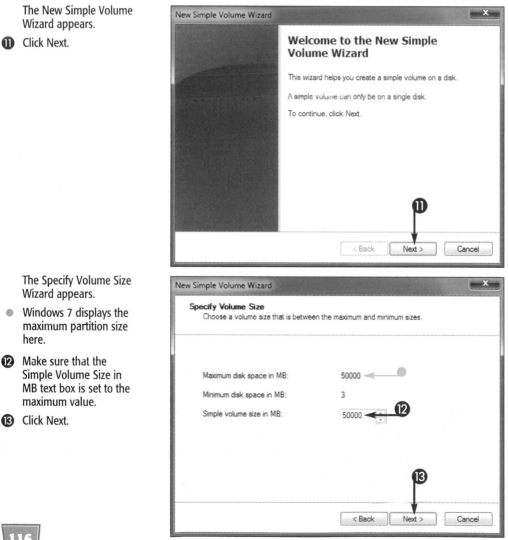

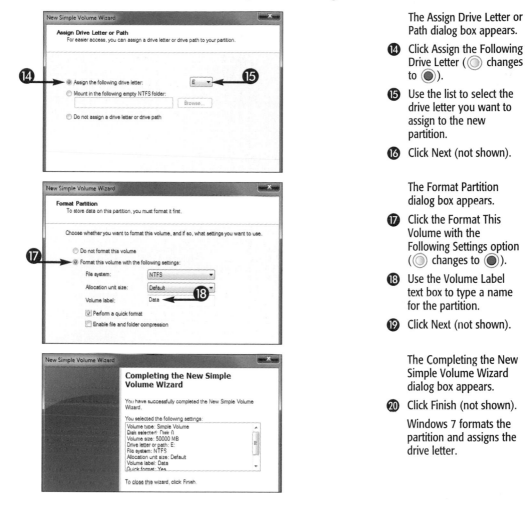

The Assign Drive Letter or Path dialog box appears.

⑭ Click Assign the Following Drive Letter (◎ changes to ◉).

⑮ Use the list to select the drive letter you want to assign to the new partition.

⑯ Click Next (not shown).

The Format Partition dialog box appears.

⑰ Click the Format This Volume with the Following Settings option (◎ changes to ◉).

⑱ Use the Volume Label text box to type a name for the partition.

⑲ Click Next (not shown).

The Completing the New Simple Volume Wizard dialog box appears.

⑳ Click Finish (not shown).

Windows 7 formats the partition and assigns the drive letter.

TIPS

Try This!

It is customary for two partitions on the same hard drive to use consecutive drive letters. However, Windows 7 probably assigned your new partition a letter other than D because D is probably taken already. To work around this problem, assign a different drive letter to the current drive D and then assign D to your new partition. See "Assign a Different Letter to a Disk Drive," earlier in this chapter.

Reverse It!

If you want to return to using a single partition, you need to first delete the extended partition. Follow steps 1 to 4 to open the Disk Management snap-in, right-click the extended partition, and then click Delete This Volume. When Windows 7 asks you to confirm, click Yes. Now right-click drive C and then click Extend Volume. In the Extend Volume Wizard, click Next, click Next, and then click Finish.

Enriching Your Windows 7 Media Experience

Windows 7 was designed from the ground up to offer you a rich media experience. Whether you are dealing with drawings, photos, sounds, audio CDs, downloaded music files, or DVDs, the tools built into Windows 7 enable you to play, edit, and even create media.

The downside to having a rich media environment at your fingertips is that the media tools themselves are necessarily feature-laden and complex. The basic operations are usually easy enough to master, but some of the more useful and interesting features tend to be in hard-to-find places. This chapter helps you take advantage of many of these off-the-beaten-track features by showing you how to find and use them.

For example, you discover lots of useful image tips and tricks, including how to create custom file names for imported images, repair image defects such as incorrect exposure and red eye, and open images for editing by default.

On the audio front, you figure out how to adjust the settings Windows Media Player uses to rip audio tracks from a CD, how to share your media library with other people on your network, how to set up an automatic playlist, and how to add sounds to Windows 7 events.

Quick Tips

Create Custom Names for Imported Images

You can create more meaningful file names for your imported images by configuring Windows Live Photo Gallery (available from http://download.live.com) to use a custom name that you specify during each import operation.

When you import images from a device such as a digital camera, Windows Live Photo Gallery launches the Import Photos and Videos tool to handle the job. By default, this tool preserves the existing file names of the images. However, most devices supply images with cryptic file names, such as IMG_1083 and scan001. These nondescript names can make it more

difficult to find and work with images, particularly if you use the Details view in the Pictures folder.

To work around this problem, you can configure the Import Photos and Videos tool to apply a custom file name to your imported images. This custom file name is based on a word or short phrase that you specify during the import operation. For example, if you specify Bahamas Vacation as the import name, then your imported images will be called Bahamas Vacation 001, Bahamas Vacation 002, and so on.

---

① Click Start.

② Click All Programs.

Note: *After you click All Programs, the command name changes to Back.*

③ Click Windows Live.

④ Click Windows Live Photo Gallery.

Windows Live Photo Gallery appears.

⑤ Click File.

⑥ Click Options.

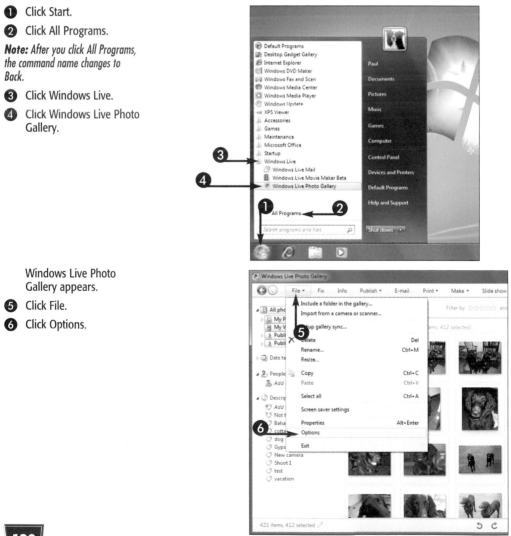

The Windows Live Photo Gallery Options dialog box appears.

⑦ Click the Import tab.

⑧ In the Settings For list, click here and then click the type of device you want to work with.

⑨ In the File Name list, click here and then click Name.

⑩ Repeat steps 8 and 9 to apply the event tag file name to imports from other devices.

⑪ Click OK.

Windows Live Photo Gallery puts the new settings into effect.

Did You Know?

You can configure Windows 7 to always launch the Import Photos and Videos tool when you connect your digital camera. In the Import tab, click the Change Default Autoplay Options link to display the AutoPlay window. In the Pictures list, click the down arrow (▼) and then click Import Pictures and Videos Using Windows Live Photo Gallery. Click Save.

More Options!

If you always clear the memory card in your digital camera after you import the images, you can have the Import Photos and Videos tool do this for you automatically. In the Import tab, click the Delete Files from Device after Importing check box (☐ changes to ☑).

You can use Windows Live Photo Gallery to improve the look of digital photos and other images. Windows Live Photo Gallery includes a special Fix window that offers a number of tools to repair various image attributes, including the exposure, colors, and red eye.

For the exposure, Windows Live Photo Gallery can adjust both the brightness of the image and the image contrast, which is the relative difference between the lightest and darkest areas in the image.

For the color, Windows Live Photo Gallery can adjust the color temperature (the relative warmth of the colors, where cooler means bluer and hotter means redder), the tint, and the saturation (the percentage of hue in each color).

Windows Live Photo Gallery also enables you to crop an image to remove unwanted subjects or to ensure that the main subject is centered in the photo.

Windows Live Photo Gallery maintains a backup of the original photo, so you can always reverse any adjustments you make.

① Click Start.

② Click All Programs.

Note: After you click All Programs, the command name changes to Back.

③ Click Windows Live.

④ Click Windows Live Photo Gallery.

Windows Live Photo Gallery appears.

⑤ Click the image you want to repair.

⑥ Click Fix to open the Fix window.

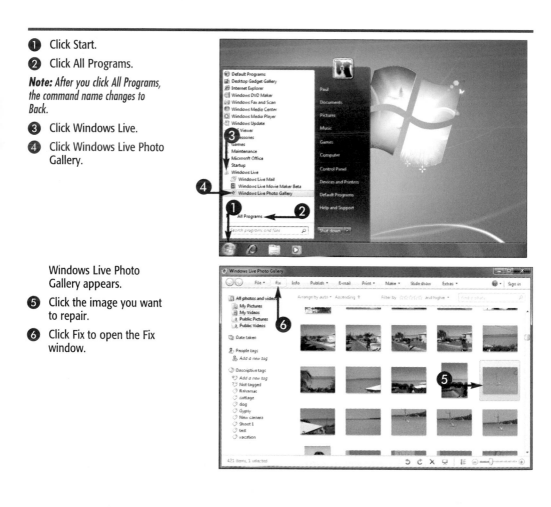

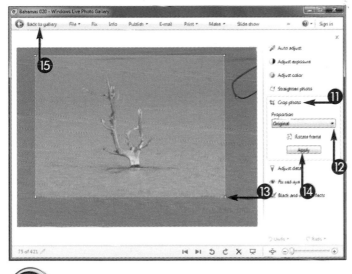

7 To change the exposure, click Adjust Exposure and then drag the displayed sliders.

8 To change the color, click Adjust Color and then drag the Color Temperature, Tint, and Saturation sliders.

● You can click Auto Adjust to have Photo Gallery make the adjustments for you.

9 To straighten a photo, click Straighten Photo and then drag the slider.

10 To remove red eye from a photo, click Fix Red Eye.

11 To crop the picture, first click Crop Photo.

12 Click here and then click the dimensions you want.

13 Drag the handles to set the new size of the image.

14 Click Apply.

15 When you are done, click Back to Gallery, and Windows Live Photo Gallery applies the repairs.

TIPS

More Options!

When you crop an image, Photo Gallery assumes you want the cropped version to have the same relative height and width of the original. If you do not want this, click the down arrow (▼) in the Proportion list and then click Custom. If you are cropping for a photo printout, click one of the standard sizes, such as 5 x 7, instead.

Reverse It!

The Photo Gallery always keeps a backup copy of the original image, just in case. To undo all your changes and get the original image back, click the image and then click Fix. In the Fix window, click Revert and then click Revert to Original (or press Ctrl+R). When Windows Live Photo Gallery asks you to confirm, click Revert.

Open Your Images for Editing by Default

You can configure Windows 7 to always open an image file in a graphics program for editing when you double-click the file.

For most document types, when you double-click a file, the file opens in an appropriate program for editing. For example, if you double-click a text document, Windows 7 opens the file in the Notepad text-editing program. Similarly, if you double-click a Rich Text Format document, the file opens in WordPad or Word depending on your computer's settings.

Unfortunately, Windows 7 is inconsistent when it comes to graphics files. For example, if

you double-click a bitmap image, the file does not open in the Paint graphics program. Instead, in many cases Windows 7 loads the file into the Windows Photo Viewer, which only allows you to view the file; you cannot edit the image. This choice is not only inconsistent, but also frustrating because now you must close the Windows Photo Viewer and open the file in Paint.

Fortunately, you can fix the problem by forcing Windows 7 to open an image file in Paint or some other graphics program when you double-click the file.

---

① Click Start.

② Click Default Programs.

The Default Programs window appears.

③ Click Set Your Default Programs.

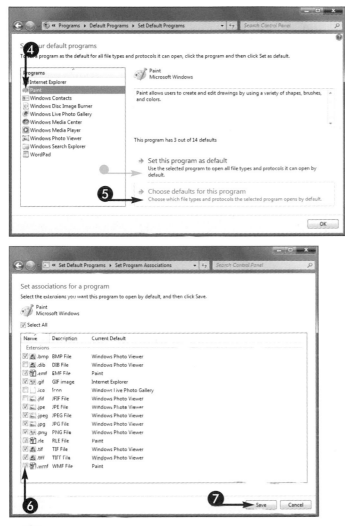

The Set Default Programs window appears.

④ Click Paint.

Note: *If you have other graphics programs installed on your computer, click the program you prefer to use for editing this file type.*

⑤ Click Choose Defaults for This Program.

● If you want to use the selected program to open all image files by default, click Set This Program as Default, instead, and then skip the rest of the steps.

The Set Program Associations window appears.

⑥ Click the check box beside each image type you want to open in the selected program (☐ changes to ☑).

⑦ Click Save.

When you now double-click any of the image file types you selected in step 6, the file opens for editing in the program you selected in step 4.

Preview It!

If you want to load an image into the Windows Photo Viewer in the future, you can still do it. Right-click the image, click Open With, and then click Windows Photo Viewer. To close the Viewer and load the image into Paint, click Open and then click Paint.

More Options!

What happens if you have a third-party graphics program that you prefer to use, but the program does not appear in the Set Default Programs window? Right-click an image, click Open With, and then click Choose Default Program. In the Open With dialog box, click Browse and then use the new Open With dialog box to locate the graphics program. Click the program and then click Open.

Compress Your Image Files

You can compress one or more of your large image files into a smaller format, either to save space or to upload to a Web site.

Image files are often quite large. Complex bitmap images and photo-quality images from a digital camera or scanner run to several megabytes or more. A large collection of such files can easily consume gigabytes of hard drive space. If you are running low on hard drive space, but you do not want to delete any of your image files, compressing those files into smaller versions can help.

Similarly, you may need to upload one or more of your image files to a Web site. You not only have to compress Web images so that users with slow connections can load them in a reasonable time, but you must also convert the images to a format that all Web browsers can work with.

In this task, you learn a trick that enables you to compress images and convert them to the Web-friendly JPEG format.

---

1. Search for or open the folder that contains the images you want to compress.

2. Select the images.

   • For comparison purposes later on, note the total size of the selected images.

3. Click E-mail.

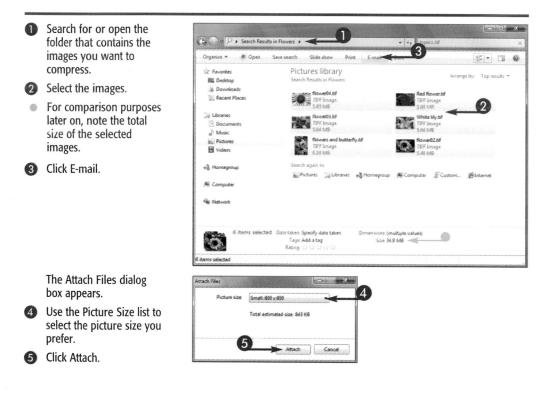

The Attach Files dialog box appears.

4. Use the Picture Size list to select the picture size you prefer.

5. Click Attach.

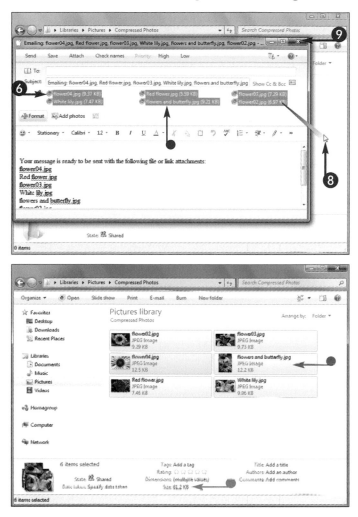

An e-mail message window opens with the compressed and converted images as attachments.

⑥ Click any attached file.

⑦ Press Ctrl+A.

● Windows selects all the files.

⑧ Click and drag the selected attachments and drop them inside a folder.

Note: *If you want to replace the original files, drop the compressed files into the original folder.*

⑨ Click Close.

● The images appear in the folder.

● The images are now compressed and take up less space on your hard drive.

Note: *If you still have the original images, either delete them or archive them to a removable drive.*

TIPS

More Options!

If your goal is to save hard drive space, you can place infrequently used images in a compressed folder. This is a special folder that shrinks the images as much as possible. When you want to work with one of the original files, you can extract it from the compressed folder at any time. To create the compressed folder, select the images and then click File, Send To, and Compressed (Zipped) Folder. Delete the original images after Windows 7 creates the compressed folder.

Check It Out!

For maximum control over compressing image files, you can use a third-party graphics program, such as Paint Shop Pro (available from www.corel.com) or the free programs IrfanView (www.irfanview.com) or Easy Thumbnails (www.notetab.com).

Customize a Media Folder by Applying a Template

You can customize a folder according to the type of media it contains, giving you easier access to some of the Windows 7 features related to that type of media.

Windows 7 is designed to make certain features and tasks available only when it makes sense. This means that the interface changes depending on what type of file, folder, or other object you are working with. For example, consider the toolbar, which appears below the address bar in any folder window. The toolbar displays a collection of links that run tasks related to the folder or to any selected file within the folder.

For example, when you open the Pictures library, the toolbar includes a command named Slide Show. Similarly, if you select a music file in the Music library, the toolbar includes Play and Play all commands.

You can access this very useful feature in any of your folders by applying the appropriate folder template, as described in this task.

① Click the folder you want to customize.

② Click Organize.

③ Click Properties.

The folder's Properties dialog box appears.

④ Click the Customize tab.

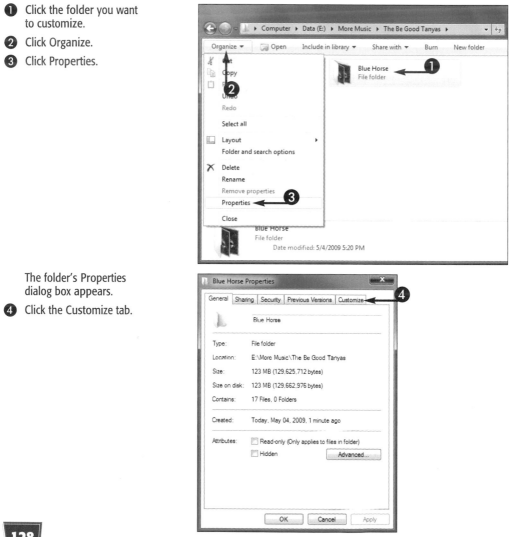

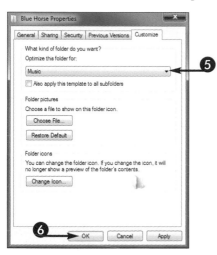

5 Click here and then click the template you want to apply to the folder.

6 Click OK.

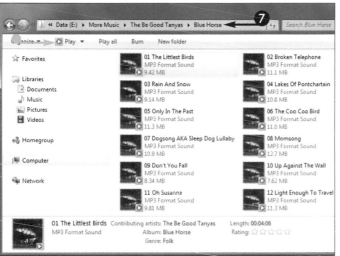

Windows 7 applies the template to the folder and its subfolders.

7 Open the folder.

● The toolbar now shows tasks related to the type of folder template you selected.

TIPS

More Options!
If you have subfolders that contain similar files, you do not have to open each folder and apply the template. Instead, follow steps 1 to 4 to select a template for the main folder, and then click the Also Apply This Template to All Subfolders check box (☐ changes to ☑).

Customize It!
To remind yourself of the template that you have applied to a folder, you should change the folder's icon to one that reflects the template type. Follow steps 1 to 4 to select a template for the main folder, and then click Change Icon. In the Change Icon dialog box, click the icon you want and then click OK.

Create an
Automatic Playlist

You can create a playlist that Media Player maintains automatically based on the criteria you specify.

You normally create a playlist by clicking and dragging music files to the playlist. However, you can also create a playlist based on the properties that Media Player maintains for each file. These properties include Album Artist, Genre, Composer, and Rating, to name just a few. So, for example, you could create a playlist that includes every music file where the Genre property equals Folk.

You create a property-based playlist by specifying the playlist *criteria*, which consists of three factors: the property, the property value, and an operator that relates the two. The most common operators are Is, Is Not, and Contains. For the folk music example, the criteria would be the following: Genre Is Folk.

The best part about property-based playlists is that they are automatic. This means that after you set up the playlist, Media Player automatically populates the playlist with all the music files that meet your criteria.

 In Windows Media Player, click the arrow beside Create Playlist.

2 Click Create Auto Playlist.

The New Auto Playlist dialog box appears.

3 Type a name for the playlist.

4 Click here to display the menu of properties.

5 Click a property.

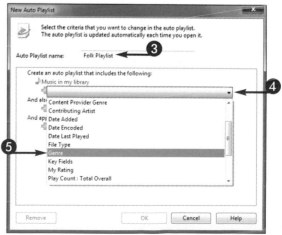

6 Click here to choose an operator.

7 Click here and then click the criteria you want to use.

8 Click OK.

● Media Player adds your playlist to Playlists.

● Media Player populates the playlist based on your criteria.

TIPS

More Options!

You can place restrictions on your automatic playlists so that they do not become too large. Open the Playlists branch, right-click your automatic playlist, and then click Edit to display the Edit Auto Playlist dialog box. Pull down the list named And Apply the Following Restrictions to the Auto Playlist, and then click Limit Number of Items, Limit Total Duration To, or Limit Total Size To. Fill in the limit, and then click OK.

Remove It!

If you no longer need your automatic playlist, you should delete it so that Media Player does not keep updating it and to reduce clutter in the Playlists branch. Right-click the playlist and then click Delete. In the confirmation dialog box that appears, click Delete from Library and My Computer, and then click OK.

Windows Media Player gives you lots of control over the copying — or *ripping* — of tracks from an audio CD by enabling you to select a format and a bit rate.

The *format* is the audio file type you want to use to store the ripped tracks on your computer. You have five choices:

The Windows Media Audio format compresses audio by removing extraneous sounds not normally detected by the human ear.

The Windows Media Audio (variable bit rate) format changes the compression depending on the audio data: If the data is more complex, it uses less compression to keep the quality high.

The Windows Media Audio Lossless format does not compress the audio tracks.

The MP3 format also compresses the audio files to make them smaller, but MP3s are generally about twice the size of WMA files.

The WAV format is an uncompressed audio file format compatible with all versions of Windows.

The *bit rate* determines the quality of the rip and is measured in kilobits per second (Kbps). The higher the bit rate, the better the quality, but the more hard drive space each track uses.

USE THE RIP SETTINGS MENU

① Insert an audio CD.

② In Windows Media Player, click the audio CD.

③ Click Rip Settings.

④ Click Format.

Windows Media Player displays the available audio file formats.

⑤ Click the format you want to use.

⑥ Click Rip Settings.

⑦ Click Audio Quality.

Windows Media Player displays the available bit rates.

Note: *The available bit rates depend on the audio file format you chose in step 5. Note that some formats use a fixed bit rate that you cannot change.*

⑧ Click the bit rate you want to use.

Windows Media Player uses the new settings the next time you rip tracks from an audio CD.

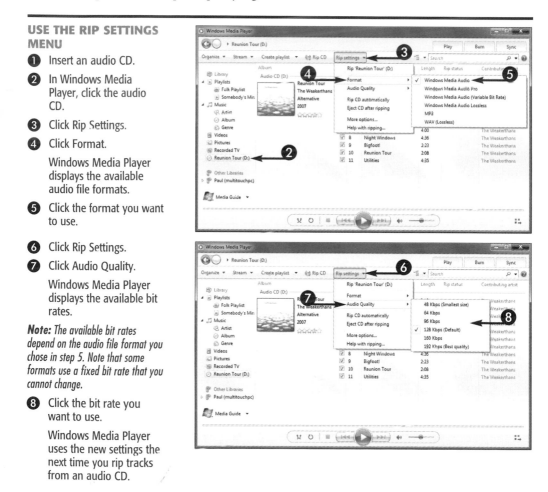

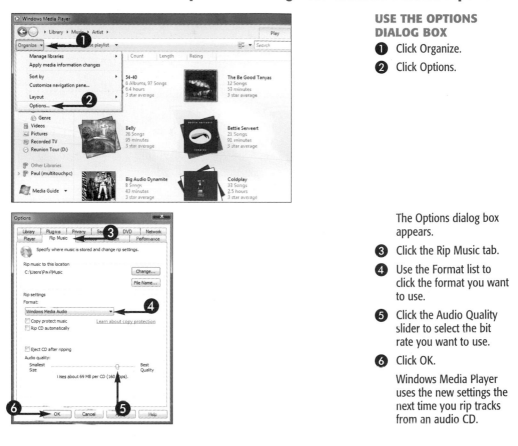

USE THE OPTIONS DIALOG BOX

① Click Organize.

② Click Options.

The Options dialog box appears.

③ Click the Rip Music tab.

④ Use the Format list to click the format you want to use.

⑤ Click the Audio Quality slider to select the bit rate you want to use.

⑥ Click OK.

Windows Media Player uses the new settings the next time you rip tracks from an audio CD.

TIP

Did You Know?

The bit rate determines the size of each ripped track. There are 8 bits in a byte, 1,024 bytes in a kilobyte, and 1,024 kilobytes in a megabyte. The following table lists the bit rates for the Windows Media Audio format and how much drive space it uses:

Bit Rates and Drive Space for the WMA Format		
Bit Rate (Kbps)	**KB/Minute**	**MB/Hour**
48	360	22
64	480	28
96	720	42
128	960	56
160	1,200	69
192	1,440	86

Customize the Data Displayed by Media Player

You can see just the information you want for every media file by customizing the Media Player view to show the specific media details you prefer.

Windows Media Player keeps track of a great deal of information for all your media files. For music files, Media Player keeps track of standard properties, such as the album title, artist, and the track names and lengths. However, Media Player also stores more detailed information, such as the genre, release date, bit rate, file format, and size.

For videos, Media Player stores standard properties, such as the title, length, and size, but also in some cases more detailed information, such as number of frames per second and the bit rate for both the video and audio tracks. For some commercial videos, you can also view the director, actors, and studio. These properties are called *metadata* because they are all data that describe the media. You can customize any of the Media Player folders to display the Details view, which shows the metadata. Further, you can customize the specific metadata columns that Media Player displays in each view.

SWITCH TO DETAILS VIEW

① In Windows Media Player, click here to open the View Options menu.

② Click Details.

Media Player switches to Details view.

CUSTOMIZE COLUMNS

① Click Organize.

② Click Layout.

③ Click Choose Columns.

The Choose Columns dialog box appears.

④ Click the deactivated check boxes of the columns you want to view (☐ changes to ☑).

⑤ Click to uncheck the activated check boxes of the columns you do not want to view (☑ changes to ☐).

⑥ To move the selected column to the left in Details view, click Move Up.

⑦ To move the selected column to the right in Details view, click Move Down.

⑧ Click OK.

● Media Player updates the view to display the columns you selected.

TIPS

More Options!

You can see more columns in Details view if you reduce the width of each column so that it is just wide enough to display its data. The easiest way to do this is to position the mouse pointer over the right edge of the column's header — ↳ changes to ✛ — and then double-click.

More Options!

You can change the order of the Details view columns without displaying the Choose Columns dialog box. Instead, use your mouse to click and drag the column header to the left or right and then drop it in the new position.

You can listen to the songs and view the photos and videos in your Media Player library on another device by sharing your library over a wired or wireless network.

If you have spent a great deal of time ripping audio CDs, downloading music files, adding other media to your library, and organizing the library, you probably do not want to repeat all that work on another computer. If you have a wired or wireless network, however, you can take advantage of the library work you have

done on one computer by sharing — or *streaming* — that library over the network. This enables any other computer using Windows 7 to include your media in that machine's Media Player library. This also applies to other user accounts on your computer. Those users can log on and then access your shared library.

Your shared library is also available to other media devices on the network, such as an Xbox 360 or a networked digital media receiver.

TURN ON MEDIA STREAMING

 In Windows Media Player, click Stream.

 Click Turn On Media Streaming.

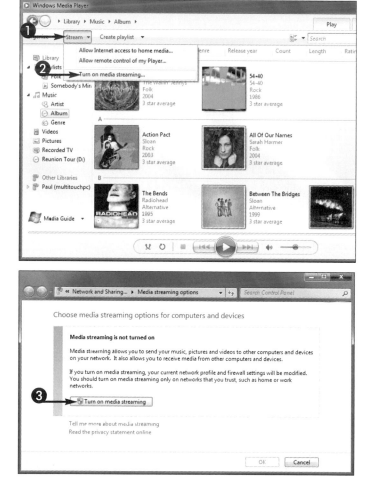

The Media Streaming Options window appears.

 Click Turn On Media Streaming.

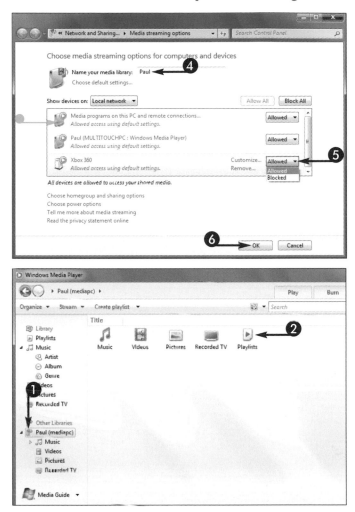

Media Player turns on media streaming and displays the streaming options.

④ Type a name for your media library.

● Media Player displays a list of the devices that can access your media library.

⑤ For each device, click Allowed if you want the device to access your media library; otherwise, click Blocked.

⑥ Click OK.

ACCESS A SHARED MEDIA LIBRARY

① In Media Player's navigation pane, click the name of the library you want to access.

② Double-click the type of media you want to play.

Note: Although other computers can usually see the shared library within a few seconds, the media in the shared library may take several minutes to appear.

More Options!
To restrict the media you share, click Stream and then click More Streaming Options. To set restrictions for all devices, click Choose Default Settings; otherwise, click a device and then click Customize. Under Star Rating, click Only (◯ changes to ◉) and then click a rating. Under Choose Parental Ratings, click Only (◯ changes to ◉), and then click the check boxes of the ratings you do not want to share (☑ changes to ☐).

More Options!
You can also allow network devices to control your local Media Player, which enables those devices to add music and other media to your library. To set this up, click Stream and then click Allow Remote Controls of My Player. In the Allow Remote Control dialog box, click Allow Remote Control on This Network.

You can customize various aspects of Media Player's navigation pane to suit the way you use Media Player.

The navigation pane on the left side of the Media Player window gives you a quick way to switch from one Media Player library to another. However, the navigation pane is also an easy way to use media properties to get different views of your media. For example, by default the Music section of the navigation pane includes three subsections: Artist, Album,

and Genre. When you click one of these subsections, you see your music organized by the corresponding property values (artist name, album title, or genre). You can customize the navigation to show other music properties, such as Rating and Year, as well as properties for the other sections: Videos, Pictures, and Recorded TV.

Media Player also enables you to customize the navigation pane to show all your playlists and to hide the Other Media section.

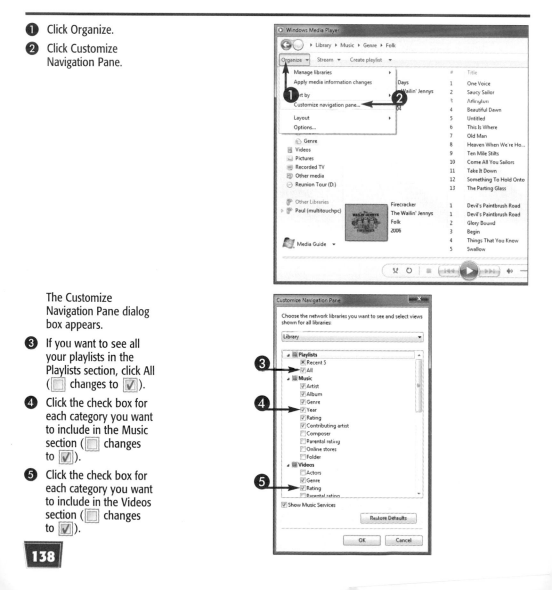

① Click Organize.

② Click Customize Navigation Pane.

The Customize Navigation Pane dialog box appears.

③ If you want to see all your playlists in the Playlists section, click All (☐ changes to ☑).

④ Click the check box for each category you want to include in the Music section (☐ changes to ☑).

⑤ Click the check box for each category you want to include in the Videos section (☐ changes to ☑).

6 Click the check box for each category you want to include in the Pictures section (☐ changes to ☑).

7 Click the check box for each category you want to include in the Recorded TV section (☐ changes to ☑).

8 Click Other Media to hide this section (☑ changes to ☐).

9 Click OK.

● Media Player applies the new settings to the navigation pane.

10 Click and drag the divider to change the width of the navigation pane as needed.

Remove It!

By default, the navigation pane includes a section called Other Libraries that displays the media libraries shared by other Media Player users on your network. If you do not want to see a particular library in your navigation pane, right-click that library and then click Remove from List. Media Player hides the library.

Remove It!

If you do not want to see the navigation pane's Other Libraries section at all, follow steps 1 and 2 to display the Customize Navigation Pane dialog box. In the list at the top of the dialog box, choose Other Libraries. Click the Show Other Libraries check box (☑ changes to ☐), and then click OK. Media Player no longer displays the Other Libraries section in the navigation pane.

Add Sounds to Windows 7 Events

You can associate sound files with specific Windows 7 occurrences, such as minimizing a window or starting a program. This not only adds some aural variety to your system, but it can also help novice users of your computer follow and understand what is happening on the screen.

In Windows 7, a *program event* is an action taken by a program or by Windows 7 itself in response to something. For example, if you click a window's Minimize button, the window minimizes to the taskbar. Similarly, if you click an item in a program's menu bar, the menu drops down. Other events, like an error message, a low notebook battery alarm, or a notification of the arrival of a new e-mail message, are generated internally by a program or by Windows 7.

Windows 7 has certain sounds associated with all of these events and many others. Some of these sounds, such as the music you hear when Windows 7 starts up, are purely decorative "ear candy." Other sounds, such as the sharp tone that sounds when an error message appears, are more useful. Whether your goal is aural decoration or usefulness, you can augment or change the existing Windows 7 sounds.

---

① Click Start.

② Type **system sound**.

③ Click Change System Sounds.

The Sound dialog box appears with the Sounds tab displayed.

④ Click the Windows 7 event you want to work with.

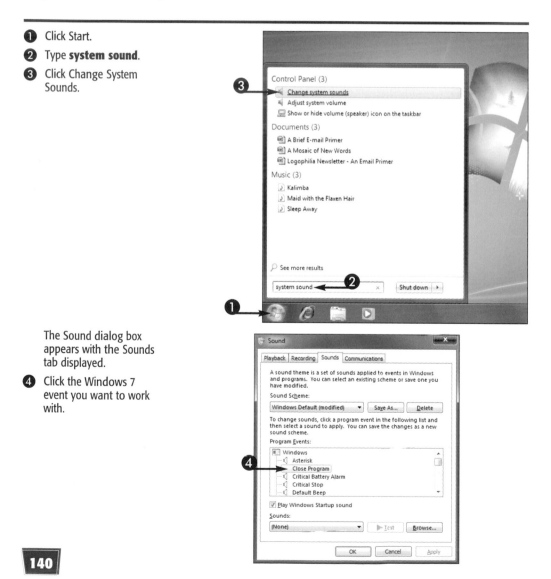

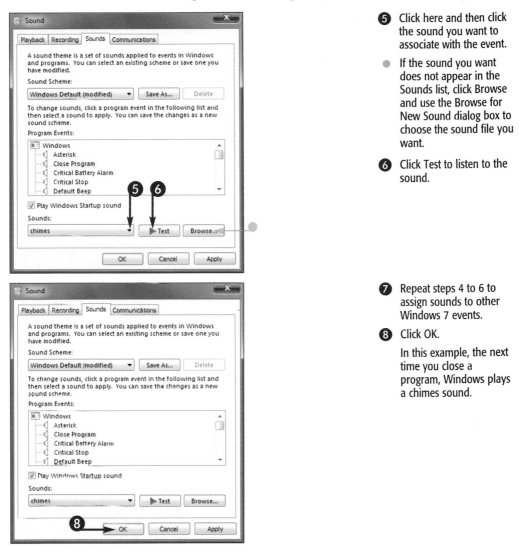

5 Click here and then click the sound you want to associate with the event.

● If the sound you want does not appear in the Sounds list, click Browse and use the Browse for New Sound dialog box to choose the sound file you want.

6 Click Test to listen to the sound.

7 Repeat steps 4 to 6 to assign sounds to other Windows 7 events.

8 Click OK.

In this example, the next time you close a program, Windows plays a chimes sound.

More Options!

You can save your selected sounds as a *sound scheme*, a collection of sound files associated with Windows 7 events. In the Sounds tab of the Sound dialog box, after you have made your sound selections, click Save As, type a name for the sound scheme, and then click OK.

Remove It!

If you tire of your sound scheme and prefer to return Windows 7 to its original sound settings, follow steps 1 to 4 to open the Sound dialog box. Click ▼ in the Sound Scheme list and then click Windows Default. If you prefer no sounds at all, click No Sounds. Click OK.

Chapter

6

Maximizing Windows 7 Performance

Whether you use Windows 7 at work or at home, you probably want to spend your computer time creating documents, sending and receiving e-mail, browsing the Web, playing games, and doing other useful and fun activities. You probably do *not* want to spend your time wrestling with Windows 7 or waiting for it to finish its tasks.

Using a few simple techniques, you can make working with Windows 7 faster and more convenient. For example, instead of wasting time logging on to Windows 7, you can configure the system to log you on automatically.

Also, you can work with a few settings to ensure Windows 7 is working quickly and

efficiently. For example, you can speed up your display by reducing the number of visual effects Windows 7 uses to draw screen elements, and by using a USB Flash drive to boost performance.

Sometimes getting the most out of Windows 7 is a simple matter of taking care of the little details. For example, you can make Windows 7 a little more efficient by configuring it to automatically move the mouse pointer to the default button in a dialog box, and to not prompt you for confirmation when you delete a file.

This chapter introduces you to these and many other techniques for maximizing your Windows 7 productivity.

Quick Tips

You can configure your Windows 7 system to start faster by bypassing the Welcome screen and logging on your user account automatically.

When you start your computer, your system first tests various components during the *power on self test* (POST) routine, and then Windows 7 loads its components into memory. You eventually end up at the Welcome screen, where you must click your user icon (if your system has multiple user accounts) and then type your account password. Only then does

Windows 7 finish loading and display the desktop.

Logging on is not an onerous task, but it does slow down the startup a bit. This is particularly true if you want to power on your computer and then go perform some other task while the system boots, because you must return to the PC to perform the logon.

To save the time it takes to log on, and to enable Windows to completely load the system without requiring any input from you, you can configure Windows 7 to automatically log on your user account.

① Click Start.

② Click All Programs.

Note: *When you click All Programs, the command name changes to Back.*

③ Click Accessories.

④ Click Run.

The Run dialog box appears.

Note: *You can also display the Run dialog box by pressing Windows key+R.*

⑤ Type **control userpasswords2**.

⑥ Click OK.

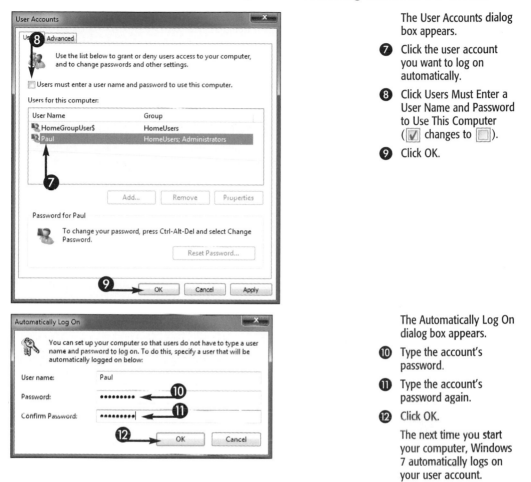

The User Accounts dialog box appears.

7 Click the user account you want to log on automatically.

8 Click Users Must Enter a User Name and Password to Use This Computer (☑ changes to ☐).

9 Click OK.

The Automatically Log On dialog box appears.

10 Type the account's password.

11 Type the account's password again.

12 Click OK.

The next time you start your computer, Windows 7 automatically logs on your user account.

Caution!

Many forms of Windows 7 security — including User Account Control, file encryption, local file security, and network file sharing — assume that the logged-on user is a trusted user who has provided the proper logon credentials to access the system. This task's technique bypasses that logon, so use it only if no other person has physical access to your computer.

Try This!

If you have other accounts on your system, you can still log on one of them. Wait until your account logs on automatically and you see the desktop. Click Start, click the arrow beside the Shut Down button, and then click either Switch User (to keep your account logged on), or Log Off (to log off your account). Either way, you end up at the Welcome screen where you can log on the other account.

You can turn off some or all of the visual effects that Windows 7 uses to display screen elements. This reduces the load on your computer, which improves the overall performance of your machine.

These visual effects include the animation Windows 7 uses when you minimize or maximize a window. For example, when you minimize a window, it appears to shrink down to the taskbar. Such effects are designed to help novice users better understand what is happening on their computer.

For graphics in general, and the visual effects in particular, performance is mostly determined

by the amount of memory on the *graphics adapter*. This is a circuit board inside your computer that processes the graphical data generated by Windows 7 and displayed on your monitor. The more memory on the adapter, the faster it can process the visual effects.

Most new computers have a decent amount of adapter memory — at least 32MB — so turning off visual effects has little impact on performance. If your adapter has 8MB or less, turning off visual effects can improve performance.

1 Click Start.

2 Type **advanced**.

3 Click View Advanced System Settings.

The System Properties dialog box appears with the Advanced tab displayed.

4 In the Performance area, click Settings.

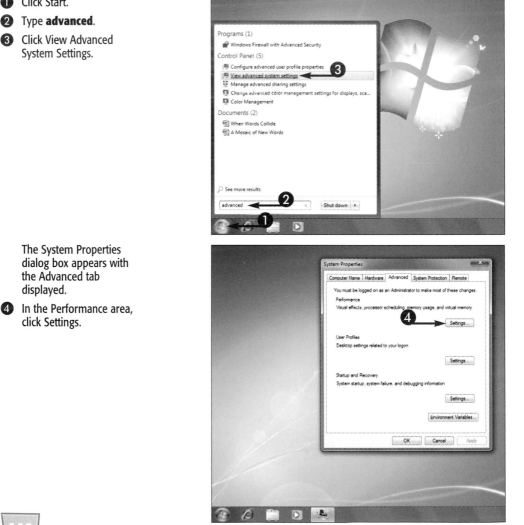

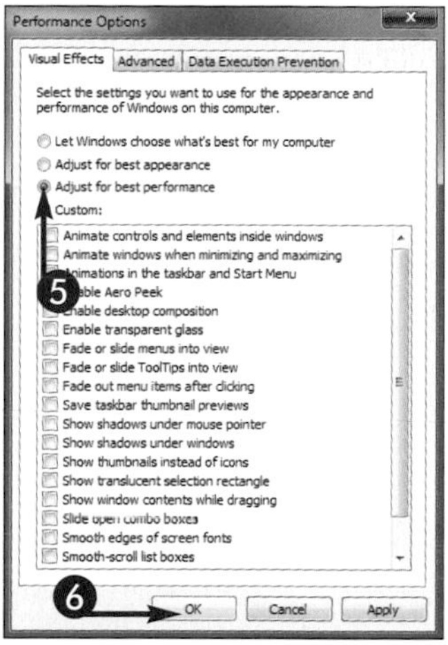

The Performance Options
dialog box appears.

⑤ Click the Adjust for Best
Performance option
(◯ changes to ◉).

⑥ Click OK to return to the
System Properties dialog
box.

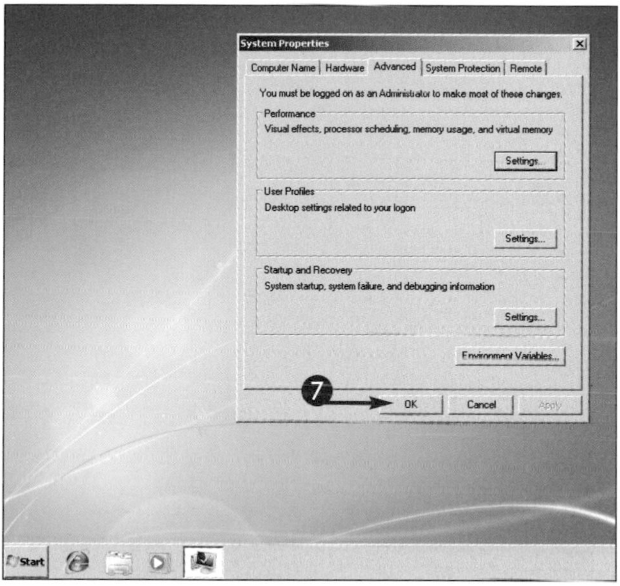

Windows 7 turns off the
visual effects.

⑦ Click OK.

Windows 7 closes the
System Properties dialog
box.

TIPS

Customize It!

If you prefer to turn off only certain
visual effects, click the Adjust for
Best Appearance option in step 7
(◯ changes to ◉) to ensure all the
effects are activated. Click the Custom
option (◯ changes to ◉) and then
click the check box for each visual effect
you want to turn off (☑ changes to ☐).

Did You Know?

If you do not know how much memory
your graphics adapter has, Windows 7 can
tell you. Click Start, type **system info**, and
then click System Information. In the
System Information window, double-click
Components and then click Display. The
Adapter RAM value tells you the amount of
memory in your graphics adapter.

You can negotiate many dialog boxes much more quickly by customizing Windows 7 to automatically move the mouse pointer over the default dialog box button.

Most dialog boxes define a *default button*, which is most often the button that dismisses the dialog box and puts the dialog box settings into effect. The most common default dialog box button is the OK button.

Windows 7 makes it easy for you to find the default button by making the button glow while the dialog box is open. That is, the button's blue color gradually fades in and out.

Many dialog boxes do nothing more than provide you with information or a warning. In most of these cases, the only thing you need to do with the dialog box is click the default button. You can get past such dialog boxes much more quickly if you configure Windows 7 to use the Snap To feature, which automatically moves the mouse pointer over the default button, because then all you have to do is click to dismiss the dialog box. If the dialog box requires more complex input from you, you still save time because the mouse pointer is already inside the dialog box.

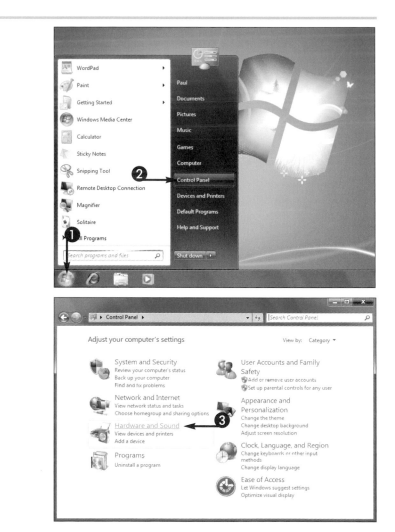

① Click Start.

② Click Control Panel.

The Control Panel window appears.

③ Click Hardware and Sound.

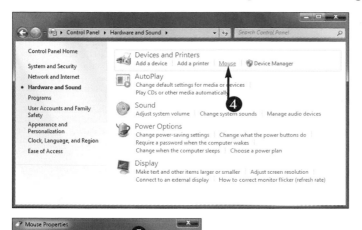

The Hardware and Sound window appears.

④ Click Mouse.

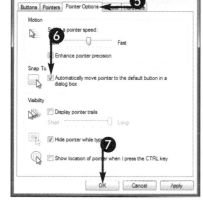

The Mouse Properties dialog box appears.

⑤ Click the Pointer Options tab.

⑥ Click the Automatically Move Pointer to the Default Button in a Dialog Box check box (☐ changes to ☑).

⑦ Click OK.

Windows 7 automatically moves the mouse pointer to the default button each time you open a dialog box.

Caution!

When the Snap To feature is activated, it is easy to get into the habit of quickly clicking whenever a notification dialog box appears. However, if you click too quickly, you may miss the message in the dialog box, which could be important. Remember to read all dialog box messages before clicking the default button.

More Options!

If you have excellent mouse control, another option that can save time in the long run is to increase the pointer speed, which enables you to get from one part of the screen to another much more quickly. Follow steps 1 to 5 to display the Pointer Options tab, click and drag the Select a Pointer Speed slider towards Fast, and then click OK.

If you add a USB flash drive to your computer, Windows 7 can use the memory on that drive to improve the performance of your system.

Windows 7 uses a technology named SuperFetch to boost system performance. SuperFetch tracks the programs and data you use over time to create a kind of profile of your hard drive usage. Using this profile, SuperFetch can then anticipate the data that you might use in the near future. It would then load (fetch) that data into memory ahead of time. If that data was indeed what your system required, performance would increase because Windows 7 would not have to retrieve the data from your hard drive.

However, SuperFetch goes even further by also using Windows 7's new ReadyBoost technology. If you insert a USB 2.0 flash drive (also called a memory key) into your system, Windows 7 asks you if you want to use the device to speed up your system. If you elect to do this, ReadyBoost uses that drive's capacity as storage for the data that SuperFetch anticipates you will require. This frees up the system memory that SuperFetch would otherwise use for storage, and more available memory means better performance for Windows 7 and your programs.

---

① Insert a flash drive into a USB port on your computer.

The AutoPlay dialog box appears.

② Click Speed Up My System Using Windows ReadyBoost.

Windows 7 displays the ReadyBoost tab of the device's Properties dialog box.

③ Click Use This Device (○ changes to ●).

● If you want Windows 7 to use the entire drive for ReadyBoost, click Dedicate This Device to ReadyBoost, instead (○ changes to ●), and then skip to step 5.

④ Click and drag the slider to set the amount of drive memory Windows 7 sets aside for ReadyBoost.

● You should set the drive space value to the value that Windows 7 recommends.

⑤ Click OK.

Windows 7 configures ReadyBoost to use the flash drive's memory.

TIPS

Did You Know?

If you have two USB flash drives and your computer has two available USB ports, you can insert both flash drives and tell Windows 7 to use them both to speed up your system. You should also know that you probably will not see much improvement in performance if your system has at least 1GB of RAM, because ReadyBoost does not need extra space when it has that much memory available.

Reverse It!

If you decide later on that you want to use the flash drive's full capacity for file storage, you can tell Windows 7 not to use the drive to augment ReadyBoost. Click Start, Computer, click the flash drive, and then click Properties. Click the ReadyBoost tab and then click the Do Not Use This Device option (○ changes to ◉). Click OK to put the new setting into effect.

If you need to perform advanced tasks in a program, you may need to run that program with elevated privileges.

Windows 7 implements a security model named *user account control* (UAC). The basic idea behind this security strategy is that you have permission to perform only a few day-to-day Windows tasks, such as moving and copying files. For more ambitious tasks that could affect the security of the system, Windows 7 asks you to provide credentials to prove that the task is not being performed by a virus program or other malicious software.

The credentials you provide depend on the type of account you have. If you have an administrator account, you click Yes in the User Account Control dialog box; if you have a Standard user account, you have to provide an administrator password.

However, this security model falls short when you need to perform certain actions. For example, if you edit a file in one of the Windows 7 protected folders, you receive a Permission Denied error when you try to save your changes.

To work around such problems, you need to start the program you are using with elevated privileges. This tells Windows 7 to run the program as though you were using the Administrator account, the highest-level account on your system, and the only account that does not need to provide credentials.

① Click Start.

② Click All Programs.

Note: When you click All Programs, the command name changes to Back.

③ Open the Start menu folder that contains the icon of the program you want to run.

● For example, to run the Command Prompt elevated, click Accessories.

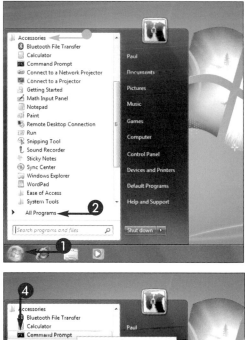

④ Right-click the program icon (for example, the Command Prompt icon).

⑤ Click Run as Administrator.

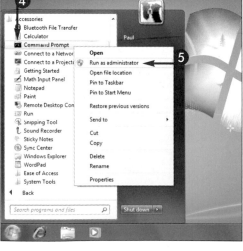

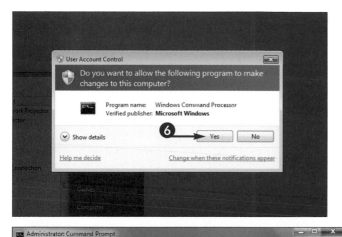

The User Account Control dialog box appears.

⑥ Click Yes.

If you have a Standard user account, you must also type the password for an administrator account.

● Windows 7 runs the program with elevated privileges.

TIPS

Did You Know?

If you have a program that you use frequently and you normally run it with elevated privileges, you can tell Windows 7 to always run the program elevated. Follow steps 1 to 3 in this task to find the program icon, right-click the icon, and then click Properties. Click the Compatibility tab, click the Run This Program as an Administrator check box (☐ changes to ☑), and then click OK.

Caution!

When you run a program with elevated privileges, it not only enables you to perform otherwise forbidden tasks using the program, but the program itself can perform tasks that programs are usually prevented from doing (at least until you enter your credentials to allow them access to the system). Because elevated programs can perform forbidden tasks, only elevate privileges for programs you know and trust. Otherwise, you might inadvertently give a virus or Trojan horse program complete access to your system.

You can add folders to the Windows Search engine's index, which makes your file searches in those folders run noticeably faster.

Having a lot of data is certainly not a bad thing, but *finding* the file you want among all that data can get frustrating. Fortunately, the Windows 7 Search feature can help by enabling you to search for files based on name, content, size, and more.

This works well if what you are looking for is in your main user account folder or one of its file libraries (such as the Documents, Pictures,

or Music library). This is because Windows 7 automatically *indexes* those folders, which means it keeps a detailed record of the contents of all your files. Using this index, the Search feature can find files up to a hundred times faster than without an index.

However, if you have files in a different location, Windows 7 does not index them, so searching those files is very time-consuming. You can dramatically speed up the searching of those files by adding their location to the Search index.

---

① Click Start.

② Type **index**.

③ Click Indexing Options.

The Indexing Options dialog box appears.

④ Click Modify.

The Indexed Locations dialog box appears.

⑤ Click the check box beside the folder you want to include in the index (☐ changes to ☑).

● The folder appears in the list of included locations.

⑥ Repeat step 5 to add other folders to the index.

⑦ Click OK.

⑧ Click Close.

Windows 7 includes the folder in the index and begins rebuilding the index.

TIPS

Did You Know?

If Windows 7 takes a long time to search or cannot find your files, you may need to rebuild the index. Follow steps 1 to 3 to display the Indexing Options dialog box. Click Advanced to display the Advanced Options dialog box, and then click Rebuild.

Caution!

The catalog created by the Indexing Service can use up hundreds of megabytes of hard drive space. To move the catalog to a hard drive with more space, follow steps 1 to 3 to display the Indexing Options dialog box. Click Advanced to display the Advanced Options dialog box. Click Select New, select a new location, and then click OK.

You can take advantage of the many file properties supported by Windows 7 to search for files based on the author, keywords, and other data.

In Windows 7, you can perform sophisticated searches by using a number of different properties. These file properties are called *metadata* because they are data that describe the data on your system — that is, your documents. Chapter 4 described how to add metadata.

For example, the Authors property specifies the name of the person (or people) who created a document. Similarly, the Tags property lists one or more words or phrases that describe the contents of a document. For music files, you can search on the Genre name, Album title, Artist name, and more.

You can create advanced searches that look in these and other properties for the file or files you seek.

---

① Open the folder you want to search in.

② Click inside the Search box.

● Windows 7 displays some properties associated with the current folder.

③ Click a property.

● Windows 7 displays the available property values.

④ Click the property value you want to use in your search.

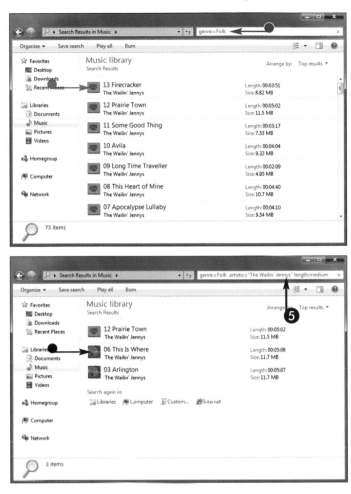

- Windows 7 adds the search criteria to the Search box.

- Windows 7 displays the files that match the property value.

⑤ Repeat steps 2 to 4 to add more metadata to your search criteria.

- Windows 7 displays the files that match all of your values.

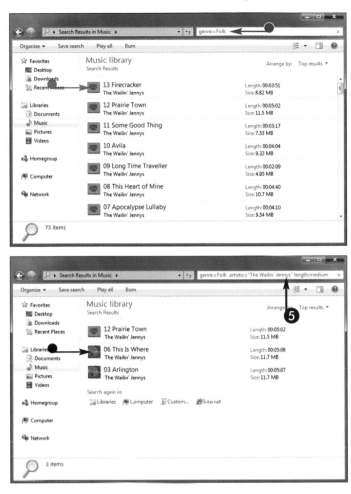

(TIPS)

More Options!

By default, Windows 7 matches only those files that satisfy all of the criteria you add to the Search box. However, there may be times when you are looking for files that match one criteria or another. For example, you might want to find music where the Genre property is Folk or Fiddle. To perform such a search, insert the word OR between the criteria, as in this example:

Genre:=Folk OR Genre:=Fiddle

More Options!

By default, Windows 7 looks for files where the property equals the value you specify. To match files where the property does not equal the value, replace the equals sign (=) with the not equals sign (<>), as in this example:

Year:=2000 Genre:<> Rock

If you are having trouble running an older program, you can customize the program's icon to run in compatibility mode so that it works properly under Windows 7.

For best performance and stability, you should try wherever possible to run programs that were designed only for Windows 7. This is not always practical, however, so it is likely that you have some older programs that came about prior to Windows 7. In most cases, those older programs should run without any problems under Windows 7. However, in some cases these older programs experience problems or fail to run in Windows 7.

The most common reason for such problems is that the older program was designed specifically to run under a particular operating system. For example, a program might have been designed for Windows 98 or Windows XP, and if the program encounters any other operating system it either refuses to run or displays frequent glitches.

You can usually work around such problems by running the program in *compatibility mode*, where Windows 7 sets up an environment that mimics the operating system for which the program was designed.

① Click Start.

② Click All Programs.

Note: *When you click All Programs, the command name changes to Back.*

③ Open the menu that contains the icon of the program you want to configure.

Note: *If the program resides on a CD, DVD, or other removable media, use Windows Explorer to open the media.*

④ Right-click the icon.

⑤ Click Properties.

The program's Properties dialog box appears.

6 Click the Compatibility tab.

7 Click the Run This Program in Compatibility Mode For check box (☐ changes to ☑).

8 Click here and then click the operating system for which the program was designed.

9 Click OK.

Windows 7 runs the program in compatibility mode each time you start it.

TIPS

More Options!
Some older programs do not run under Windows 7 because they require fewer colors than Windows 7 displays. For example, many older programs can use at most 256 colors, but the Windows 7 minimum is 65,536 colors. To fix this, follow steps 1 to 6, click the Run in 256 Colors check box (☐ changes to ☑), and then click OK.

More Options!
Another reason some older programs do not work with Windows 7 is because they expect a screen resolution of 640 x 480, and the minimum resolution under Windows 7 is 800 x 600. To solve this problem, follow steps 1 to 6, click the Run in 640 x 480 Screen Resolution check box (☐ changes to ☑), and then click OK.

You can save a step each time you delete a file by turning off the Recycle Bin's confirmation dialog box.

Each time you delete a file in Windows 7, the Confirm File Delete dialog box appears, asking if you are sure you want to send the file to the Recycle Bin. This is usually a good idea because it prevents you from accidentally deleting a file that you would prefer to keep.

However, deleting a file by accident in Windows 7 is not a huge problem because you can always open the Recycle Bin folder and then restore the file to its original folder.

Therefore, if you find the extra step of responding to the delete confirmation prompt to be unnecessary or inefficient, you can adjust the Recycle Bin's properties to turn off the confirmation prompt.

---

① Click Windows Explorer.

Windows Explorer appears.

② Click here to open the top-level folder menu.

③ Click Recycle Bin.

The Recycle Bin folder appears.

④ Click Organize.

⑤ Click Properties.

Organize ▾
✂ Cut
📋 Copy
📋 Paste
Undo
Redo
Select all
🖿 Layout ▸
Folder and search options
✕ Delete
Rename
Remove properties
Properties
Close

🖳 Network

🗑 0 items

The Recycle Bin Properties dialog box appears.

⑥ Click Display Delete Confirmation Dialog (☑ changes to ☐).

⑦ Click OK.

When you delete a file from now on, Windows 7 will not ask you to confirm.

Recycle Bin Properties

General

Recycle Bin Location	Space Available
Data (D:)	48.8 GB
Local Disk (C:)	183 GB

Settings for selected location

⦿ Custom size:
Maximum size (MB): 4547

◯ Don't move files to the Recycle Bin. Remove files immediately when deleted.

☐ Display delete confirmation dialog

OK   Cancel   Apply

TIPS

Try This!

If you can see your desktop, Windows 7 offers a much faster method to display the Recycle Bin's properties. Right-click the Recycle Bin icon on the desktop, and then click Properties in the shortcut menu. Windows 7 opens the Recycle Bin Properties dialog box.

More Options!

If you do not want to use the Recycle Bin at all, Windows 7 offers two methods for deleting a file immediately. If you prefer to delete a file immediately only occasionally, click the file and then press Shift+Delete. To delete all files immediately, follow steps 1 to 5 to display the Recycle Bin Properties dialog box, click the Do Not Move Files to the Recycle Bin option (◯ changes to ⦿), and then click OK.

You can customize Windows 7 to perform a specific action whenever you insert a particular type of media, such as an audio CD.

When you insert some types of media into your computer, you usually see a dialog box that gives you a list of actions you can perform on that media. For example, if you insert an audio CD, you have the choice of playing the CD in Windows Media Player, ripping the songs from the CD to Windows Media Player, playing the CD in Media Center, and so on.

This is called AutoPlay and it works for the following media types: audio CDs, DVD movies, enhanced audio CDs and DVDs, software and games, pictures, video files, audio files, blank CDs, DVDs, and BDs (Blu-ray discs), Blu-ray movies, audio DVDs, video CDs, and Super Video CDs.

If you always select the same action for a particular media type, you can bypass the AutoPlay dialog box and have Windows 7 perform that action automatically.

① Click Start.

② Click Default Programs.

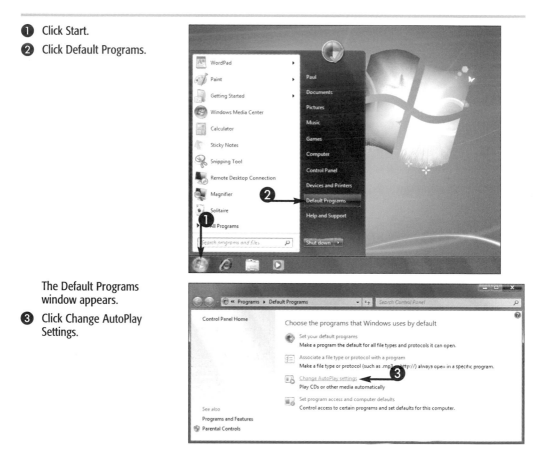

The Default Programs window appears.

③ Click Change AutoPlay Settings.

The AutoPlay window appears.

④ Click Use AutoPlay for All Media and Devices (☐ changes to ☑).

⑤ For the media type you want to configure, click the down arrow and then click the default action that you want Windows 7 to perform when you insert the media.

⑥ Repeat step 5 for the other media you want to configure.

⑦ Click Save.

Windows 7 performs the default actions you chose whenever you insert the configured media.

TIPS

Reverse It!

If you do not like the default action you have chosen for a media type, follow steps 1 to 3 to display the AutoPlay window. Click the down arrow (▼) for the media type, and then click Ask Me Every Time. If you prefer to reset all the media, scroll down to the bottom of the AutoPlay window and then click Reset All Defaults. Click Save.

Remove It!

If you prefer that Windows 7 not take any action when you insert any type of media, you can turn off the AutoPlay feature. Follow steps 1 to 3 to display the AutoPlay window and then click the Use AutoPlay for All Media and Devices check box (☑ changes to ☐). Click Save.

You can ensure that a device is working at optimum performance by updating the device's driver to the latest version.

Windows 7 acts as a go-between for you and your programs and the hardware devices on your system. For example, when you press a key on your keyboard, Windows 7 accepts the keystroke and either displays it on-screen (if you are typing) or runs a command (if you pressed a shortcut key).

Windows 7 communicates with a hardware device by using a small program called a *device driver*, and this communication works two

ways: from the device and to the device. For example, a keyboard uses its device driver to let Windows 7 know what key you pressed.

Hardware manufacturers often create new versions of their device drivers to fix problems and improve the device's performance. For these reasons, it is a good idea to always use the latest device drivers for your system's hardware. After you download a new driver from the manufacturer's Web site, you then need to update the existing driver on your system.

① Click Start.

② Click Control Panel.

The Control Panel window appears.

③ Click System and Security.

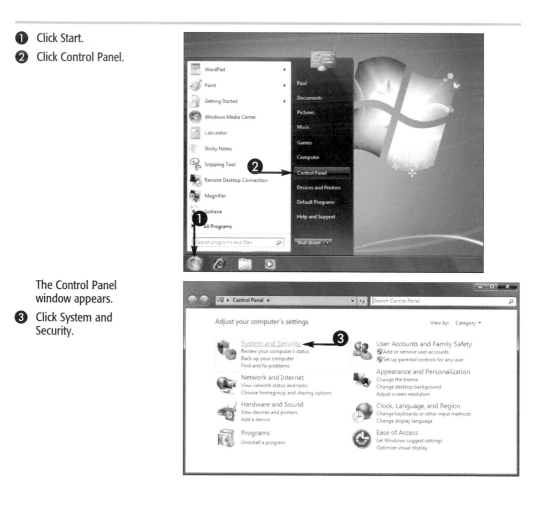

The System and Security window appears.

④ Click Device Manager.

The Device Manager window appears.

⑤ Click the device you want to update.

TIPS

Did You Know?

Windows Update monitors your hardware to look for newer device drivers, and then makes those drivers available to you. To check for available driver updates, click Start, click All Programs, and then click Windows Update. If you see a link named *X* Optional Updates Are Available, click that link, click the check box beside each driver you want to install (☐ changes to ☑), and then click OK.

Did You Know?

If you have a device that is performing slowly or is having problems, the cause may be a corrupted device driver file. In most cases, you can fix this problem by reinstalling the device's driver. Follow the steps in this task and, when it is time to select the driver, select the original driver, which is usually on the CD that came with the device.

continued

Most device manufacturers offer a Web site where you can download the latest drivers, but it helps to know how to navigate these sites.

Look for an area of the site dedicated to driver downloads. The good sites have links to areas named Downloads or Drivers, but it is far more common to first have to go through a Support or Customer Service area.

Go through each step the site provides. For example, it is common to have to select an overall driver category, and then a device

category, and then a line category, and then the specific model you have.

When you get to the device's download page, be careful which file you choose. Make sure that it is a Windows 7 driver, and make sure that you are not downloading a utility program or some other non-driver file.

When you finally get to download the file, save it to your computer. The best location is your user account's Downloads folder.

⑥ Click the Update Driver
Software button.

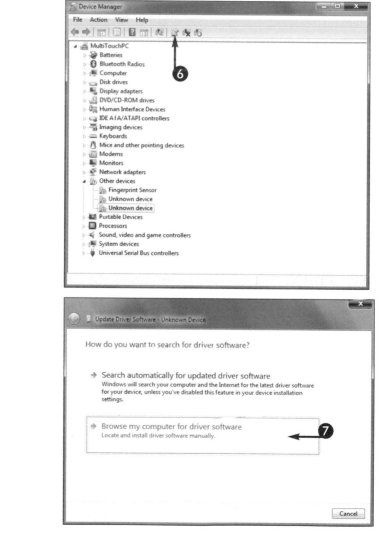

The Update Driver
Software dialog box
appears.

⑦ Click Browse My
Computer for Driver
Software.

Note: *If you have a CD with the device driver, insert the disc and click Search Automatically for Updated Driver Software, instead.*

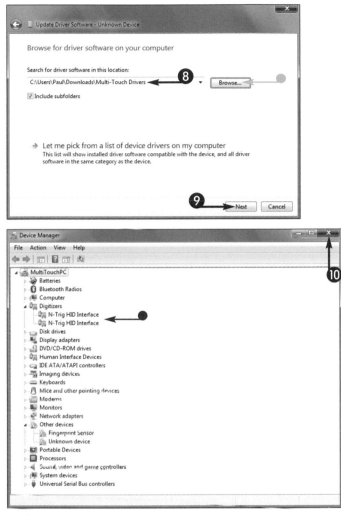

The Browse for Driver Software on Your Computer dialog box appears.

⑧ Type the location of the folder where you saved the downloaded driver.

● Alternatively, click Browse, use the Browse for Folder dialog box to select the folder, and then click OK.

⑨ Click Next.

● Windows 7 installs the driver.

⑩ Click the Close button to close Device Manager.

Windows 7 now uses the updated device driver.

TIPS

Reverse It!
The latest device drivers are usually the most stable and bug-free. However, you may occasionally find that updating a device driver causes problems. In that case, you need to *roll back* the driver to the previous version. Follow steps 1 to 4 to display Device Manager, and then double-click your device. Click the Driver tab and then click the Roll Back Driver button.

Remove It!
When you remove a device from your system, Windows 7 usually recognizes that the device is no longer part of the system and it uninstalls the device's driver. However, Windows 7 sometimes does not realize the device is gone and continues to load the driver. If this happens, follow steps 1 to 4 to display Device Manager, right-click the device, and then click Uninstall.

If you find that you often need to restart your computer, you can configure Windows 7 with a shortcut that enables you to restart your system with just a single mouse click.

If you have a program that you use regularly, you can access the program more quickly by creating a shortcut. A *shortcut* is a special file that points to a program. When you launch the shortcut, Windows 7 automatically loads that program.

In particular, Windows 7 has a command that you can run to restart your computer, and you

can create a shortcut for that command. Running the shortcut is a bit faster than the standard method for restarting Windows 7, which requires clicking Start, clicking the arrow beside the Shut Down command, and then clicking Restart.

Even better, by pinning the restart shortcut to your Windows 7 taskbar, you can run the command with just a single click.

① Right-click the desktop.

② Click New.

③ Click Shortcut.

The Create Shortcut Wizard appears.

④ In the text box, type **shutdown /r /t 0**.

⑤ Click Next.

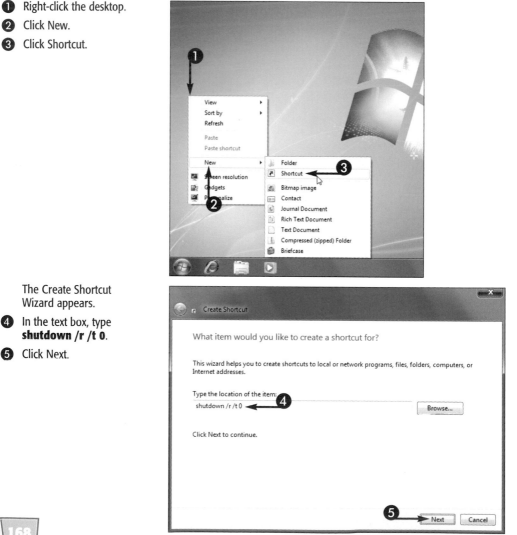

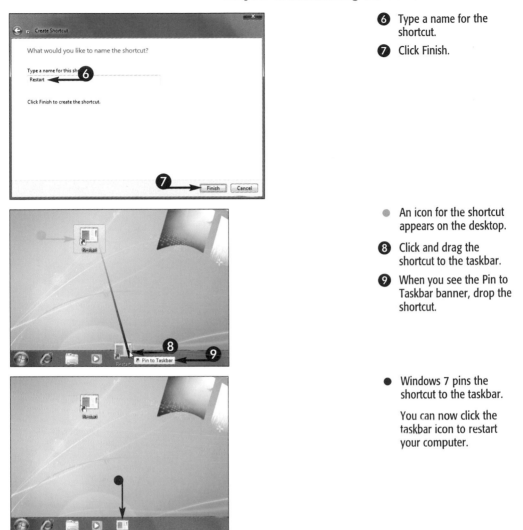

6 Type a name for the shortcut.

7 Click Finish.

● An icon for the shortcut appears on the desktop.

8 Click and drag the shortcut to the taskbar.

9 When you see the Pin to Taskbar banner, drop the shortcut.

● Windows 7 pins the shortcut to the taskbar.

You can now click the taskbar icon to restart your computer.

Try This!

If you find that you shut down your computer more often than you restart it, you can create a one-click shutdown shortcut, instead. Follow steps 1 to 3 to begin a new shortcut, type **shutdown /s /t 0** in the first Create Shortcut Wizard dialog box, then follow steps 5 to 9 to complete the shortcut and pin it to the taskbar.

More Options!

Windows 7 applies a generic shortcut icon to your new shortcut. To apply a more representative icon, right-click the shortcut, click Properties, click the Shortcut tab, and then click Change Icon. Click OK to open the Change Icon dialog box, click the icon you want to use, and then click OK in the open dialog boxes.

Chapter

7

Tapping Into the Power of Internet Explorer

The World Wide Web is arguably the most impressive of the various services accessible via the Internet. With *billions* of pages available covering practically every imaginable topic, the Web is one of our greatest inventions and an unparalleled source of information.

One problem with the Web, though, is actually getting at all that information. With so much online ground to cover, you want a reliable and efficient means of transportation. For the World Wide Web, the vehicle of choice is the Web browser, and in Windows 7, the default Web browser is Internet Explorer. This program is fairly easy to use if all you do is click links and type Web site addresses. But to get the most out of the Web, you can tap

into the impressive array of features and options that Internet Explorer offers.

This chapter helps you do just that by taking you through a few truly useful tips and tricks that unleash the power of Internet Explorer. You learn how to take advantage of Internet Explorer's tabs feature; disable Internet Explorer add-ons; subscribe to Web feeds; use your favorite search engine with Internet Explorer; save sites longer for easier surfing; view pop-up windows for specific sites; and more.

Some versions of Windows 7, particularly those sold in the European Union, do not include the Internet Explorer Web browser. To obtain Internet Explorer, contact your computer manufacturer or Microsoft.

Quick Tips

Automatically Switch to New Tabs

You can make the Internet Explorer tab feature much more convenient by configuring the program to automatically switch to new tabs as you create them. Before Internet Explorer 7, if you wanted to open multiple Web sites at once, you had to open multiple copies of the Internet Explorer window.

The latest versions of Internet Explorer, including the version that comes with Windows 7, support *tabbed browsing*, which means you can open multiple Web sites at once

in a single browser window. Each site appears in its own tab, and you can switch from one site to another just by clicking the tabs.

To open a site in a new tab, you right-click the link and then click Open in New Tab. Internet Explorer creates the tab and then opens the Web page in the tab. However, to see the page, you must then click the tab. It is more efficient to have Internet Explorer automatically switch to a new tab when you create it.

① Click Tools.

② Click Internet Options.

The Internet Options dialog box appears.

③ Click the General tab.

④ In the Tabs group, click Settings.

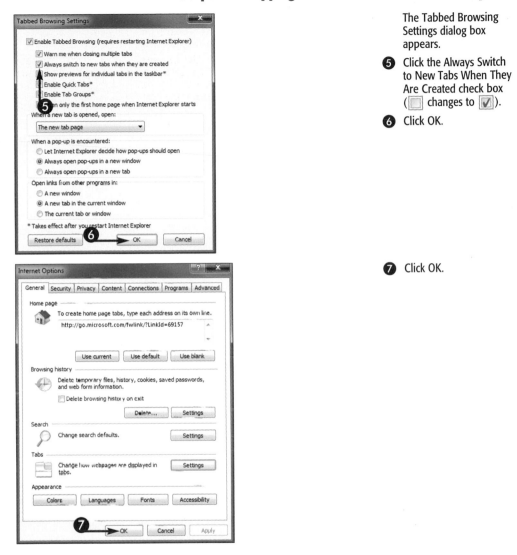

The Tabbed Browsing Settings dialog box appears.

⑤ Click the Always Switch to New Tabs When They Are Created check box (☐ changes to ☑).

⑥ Click OK.

⑦ Click OK.

Did You Know?

If you want to automatically switch to a new tab only occasionally, you do not have to follow the steps in this task. Instead, press and hold both Shift and Ctrl and then click the link. Internet Explorer loads the page in a new tab and then automatically switches to that tab.

More Options!

When you create a new tab by clicking the New Tab button or pressing Ctrl+T, Internet Explorer displays the New Tab page. To load your home page, instead, follow steps 1 to 4, use the When a New Tab Is Opened, Open list to click Your First Home Page, and then click OK.

You can easily view and switch between the Web pages open in your tabs by using the Internet Explorer Quick Tabs feature. Opening multiple pages in a single Internet Explorer window using tabs is convenient. However, tabs do suffer from one drawback. Depending on the width of your monitor and the screen resolution you are using, Internet Explorer can display only a limited number of tabs. For example, when Internet Explorer is maximized on a monitor running at 1024 x 768 screen resolution, the program can display a maximum of nine tabs.

If you have more tabs open than Internet Explorer can display, the program adds arrow buttons to scroll left and right through the tabs. But scrolling is not always convenient because each tab gives you only a minimum amount of information.

When you are dealing with a large number of tabs, a faster way to navigate the tabs is to use the Internet Explorer Quick Tabs feature, which displays a thumbnail image of each open Web page. You can then click the thumbnail of the page you want to immediately switch to that tab.

---

1 Open pages in two or more tabs.

2 Click the Quick Tabs button.

Note: *You can also select the Quick Tabs button by pressing Ctrl+Q.*

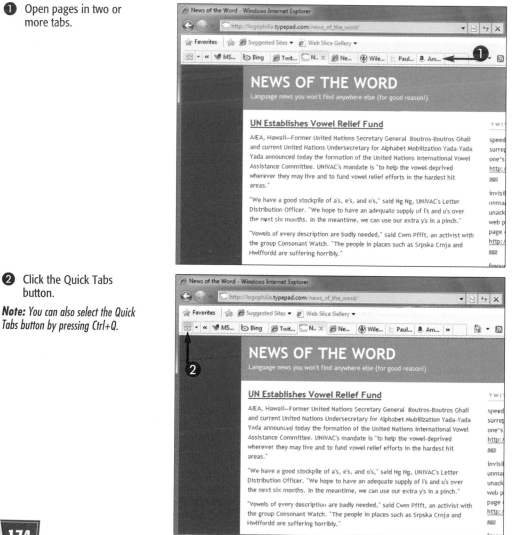

Internet Explorer displays thumbnail images of the Web pages in each tab.

③ Click the Web page you want to view.

Internet Explorer switches to the tab that contains the Web page you selected.

TIPS

More Options!

Internet Explorer also maintains a Tab List, which is a list of the names of the Web pages you have open in the current Internet Explorer window. To display the Tab List, click the down arrow to the right of the Quick Tabs button. (Note that you can only display the Tab List if you have at least two tabs open.) You can then click a page name to switch to that tab.

Remove It!

If you find that you do not use the Quick Tabs feature, you can turn it off to make room for more tabs. Click Tools and then click Internet Options to display the Internet Options dialog box. In the General tab, click Settings in the Tabs group and then click the Enable Quick Tabs check box (✓ changes to ☐). Click OK in the open dialog boxes and then restart Internet Explorer.

Open Multiple Pages When You Start Internet Explorer

If you regularly view several different pages at the start of each Internet Explorer session, you can save time by opening those pages automatically each time you start Internet Explorer.

In Internet Explorer, the *home page* is the page that the browser displays automatically when you first start the program. The default Internet Explorer home page is MSN.com, but most people change that to a page that they use regularly.

However, you may have more than one page that you open after Internet Explorer starts. For example, you may open a portal page such as MSN or Yahoo, a search page such as Google, your company's external or internal Web site, a news page, one or more blogger pages, and so on. Opening each new tab and navigating to the appropriate page can take time.

The Windows 7 version of Internet Explorer enables you to define multiple home pages. Internet Explorer automatically opens each home page in its own tab when you launch the program.

---

① Open the Web page that you want to add as a home page.

② Click the Home menu.

③ Click Add or Change Home Page.

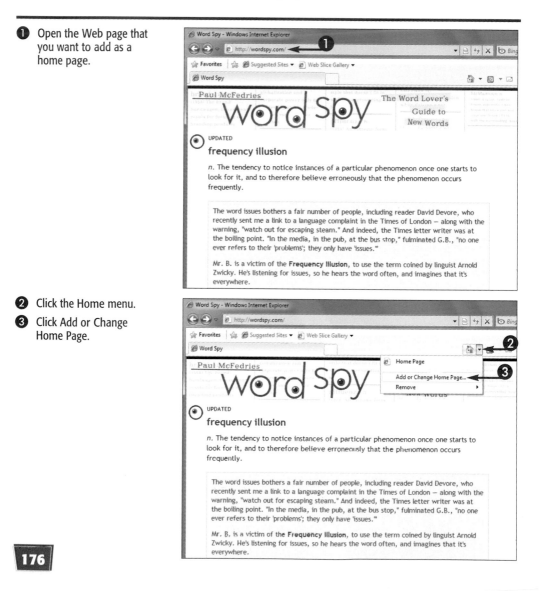

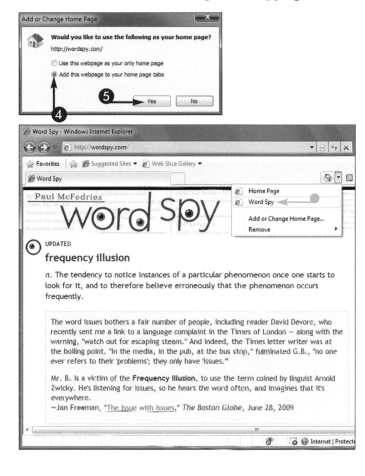

The Add or Change Home Page dialog box appears.

④ Click the Add This Webpage to Your Home Page Tabs option (○ changes to ●).

⑤ Click Yes.

● Internet Explorer adds the page to the Home list.

TIPS

More Options!

If you do not currently have access to the Internet, you can still add a site as a home page. Click Tools and then click Internet Options to display the Internet Options dialog box. In the General tab, click the last item in the Home Page list, press End, and then press Enter to start a new line. Type the address of the new home page and then click OK.

Remove It!

If you have set up a site as one of your Internet Explorer home pages, but you no longer visit that site, you should remove it to reduce the time it takes for Internet Explorer to launch. Click the Home menu, click Remove, and then click the home page that you want to delete. When Internet Explorer asks you to confirm, click Yes.

You can solve some Internet Explorer problems and make the program faster and more efficient by disabling one or more add-ons.

An add-on is an extra feature — such as a toolbar or a control — that does not come with Internet Explorer, but is installed separately. Although Microsoft makes some Internet Explorer add-ons, most come from third-party developers.

Add-ons can be extremely useful and can enhance not just Internet Explorer, but also your surfing experience. However, add-ons occasionally cause problems, either because they were not programmed for the version of Internet Explorer you are using, or because there is a bug or other error in the add-on.

In such cases, the add-on may cause Internet Explorer to operate slowly, or it may cause the program to crash or fail to start. You can often fix such behavior by disabling the add-on causing the problem.

You may also want to disable an add-on that is cluttering the Internet Explorer window or is otherwise interfering with your Web surfing.

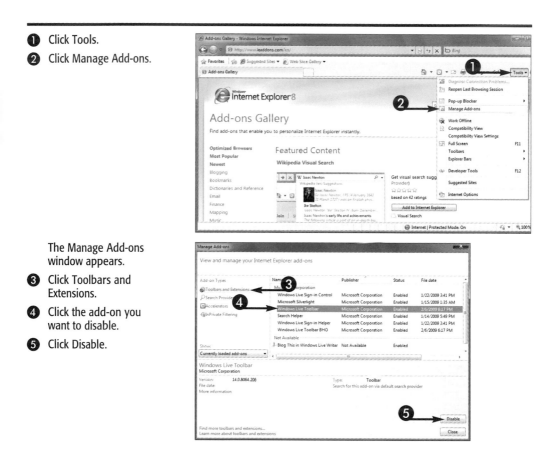

1 Click Tools.

2 Click Manage Add-ons.

The Manage Add-ons window appears.

3 Click Toolbars and Extensions.

4 Click the add-on you want to disable.

5 Click Disable.

The Disable Add-on dialog box appears.

 If you want to disable any other add-ons made by the same company, click the check box beside each add-on (☐ changes to ☑).

⑦ Click Disable.

⑧ Click Close.

⑨ Shut down and restart Internet Explorer.

Internet Explorer does not load the add-on when it restarts.

Try This!

If you are having problems with Internet Explorer, but you are not sure whether an add-on is at fault, try running the program without any add-ons. Click Start, type **add-on**, and then click Internet Explorer (No Add-ons) in the search results. This runs Internet Explorer with all add-ons disabled. If Internet Explorer runs fine, you know an add-on is causing the problem.

Reverse It!

You might decide you want to use a disabled add-on again. For example, you might need the add-on's functionality, or you might realize that it is not causing any problems with Internet Explorer. To enable the add-on, follow steps 1 to 3, click the add-on, click Enable, and then click Enable again in the Enable Add-on dialog box.

Subscribe to a Web Feed to See New Site Content

You can keep up-to-date with a Web site by subscribing to its Web feed, which displays the latest site content.

Some Web sites remain relatively static over time, so you only need to check in every once in a while to see if anything is new. Some Web sites change content regularly, such as once a day or once a week, so you know in advance when to check for new material. However, many sites — particularly blogs — change the content frequently, although not at a regular interval. For these sites, keeping up with new

content can be time-consuming, and it is easy to miss new information.

To solve these problems, many Web sites now maintain Web feeds, which are also called RSS feeds (RSS stands for Really Simple Syndication). A *Web feed* is a special file that contains the most recent information added to the site. You can use Internet Explorer to subscribe to a site's Web feed. This makes it easy to view the feed any time that you want to see the site's new content.

SUBSCRIBE TO A WEB FEED

① Navigate to the site you want to work with.

● If the site has at least one Web feed, the Feeds button becomes activated.

② Click the down arrow to display the Feeds list.

③ Click the feed you want to view.

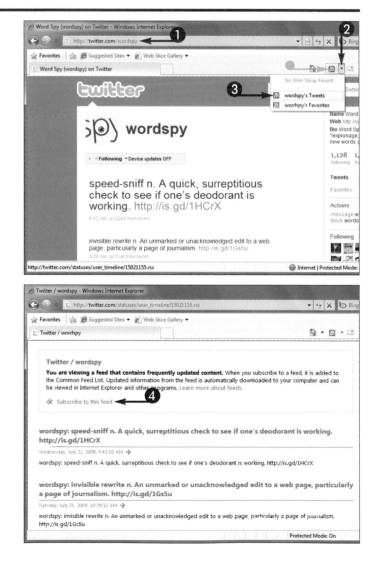

Internet Explorer displays the feed.

④ Click Subscribe to This Feed.

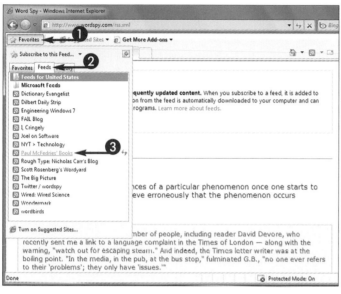

The Subscribe to This Feed dialog box appears.

⑤ Type a new name for the feed (this is optional).

⑥ Click Subscribe.

Internet Explorer subscribes to the feed.

VIEW A WEB FEED

① Click Favorites.

② Click Feeds.

Internet Explorer displays the feeds.

Note: You can also display the Feeds list by pressing Ctrl+J.

③ Click the feed you want to view.

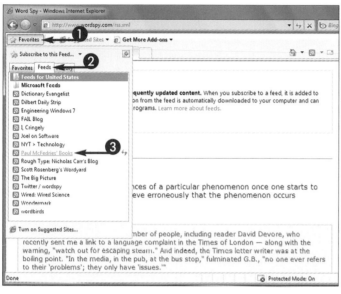

TIPS

More Options!
Instead of subscribing to a feed, you can subscribe to a Web slice using Internet Explorer 8. A Web slice is a specific section of a Web page that the site makes available. When a slice is available, the green Add Web Slices button (🔲) appears rather than the RSS feed button (🔲). Click 🔲 and then click Add to Favorites Bar to add the slice.

More Options!
Internet Explorer activates the Feeds button when it finds a feed on a site. If you want a stronger indication that a feed is available, click Tools and then click Internet Options to display the Internet Options dialog box. Click the Content tab and then click Settings in the Feeds and Web Slices group. Click the Play a Sound When a Feed or Web Slice Is Found for a Webpage check box (☐ changes to ☑). Click OK.

Set the Web Feed Refresh Frequency

You can customize the frequency with which Internet Explorer refreshes a Web feed to suit the way you work or the nature of the feed.

With most Web sites that offer a feed, the feed is updated at the same time as, or soon after, new content is posted to the site. The frequency with which this occurs varies widely: once a day, once a week, several times a day, or even several times an hour.

By default, Internet Explorer checks for an updated feed once per day. This is a reasonable schedule for a site that posts new content once or twice a day or every couple of days. However, it is not an efficient schedule for feeds updated much more or much less frequently. For example, if a feed updates only once a week, checking the feed every day is wasteful for Internet Explorer. You can make a feed more efficient or easier to read by setting up a custom refresh schedule that suits the feed.

① Click Favorites.

② Click Feeds.

③ Right-click the feed you want to view.

④ Click Properties.

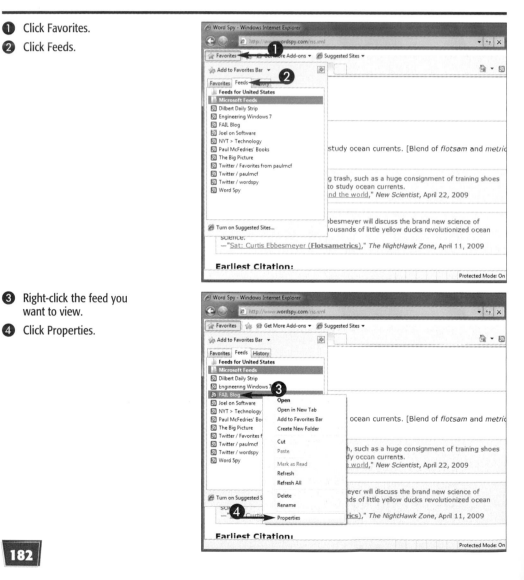

The Feed properties dialog box appears.

⑤ Click the Use Custom Schedule option (◯ changes to ◉).

Feed Properties

Name: FAIL Blog

Address: http://feeds2.feedburner.com/failblog

User name and password   Settings...

Update schedule

Your computer checks this feed or Web Slice for new updates on a specified schedule.

◯ Use default schedule

Default: 1 day   Settings...

◉ Use custom schedule

Frequency: Suggested (1440 minutes) ▾

☐ Automatically download attached files   View files

⑤

Archive

Set the maximum number of updates you want saved for this feed. Changes take effect when the feed is updated.

⑥ Click the Frequency list down arrow.

⑦ Click the frequency with which you want to check the feed.

⑧ Click OK.

Internet Explorer updates the feed's refresh frequency.

Feed Properties

Name: FAIL Blog

Address: http://feeds2.feedburner.com/failblog

User name and password   Settings...

Update schedule

Your computer checks this feed or Web Slice for new updates on a specified schedule.

◯ Use default schedule

Default: 1 day   Settings...

◉ Use custom schedule

Frequency: Suggested (1440 minutes) ▾ ⑥

☐ Automatically de | Suggested (1440 minutes)
15 minutes
30 minutes
1 hour ⑦
4 hours
1 day
1 week
Never

Archive

Set the maximum nu feed. Changes take

◯ Keep maximum items (2500)

◉ Keep the most recent items only

Number of items: 200

About feeds   ⑧   OK   Cancel

TIPS

Did You Know?

How can you tell whether a feed has new posts? The easiest method is to click the Favorites button and then click Feeds. If Internet Explorer displays a feed's title in bold text, it means the feed has new posts. Note, too, that when you position the mouse pointer over a feed, Internet Explorer displays the Refresh This Feed button (✦↑) on the right side of the Feeds pane. Click that button to have Internet Explorer check for new feed items.

More Options!

The default interval that Internet Explorer uses to check feeds for new posts is once a day. To change the default schedule, click Tools and then click Internet Options to display the Internet Options dialog box. Click the Content tab and then click Settings in the Feeds and Web Slices group. Use the Default Schedule list to click the interval you want to use, and then click OK.

Improve Searching by Adding More Search Engines

You can make your Web searches more powerful by adding your favorite search engines to the Internet Explorer Search box.

With billions of pages, the World Wide Web is an amazing information resource. However, it can also be a frustrating resource because *finding* the page you want among those billions is a real challenge. You can ask friends and family, or you can use a site such as Yahoo.com that categorizes pages, but these strategies are often unreliable.

To find the site you want, you can take advantage of the various search engines that enable you to find Web pages based on the search text you provide. The Internet Explorer Search box uses the Bing site to perform its searches.

If you have a search engine other than Bing that you prefer above all others, you may decide that it is worth the extra effort to navigate to that site instead of using Bing via the Internet Explorer Search box. However, you can have it both ways. You can configure Internet Explorer to use your favorite search engine via the Search box.

---

1 Click the Search menu.

2 Click Find More Providers.

The Add-ons Gallery: Search Providers Web page appears.

3 Locate the search engine you want to use and then click Add to Internet Explorer.

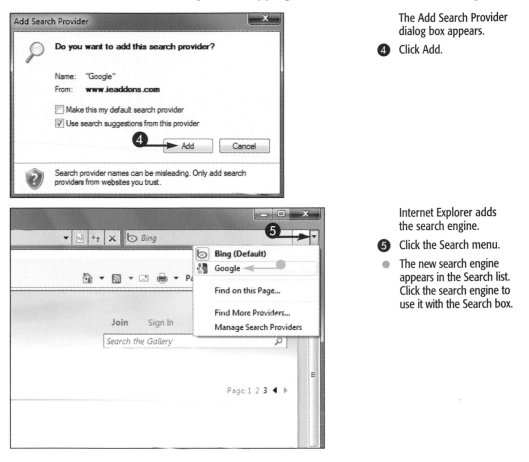

The Add Search Provider dialog box appears.

④ Click Add.

Internet Explorer adds the search engine.

⑤ Click the Search menu.

● The new search engine appears in the Search list. Click the search engine to use it with the Search box.

More Options!

The search engine that Internet Explorer uses in the Search box when you first start the program is called the *default search provider*. The default is Bing, but you can change it to one of your added search engines. Click the Search menu and then click Manage Search Providers. In the Manage Add-ons window, click the search engine you want to use and then click Set as Default. Click Close.

Remove It!

If you add a search engine and later decide you do not want to use it, you should delete it to avoid cluttering the Search list. To remove a search engine, click the Search menu and then click Manage Search Providers. In the Manage Add-ons window, click the search engine you want to delete and then click Remove. Click Close.

Save Web Sites Longer to Surf More Efficiently

You can improve the efficiency of your Web surfing by increasing the number of days that Internet Explorer maintains a record of the sites you have visited.

When you navigate to a Web page, Internet Explorer adds the page's title and address to the History list, which is part of the Favorites Center. The History list is an important Internet Explorer feature because it enables you to easily and quickly return to a page that you have previously visited. The History list

also enables you to view the pages that you have visited most often, so it gives you an easy way to see which pages are your favorites.

By default, Internet Explorer keeps a page in the History list for 20 days before removing it. However, you may find that you often want to revisit pages after the 20-day period has expired. In that case, you can configure Internet Explorer to save pages in the History list for a longer period. The maximum number of days you can save pages is 999.

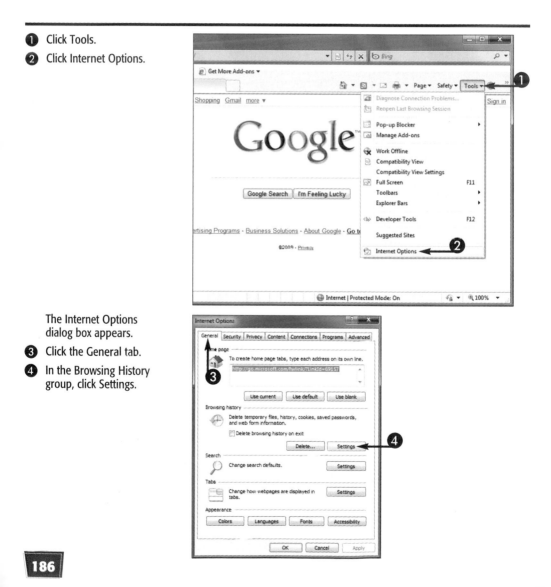

① Click Tools.

② Click Internet Options.

The Internet Options dialog box appears.

③ Click the General tab.

④ In the Browsing History group, click Settings.

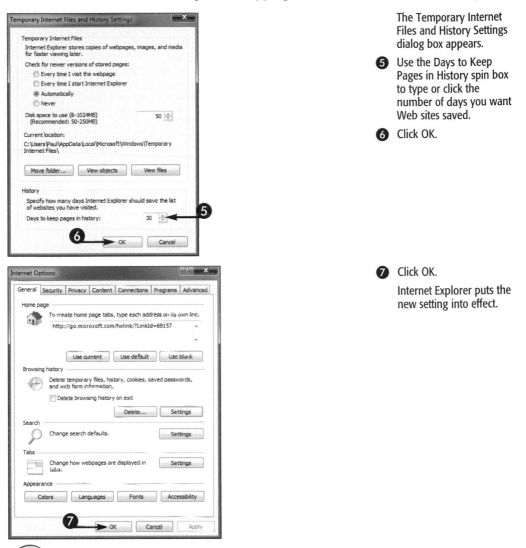

The Temporary Internet Files and History Settings dialog box appears.

⑤ Use the Days to Keep Pages in History spin box to type or click the number of days you want Web sites saved.

⑥ Click OK.

⑦ Click OK.

Internet Explorer puts the new setting into effect.

Try This!
To work with the History list, click the Favorites button and then click History. (You can also press Ctrl+H.) The History list organizes your visited sites into date categories such as Today, Yesterday, Last Week, and Last Month. Click a category, click the site you want to work with, and then click the specific page you want to visit.

Did You Know?
You can sort the History list in various ways. The default sort order is By Date. To change this, display the Favorites Center, click the History menu, and then click By Site, By Most Visited, or By Order Visited Today. You can also click Search History to perform a search on the history entries.

Always Check for Newer Versions of Web Pages

You can ensure that you are always seeing the most up-to-date version of each Web page by configuring Internet Explorer to always check for newer versions of its stored pages.

In the same way that a disk cache stores frequently used data for faster performance, Internet Explorer also keeps a cache of files from Web pages you have visited recently. This cache is a special folder called Temporary Internet Files. When you visit a page, Internet Explorer stores copies of the Web page code, images, and other media in Temporary

Internet Files. Internet Explorer then uses these saved files to display that Web page quickly the next time you surf to the page or if you view the page while you are offline.

However, there is a chance that the Web page may have changed since your last visit, so Internet Explorer may show the older version of the page. To prevent this from happening, configure Internet Explorer to always check to see if the current page files are newer than the stored page files.

---

① Click Tools.

② Click Internet Options.

The Internet Options dialog box appears.

③ Click the General tab.

④ In the Browsing History group, click Settings.

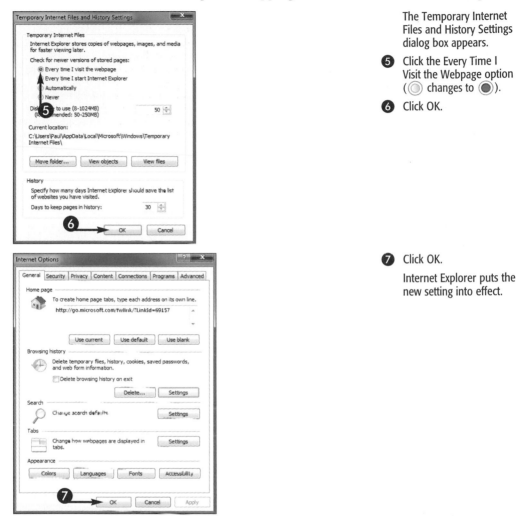

The Temporary Internet Files and History Settings dialog box appears.

⑤ Click the Every Time I Visit the Webpage option (◯ changes to ◉).

⑥ Click OK.

⑦ Click OK.

Internet Explorer puts the new setting into effect.

More Options!

If you have lots of free disk space, you can make your surfing even faster by configuring Internet Explorer to cache more data in the Temporary Internet Files folder. Follow steps 1 to 4 to open the Temporary Internet Files and History Settings dialog box, and then use the Disk Space to Use spin box to increase the size of the cache.

More Options!

If your computer has a second hard drive and your main hard drive is running low on free space, you can move the Temporary Internet Files folder to the second drive. Follow steps 1 to 4 to open the Temporary Internet Files and History Settings dialog box, and then click Move folder. Use the Browse for Folder dialog box to select a folder on the second hard drive, and then click OK.

View Pop-Ups from a Specific Web Site

You can improve your surfing experience by configuring Internet Explorer to view the pop-up ads for certain Web sites that Internet Explorer would otherwise block.

Web page advertising is a necessary evil because Webmasters often need the money from advertisers to help defray the inevitable costs of maintaining a site. Banner ads are a popular choice, but to make more of an impact, advertisers often insist that their ads appear in separate pop-up windows. These pop-ups are everywhere on the Web these days. Small personal pages may display a single

pop-up when you enter or leave the site; some commercial sites display a few pop-ups as you peruse their pages; and then there are those sites that throw out a barrage of pop-ups. Depending on your level of tolerance, pop-ups are either mildly irritating or downright annoying. Either way, pop-up ads can make surfing the Web a real chore.

However, some sites display useful information in pop-up windows, and Internet Explorer may block these windows. If so, you can add the site's address to the list of sites allowed to display pop-ups.

---

① Click Tools.

② Click Pop-up Blocker.

③ Click Pop-up Blocker Settings.

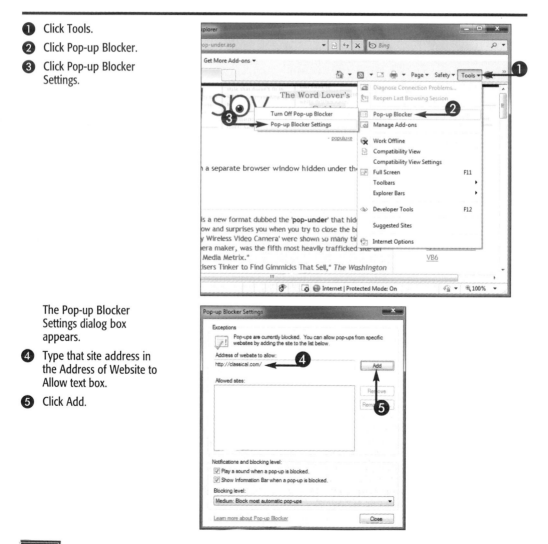

The Pop-up Blocker Settings dialog box appears.

④ Type that site address in the Address of Website to Allow text box.

⑤ Click Add.

Pop-up Blocker Settings

Exceptions

Pop-ups are currently blocked. You can allow pop-ups from specific websites by adding the site to the list below.

Address of website to allow:

Add

Allowed sites:

*.classical.com

Remove

Remove all...

Notifications and blocking level:

☑ Play a sound when a pop-up is blocked.

☑ Show Information Bar when a pop-up is blocked.

Blocking level:

Medium: Block most automatic pop-ups

Learn more about Pop-up Blocker

Close

- Internet Explorer includes the address in the Allowed Sites list.

6 Repeat steps 4 and 5 to add other sites to the Allowed Sites list.

Pop-up Blocker Settings

Exceptions

Pop-ups are currently blocked. You can allow pop-ups from specific websites by adding the site to the list below.

Address of website to allow:

Add

Allowed sites:

*.classical.com
*.nytimes.com

Remove

Remove all...

Notifications and blocking level:

☑ Play a sound when a pop-up is blocked.

☑ Show Information Bar when a pop-up is blocked.

Blocking level:

Medium: Block most automatic pop-ups

Learn more about Pop-up Blocker

Close

7 Click Close.

8 Restart Internet Explorer.

The next time you visit the site, Internet Explorer displays its pop-up windows.

TIPS

More Options!

Instead of typing a site's address in the Pop-up Blocker Settings dialog box, an easier method is to navigate to the site and look for the Internet Explorer Information bar that appears when the program blocks a pop-up. Click the Information Bar, click Always Allow Pop-ups from This Site, and then click Yes when Internet Explorer asks you to confirm.

More Options!

If you only want to occasionally allow pop-ups from a site, follow steps 1 to 3, use the Blocking Level list to click High: Block All Pop-ups, and then click OK. The next time you navigate to the site and want to view its pop-ups, press and hold Ctrl and Alt until the pop-up appears.

Customize the Favorites Bar for Easier Surfing

You can customize Internet Explorer's Favorites bar to provide easy one-click access to those Web sites that you visit most often.

One of Internet Explorer's most useful features is the Favorites bar, which appears beside the Favorites button. By default it consists of two buttons, each of which is associated with a Web slice. When you click a button, Internet Explorer displays the Get More Add-ons slice and the Suggested Sites slice.

However, the Links bar is fully customizable and supports not only Web slices, but also regular sites. This means you can populate the Favorites bar with new buttons associated with the sites you visit most often. This task takes you through these and other Favorites bar customizations.

CREATE A BUTTON FOR THE CURRENT WEB PAGE

1 Navigate to the page you want to add to the Favorites bar.

2 Click the Add to Favorites Bar icon.

● A new button associated with the page appears on the Favorites bar. You can click this button to navigate directly to the page.

CREATE A BUTTON FROM A WEB PAGE LINK

1 Navigate to the page that contains the link you want to add to the Favorites bar.

2 Click and drag the link text and drop it on the Favorites bar.

● A new button associated with the linked page appears on the Favorites bar. You can click this button to navigate directly to the linked page.

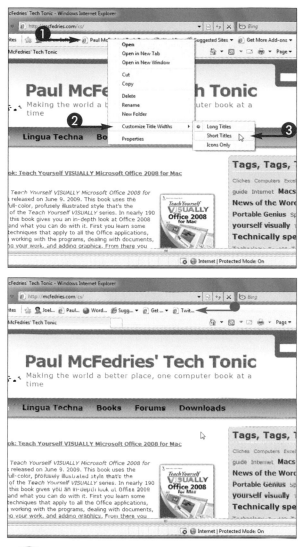

CUSTOMIZE THE TITLE WIDTHS

① Right-click any Favorites bar button.

② Click Customize Title Widths.

③ Click the width you prefer, such as Short Titles.

● Internet Explorer customizes the Favorites bar titles.

Customize It!

The positions of the Favorites bar buttons are not fixed. To move a button to another position, click and drag the button and then drop it in the position you prefer. To rename a button, right-click it, click Rename, type the new name in the Rename dialog box, and then click OK. To delete a button, right-click it, click Delete, and then click Yes when Internet Explorer asks you to confirm.

Did You Know?

If the address of one of your sites changes, you can edit the address associated with the site's Links bar button. Right-click the button and then click Properties. In the button's Properties dialog box, type the new address in the URL text box. Click OK.

Making E-mail Easier

The World Wide Web may be the most impressive of the Internet services, but it would not be hard to make the case that e-mail is the most indispensable. E-mail, which most of us have been using for only a few years, leaves us wondering how we ever managed without it. E-mail's position midway between conversation and letter writing makes it ideal for certain types of communication, and rarely can a person be found nowadays who does not rely on it.

The fact that e-mail is easy to use also helps. Even novice computer users seem to grasp the basic e-mail idea quickly and are often sending messages within minutes. But if, like most people, you use e-mail all day

long, you probably want to make it even easier. This chapter shows you how to do that. The tasks you learn here are designed to save precious seconds and minutes of everyday e-mail chores. That may not sound like much, but added up over the course of a busy e-mail day, those seconds can make the difference between leaving work on time and staying late.

Among the timesavers in this chapter, you learn how to leave messages on the server, change your message priority, create an e-mail distribution list, create a backup copy of your address book, exchange electronic business cards, and spell check your messages.

Quick Tips

Leave Your Messages on the Server

You can configure Windows Live Mail to leave your messages on the server, enabling you to retrieve a message multiple times from different computers.

When you ask Windows Live Mail to retrieve your messages, it contacts your Internet service provider's e-mail server, downloads the messages, and then deletes them from the server. However, there may be times when you do not want the messages deleted. For example, if you are working at home or on the road and want to retrieve your work messages,

it is better to leave them on the server so that you can also retrieve them when you return to the office.

Note, however, that most Internet service providers (ISPs) offer a limited amount of e-mail storage space, so you cannot leave messages on the server indefinitely. To ensure that your messages are deleted eventually, follow steps 1 to 5 and then click the Remove From Server After *x* Days check box (☐ changes to ☑), where *x* is the number of days after which you want the server messages deleted.

1. In Windows Live Mail, press Alt.

● Windows Live Mail displays the menu bar.

2. Click Tools.

3. Click Accounts.

The Accounts dialog box appears.

4. Click the account you want to work with.

5. Click Properties.

6. In the account's Properties dialog box, click the Advanced tab.

7. Click the Leave a Copy of Messages on Server check box (☐ changes to ☑).

8. Click OK.

9. Click Close in the Accounts dialog box.

Windows Live Mail leaves a copy of the messages on the server.

You can set the priority level of your outgoing message to let the recipient know whether to handle your message with high or low priority.

If you are sending a message that has important information or that requires a fast response, set the message's priority to high. When the recipient receives the message, his or her e-mail program indicates the high priority. For example, Windows Live Mail indicates high priority messages with a red exclamation mark. Alternatively, you can set the priority to low for unimportant messages so that the recipient knows not to handle the message

immediately. Windows Live Mail flags low priority messages with a blue, downward-pointing arrow.

If you are sending important information via e-mail, you may want to ensure that the message arrived safely. You can do that by sending a request for a read receipt, which is a message automatically sent to you when the recipient reads the message for the first time (although many people do not allow read receipts to be sent, for privacy reasons). In the message window, press Alt to display the menu bar, click Tools, and then click Request Read Receipt.

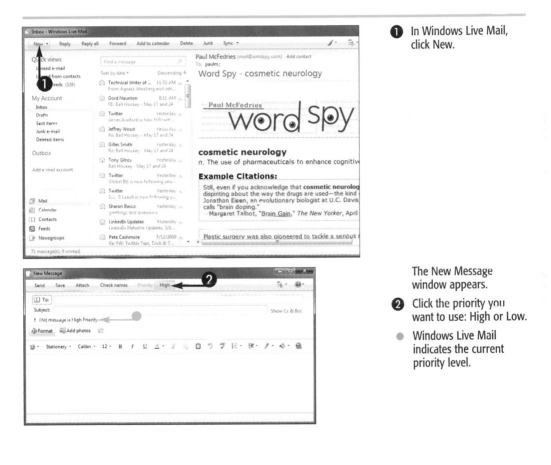

① In Windows Live Mail, click New.

The New Message window appears.

② Click the priority you want to use: High or Low.

● Windows Live Mail indicates the current priority level.

If you regularly send messages to a particular collection of people, you can organize those recipients into a category. This saves time because when you choose the category as the message recipient, Windows Live Mail sends the message to every address in the category.

Sending a message to a number of people takes time because you have to either type many addresses or select many people from your address book. If you find that you are sending

some of your messages to the same group repeatedly, you can avoid the drudgery of adding those recipients individually by creating a distribution list or, as Windows Live Mail calls it, a *contact category*.

After you add the recipients to the list, all you have to do is send the message to the category. Windows Live Mail then distributes copies of the message to every member of the category.

① In Windows Live Mail, click Contacts.

Note: You can also press Ctrl+Shift+C.

The Windows Live Contacts window appears.

② Click Create a New Category.

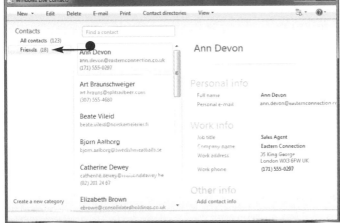

The Create a New Category dialog box appears.

③ Type a name for the category.

④ Click a contact that you want to include in the category.

● Windows Live Contacts adds the contact to the category.

⑤ Repeat step 4 for the other contacts you want to add to the category.

Note: *If you add the wrong contact by accident, you can remove it by clicking the contact name again.*

⑥ Click Save.

● Windows Live Contacts adds the category.

TIPS

Try This!
One of the best reasons to create a category is that you can send an e-mail message to each member. Normally, sending an e-mail message to multiple contacts involves typing or selecting multiple addresses. With a category, however, you send a single message to the category, and Windows Live Mail automatically sends a copy to each member. Right-click the category and then click Send E-mail.

More Options!
If you want to add new contacts to the category or delete existing contacts, right-click the category and then click Edit Category (or double-click the category). If you want to delete a category, right-click the category and then click Delete Category. When Windows Live Contacts asks you to confirm the deletion, click OK.

Protect Your Contacts by Creating a Backup Copy

You can create a backup copy of your contacts. If you have a problem with the contacts in the future, you can restore your contacts from the backup copy.

Windows Live Contacts is handy for storing e-mail addresses of people you correspond with regularly. Instead of remembering complex e-mail addresses, you simply type or select the person's name when composing a new message. However, the usefulness of Windows Live Contacts extends far beyond e-mail. For each contact, you can also store data such as

his or her home and business addresses, phone, fax, and cell numbers, spouse and children's names, gender, birthday, and more.

If you rely on Windows Live Contacts to store all this information about the people you know, then you must ensure that the data is safe. Unfortunately, if Windows Live Contacts gets corrupted, you could lose all your contact data. Just in case this happens, you can regularly create backup copies of your Windows Live Contacts data.

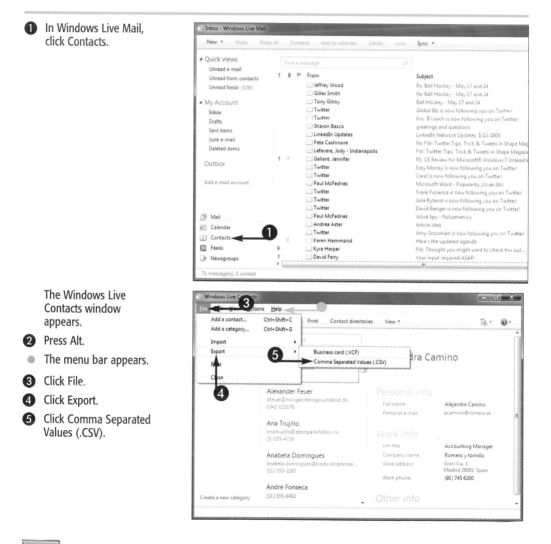

1 In Windows Live Mail, click Contacts.

The Windows Live Contacts window appears.

2 Press Alt.

● The menu bar appears.

3 Click File.

4 Click Export.

5 Click Comma Separated Values (.CSV).

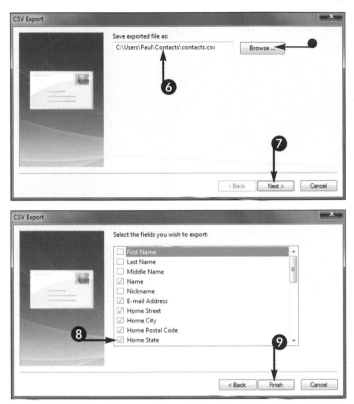

The CSV Export dialog box appears.

⑥ Type the location and name of the exported file.

Note: *Be sure to add .csv to the end of the exported file name.*

● You can also click Browse and use the Save As dialog box to select a location and type a file name.

⑦ Click Next.

⑧ Click the check boxes for each field you want to include (☑) or exclude (☐).

⑨ Click Finish.

Windows Live Mail exports the Address Book data to the file.

TIPS

Important!

If you have a problem with your Contacts folder — for example, if it does not open or does not display your contacts — you can restore it by importing the backed-up copy. In Windows Live Mail, click Contacts, press Alt, click File, Import, and then Comma Separated Values (.CSV). Type the location and name of the exported file from step 6 and click Next. Click Finish.

Did You Know?

You can also make backup copies of your Windows Live Mail messages and e-mail accounts. Press Alt to display the Windows Live Mail menu bar, click File, and then click Export. To back up your e-mail messages, click Messages, click Microsoft Windows Live Mail, and then click Next; to back up your accounts, instead, click Accounts, click your account, and then click Export.

E-mail an Electronic Business Card

You can create an electronic version of a business card that includes your name, address, and contact information. You can then attach this business card to your messages, enabling other people to easily add you to their address books.

The ritual exchange of business cards is a common sight at meetings, conferences, and cocktail parties. With the advent of e-mail, however, fewer people are meeting face-to-face, so there are fewer opportunities to swap cards. Fortunately, Windows Live Mail offers a feature that enables you to exchange business cards electronically.

An electronic business card is called a *vCard* and, just like its paper counterpart, it includes the person's name, address, phone numbers, and other contact information. If you have an item in the Contacts folder for yourself, you can use it to create a vCard, which you can then attach to your messages. The recipient can then view the attached card and easily add you to his or her address book. Similarly, you can view vCards sent to you and add the senders to your Windows Live Contacts list.

CREATE YOUR ELECTRONIC BUSINESS CARD

① In Windows Live Mail, click Contacts.

The Windows Live Contacts window appears.

Note: If you do not have a contact with your personal data, create one now.

② Press Alt.

● The menu bar appears.

③ Click File.

④ Click Export.

⑤ Click Business Card (.VCF).

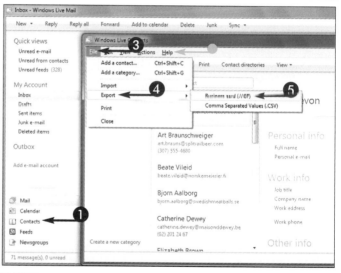

The Browse For Folder dialog box appears.

⑥ Click your user profile's Contacts folder.

⑦ Click OK.

Windows Live Contacts exports the contacts to .VCF files in the Contacts folder.

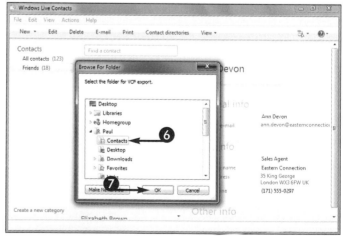

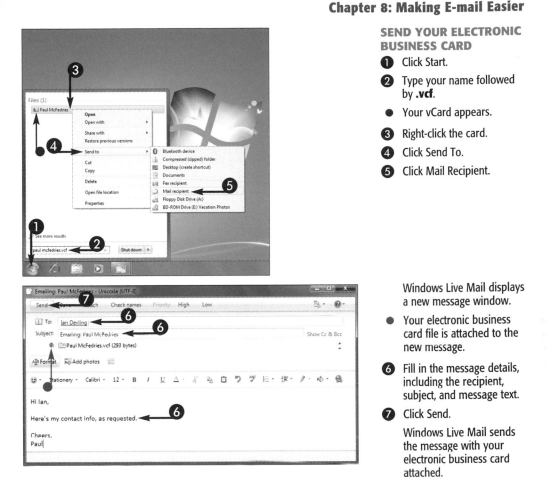

SEND YOUR ELECTRONIC BUSINESS CARD

1. Click Start.

2. Type your name followed by **.vcf**.

● Your vCard appears.

3. Right-click the card.

4. Click Send To.

5. Click Mail Recipient.

Windows Live Mail displays a new message window.

● Your electronic business card file is attached to the new message.

6. Fill in the message details, including the recipient, subject, and message text.

7. Click Send.

Windows Live Mail sends the message with your electronic business card attached.

TIPS

Try This!

You can also add your business card directly from an e-mail message that you are composing. In the e-mail message window, click Attach to display the Open dialog box. Navigate to the Contacts folder, click your vCard file, and then click Open.

Did You Know?

If you receive a message that includes a vCard, you can see the business card icon ( ) in the preview pane. Click the icon and then click Open to open the attached vCard file. To add the sender to your Contacts list, click Add Contact.

You can change the hard drive location that Windows Live Mail uses to store the contents of your message folders. This is useful if you are running out of space on the current hard drive and need to move the messages to a disk with more free space.

Windows Live Mail stores the contents of your Inbox, Outbox, Sent Items, Deleted Items, Drafts, and Junk E-mail folders, as well as any new folders you create, in a special hard drive location called the *message store*. The size of

the message store depends on a number of factors, including how often you use e-mail, how many messages you save, how often you clean out your Deleted Items folder, and so on.

However, it is not unusual for the message store to consume dozens or even hundreds of megabytes of disk space. If you are running low on disk space and your computer has another hard drive with more free space, you can give your message store room to grow by moving it to the other disk.

① In Windows Live Mail, click Menus.

② Click Options.

The Options dialog box appears.

③ Click the Advanced tab.

④ Click Maintenance.

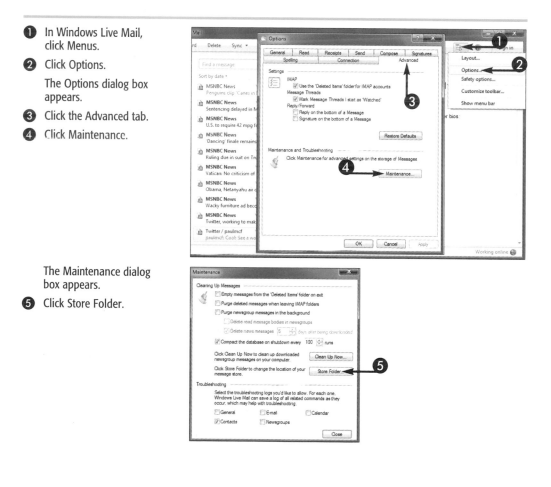

The Maintenance dialog box appears.

⑤ Click Store Folder.

The Store Location dialog box appears.

⑥ Click Change.

The Browse For Folder dialog box appears.

⑦ Click the folder you want to use as the new location.

⑧ Click OK.

⑨ Click OK.

Windows Live Mail tells you to shut down the program to put the new store location into effect.

⑩ Click OK.

⑪ Click Close.

⑫ Click OK.

⑬ Click Close to shut down Windows Live Mail and then restart the program.

Windows Live Mail moves the message store.

TIPS

Important!
To speed up the process of moving the message store, you can do some folder maintenance before performing these steps. For example, delete any messages you no longer want, including any messages in the Deleted Items folder. You can also delete any folders that you no longer use.

More Options!
Another way to save disk space with Windows Live Mail is to compact your folders to remove wasted space caused by message deletions. Follow steps 1 to 4 to display the Maintenance dialog box. Use the Compact the Database on Shutdown Every *X* Runs spin box to specify a relatively small number of runs, such as 10 or 20; the default is 100. Click Close and then click OK.

Activate the Spell Checker to Eliminate Message Errors

You can make your e-mail messages easier to read and more professional in appearance by using the Windows Live Mail built-in spell checker to catch and fix spelling errors.

Whether you use e-mail for short notes or long essays, you can detract from your message if your text contains more than a few spelling errors. Sending a message riddled with spelling mistakes can also reflect poorly on you, whether the recipient is your boss, your colleagues, a customer, or a recruiter.

To ensure your message is received in its best light, you should activate the Windows Live Mail spell checker. This tool then checks your text for errors each time you send a message and offers suggested replacements.

The spell checker often flags a word that you know is correct. This can happen with people's names, company names and products, jargon terms, and so on. If Windows Live Mail flags such a word, you can prevent it from flagging the word in the future by clicking Add in the Spelling dialog box.

① Click Menus.

② Click Options.

The Options dialog box appears.

③ Click the Spelling tab.

④ Click the Always Check Spelling Before Sending check box (☐ changes to ☑).

⑤ Click OK.

Windows Live Mail activates the spell checker.

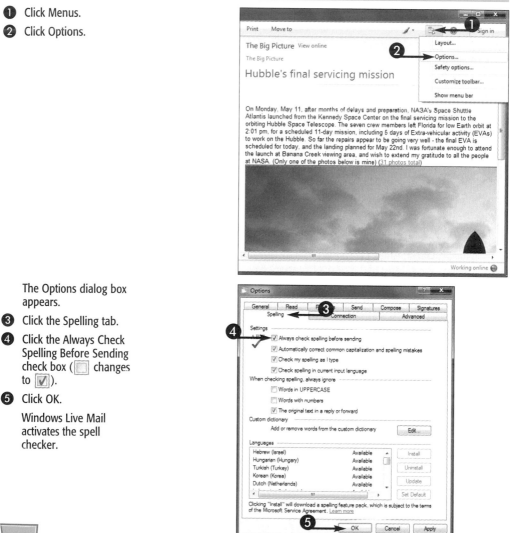

After you start Windows Live Mail, the program contacts your mail server every 30 minutes to see if any new messages have arrived. You can change the frequency with which Windows Live Mail checks for new messages to any time between 1 minute and 480 minutes. For example, you may prefer a shorter time if you are expecting an important message. Alternatively, if you want to minimize your connection time, you may prefer a much longer frequency.

Chapter 8

If you set your e-mail frequency to a value higher than the connection idle time setting, your Internet connection may be disconnected when Windows Live Mail tries to check for new messages. To work around this problem, follow steps 1 to 3 and then use the If My Computer Is Not Connected at This Time list to click Connect Only When Not Working Offline and then click OK.

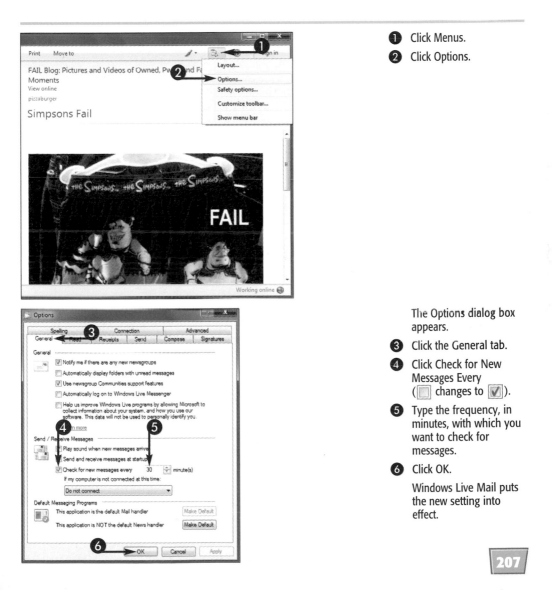

① Click Menus.

② Click Options.

The Options dialog box appears.

③ Click the General tab.

④ Click Check for New Messages Every (☐ changes to ☑).

⑤ Type the frequency, in minutes, with which you want to check for messages.

⑥ Click OK.

Windows Live Mail puts the new setting into effect.

You can define a Windows Live Mail rule by creating the rule from an existing message. In Windows Live Mail, you use rules to examine incoming messages to set certain conditions. For example, if a message has a particular word or phrase in the Subject line or body, you can move the message to a special folder. Similarly, you can check for messages with attachments and elect not to download them from the mail server.

Perhaps the most common rule condition is to use the e-mail address of the sender. You can redirect the message to a folder for that

person's messages, send out an automatic reply, or even automatically delete the message if it comes from someone from whom you do not want to have contact.

With Windows Live Mail you can quickly define such rules by creating them from an existing message. In this case, Windows Live Mail automatically sets up the sender's e-mail address as a rule condition, so you need only define the action you want to perform on messages that come from that address.

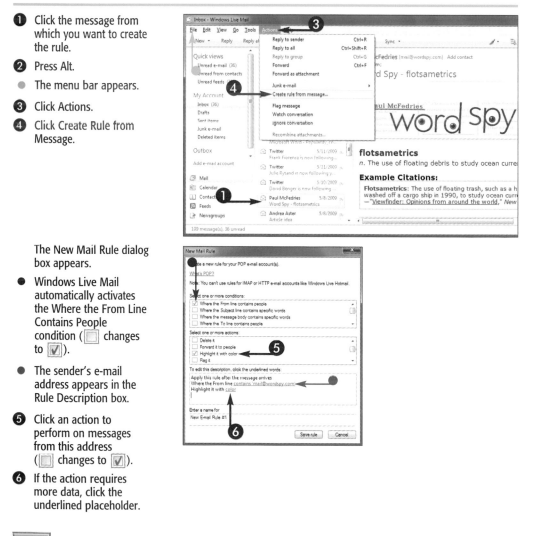

1 Click the message from which you want to create the rule.

2 Press Alt.

● The menu bar appears.

3 Click Actions.

4 Click Create Rule from Message.

The New Mail Rule dialog box appears.

● Windows Live Mail automatically activates the Where the From Line Contains People condition (☐ changes to ☑).

● The sender's e-mail address appears in the Rule Description box.

5 Click an action to perform on messages from this address (☐ changes to ☑).

6 If the action requires more data, click the underlined placeholder.

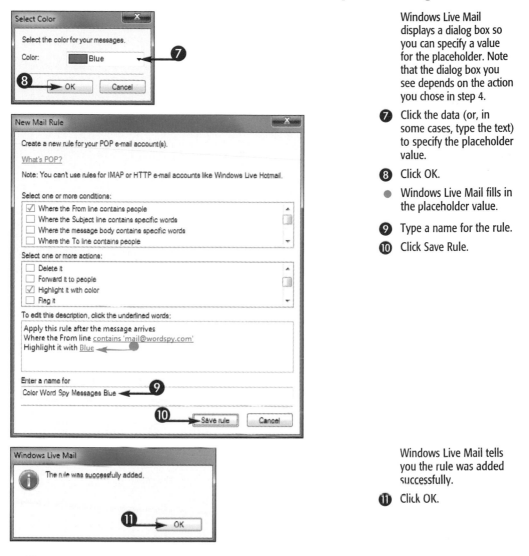

Windows Live Mail displays a dialog box so you can specify a value for the placeholder. Note that the dialog box you see depends on the action you chose in step 4.

⑦ Click the data (or, in some cases, type the text) to specify the placeholder value.

⑧ Click OK.

● Windows Live Mail fills in the placeholder value.

⑨ Type a name for the rule.

⑩ Click Save Rule.

Windows Live Mail tells you the rule was added successfully.

⑪ Click OK.

TIPS

Apply It!

After you create the rule from the message, Windows Live Mail does not apply the rule right away. To apply the rule, press Alt, click Tools, Message Rules, and then Mail. In the Message Rules dialog box, click Apply Now, click the rule you created, and then click Apply Now.

Remove It!

If you no longer require the rule, you can delete it. Press Alt, click Tools, Message Rules, and then Mail to display the Message Rules dialog box. Click the rule and then click Remove. When Windows Live Mail asks you to confirm, click Yes.

Change Your Outgoing Mail Port to Ensure Messages Get Sent

If your e-mail provider requires a different port for outgoing mail, you can configure your e-mail account to use the different port so that your message gets sent.

For security reasons, some Internet service providers (ISPs) insist that all their customers' outgoing mail must be routed through the ISP's Simple Mail Transport Protocol (SMTP) server. This usually is not a big deal if you are using an e-mail account maintained by the ISP, but it can lead to several problems if you are using an account provided by a third party (such as your Web site host). For example, your ISP might block messages sent using the

third-party account because it thinks you are trying to relay the message through the ISP's server (a technique that spammers often use).

You might think that you can solve the problem by specifying the third-party host's SMTP server in the account settings. However, this usually does not work because outgoing e-mail is sent by default through port 25; when you use this port, you must also use the ISP's SMTP server.

To work around this problem, many third-party hosts offer access to their SMTP server via a port other than the standard port 25.

---

1 In Windows Live Mail, press Alt.

● Windows Live Mail displays the menu bar.

2 Click Tools.

3 Click Accounts.

The Accounts dialog box appears.

4 Click the account you want to work with.

5 Click Properties.

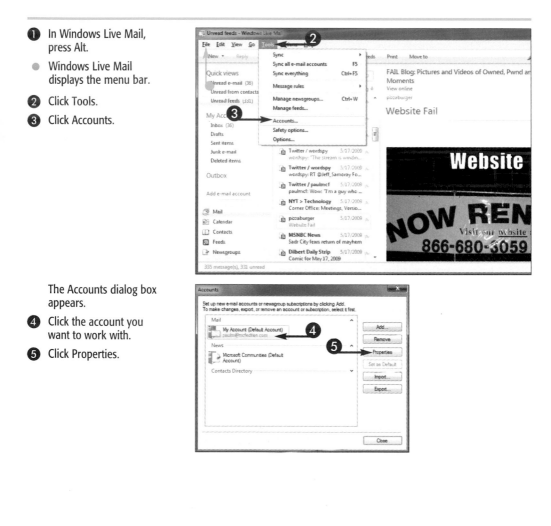

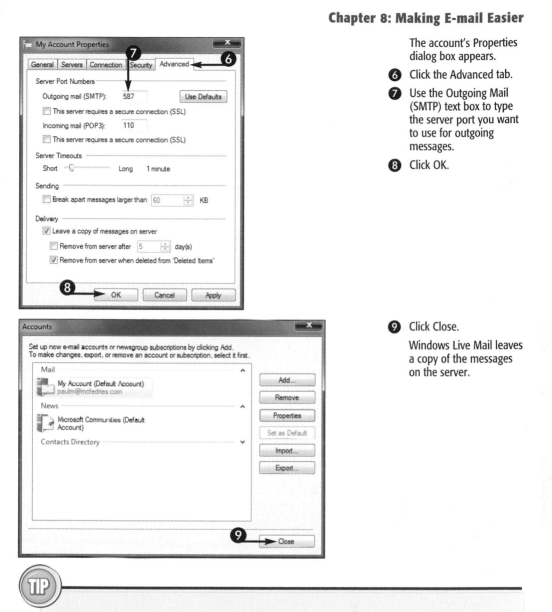

The account's Properties dialog box appears.

⑥ Click the Advanced tab.

⑦ Use the Outgoing Mail (SMTP) text box to type the server port you want to use for outgoing messages.

⑧ Click OK.

⑨ Click Close.

Windows Live Mail leaves a copy of the messages on the server.

TIP

More Options!
Another security feature now implemented by most e-mail providers is to require that each outgoing message be authenticated, which means supplying a user name and password, usually the same logon data that you use to retrieve your incoming messages. To set this up, follow steps 1 to 5, click the Servers tab, and then click My Server Requires Authentication (☐ changes to ☑) in the Outgoing Mail Server section. Click Settings to open the Outgoing Mail Server dialog box, and then select a Logon Information option, depending on the data your e-mail provider supplies. For example, if you use the same logon as you do for retrieving messages, click Use Same Settings as My Incoming Mail Server (◯ changes to ◉). Click OK.

If you use Windows Fax and Scan to receive incoming faxes, you can configure the program to send you a delivery receipt as an e-mail message each time a fax comes in.

If you receive faxes, Windows Fax and Scan is a handy program because you can configure it to automatically answer incoming fax calls. Windows Fax and Scan then displays a message telling you that a new fax has been received.

However, if Windows Fax and Scan is running on a PC other than the one you are using, you might not be in a position to see the new fax message. Instead of constantly checking the other PC for a new fax, Windows Fax and Scan has an option that enables you to have a delivery notification sent to an e-mail address that you specify. You can also configure Windows Fax and Scan to attach a copy of the fax to the e-mail message.

① Click Start.

② Click All Programs.

Note: *When you click All Programs, the command name changes to Back.*

③ Click Windows Fax and Scan.

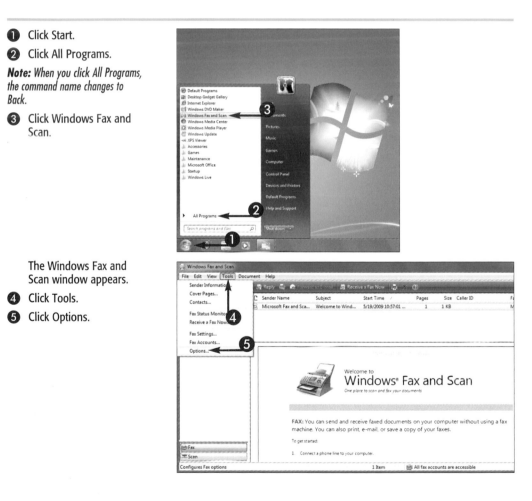

The Windows Fax and Scan window appears.

④ Click Tools.

⑤ Click Options.

The Fax Options dialog box appears.

6 Click the Receipts tab.

Fax Options

General | Receipts | Send | Compose

Send/Receive Fax Messages

☑ Play so⑥d when new messages arrive

OK | Cancel | Apply

7 Click E-mail To
(◯ changes to ◉).

8 Type the e-mail address where you want the notification sent.

Fax Options

General | Receipts | Send | Compose

D⑦ry Receipts

◯ None

◉ E-mail To: me@here.com   Address book...

☑ Use one receipt for delivery to multiple recipients

⑨ ☑ Attach a copy of the sent fax

9 Click Attach a Copy of the Sent Fax (☐ changes to ☑).

10 Click OK.

With each newly received fax, Windows Fax and Scan now e-mails you a notification and a copy of the fax.

⑩ ➤ OK | Cancel | Apply

TIPS

Important!
Before you use Windows Fax and Scan, you should create a fax account. In Windows Fax and Scan, click Tools, click Fax Accounts, click Add, click Connect to a Fax Modem, click Next, and then click Answer Automatically (or use a different answering setting, if you prefer). If you see the Windows Security dialog box, click Allow Access, and then click Close.

More Options!
Now that you are receiving fax notifications, you might want to disable the sounds that Windows Fax and Scan makes when it receives a fax. Click Tools and then click Fax Settings to open the Fax Settings dialog box. Click the Tracking tab and then click Sound Options to open the Sound Settings dialog box. Click An Incoming Call Rings (☑ changes to ☐), click A Fax Is Received (☑ changes to ☐), and then click OK.

Enhancing Internet Security and Privacy

The Internet is now the online home away from home for hundreds of millions of people around the world. The lure of all that information, entertainment, and camaraderie has proven to be simply impossible to resist.

But the Internet has also lured more than its fair share of another class of people: malicious hackers, system intruders, and con artists of every stripe. These miscreants seem to spend most of their waking hours thinking up new ways to disrupt the Internet, break into your online computer, and steal everything from your credit card number to your full identity. Thankfully, like crime in the real world, online crime is still relatively rare. However, as the newspaper headlines attest almost daily, cybercrime is a big business, and so it pays to play it safe.

This chapter helps by offering you a full suite of tasks and techniques designed to make your Internet sessions as safe as possible. You learn how to add a site to the Restricted Sites zone; delete your browsing history; configure Windows Live Family Safety to block specific Web sites; restrict Internet content; use e-mail safely and securely; and control junk e-mail.

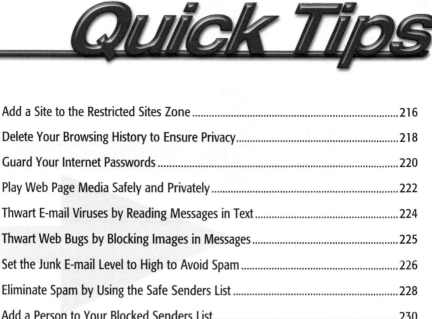

You can add a potentially dangerous Web site to Internet Explorer's Restricted Sites security zone to make your Web surfing sessions safer.

Web pages can contain small programs, scripts, and other so-called *active* content. This active content is designed to offer you a more lively and interactive experience. However, dangers are associated with such content, just as with any remote program that runs on your computer. For example, some scripts can access the data on your hard drive. Fortunately, the vast majority of sites that use such content do so responsibly and safely. However, there are

ways to use such content for nefarious purposes, and many Web pages are set up to do just that.

Therefore, it pays to be always vigilant when you are on the Web. You can do this by setting the appropriate security level for the places you visit. The security level determines what types of active content can run, either with or without your permission. The higher the level, the less active content that can run. The most secure zone is called Restricted Sites, and it is a good idea to add any potentially dangerous sites to the Restricted Sites zone.

---

① In Internet Explorer, click Tools.

② Click Internet Options.

The Internet Options dialog box appears.

③ Click the Security tab.

④ Click Restricted Sites.

⑤ Click Sites.

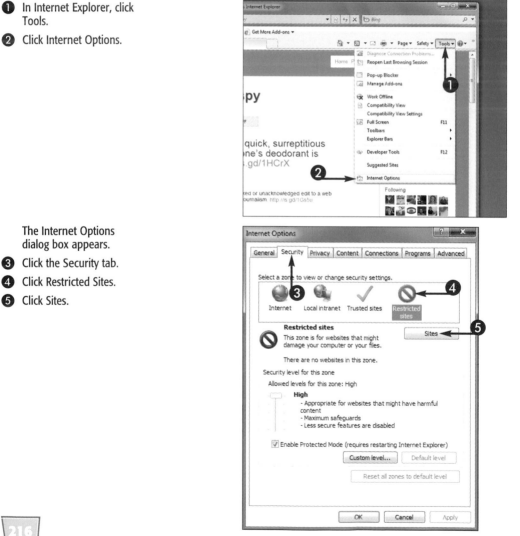

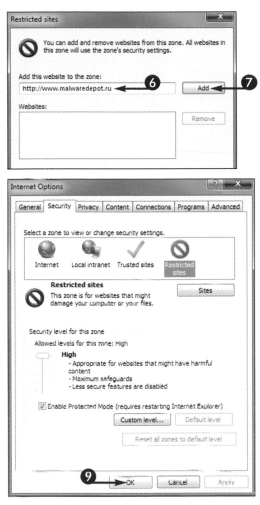

The Restricted Sites dialog box appears.

⑥ Type the address of the potentially dangerous Web site.

⑦ Click Add.

Note: *If you want to add other sites to this zone, repeat steps 6 and 7.*

⑧ Click Close (not shown).

⑨ Click OK.

Internet Explorer applies the new security settings.

TIPS

More Options!
Internet Explorer also has a Trusted Sites zone that uses the Medium security level. This level is easier to use because you see fewer warnings and more types of content appear on the page. However, safety is also a bit less than with the Internet zone, so use it only for Web sites that you trust completely. To add a site to this zone, click Trusted Sites, click Sites, type the address, and click Add.

More Options!
If other people use your computer, you may want to prevent them from downloading any files from the Web. To do this, click the Internet zone and then click Custom Level to display the Security Settings - Internet Zone dialog box. In the Settings list, scroll down to the File Download option, and then click Disable (○ changes to ●). Click OK.

To ensure that other people who have access to your computer cannot view information from sites you have visited, you can delete your browsing history.

As you visit Web sites, Internet Explorer maintains information about the sites you visit. Internet Explorer also maintains a folder called Temporary Internet Files which stores copies of page text, images, and other content so that sites load faster the next time you view them. Similarly, Internet Explorer also saves text and passwords that you have typed into forms. Internet Explorer also maintains *cookies*, which

are small text files that store information such as site preferences and site log-on data.

Saving all this data is useful because it enables you to quickly revisit a site. However, it is also dangerous because other people who use your computer can just as easily visit or view information about those sites. This can be a problem if you visit financial sites, private corporate sites, or some other page that you would not want another person to visit. You reduce this risk by deleting some or all of your browsing history.

① Click Safety.

② Click Delete Browsing History.

Note: *You can also press Ctrl+Shift+Delete.*

The Delete Browsing History dialog box appears.

③ To keep the browsing history associated with sites on your Favorites list, click Preserve Favorites Website Data (☐ changes to ☑).

④ To delete saved Web page files, click Temporary Internet Files (☐ changes to ☑).

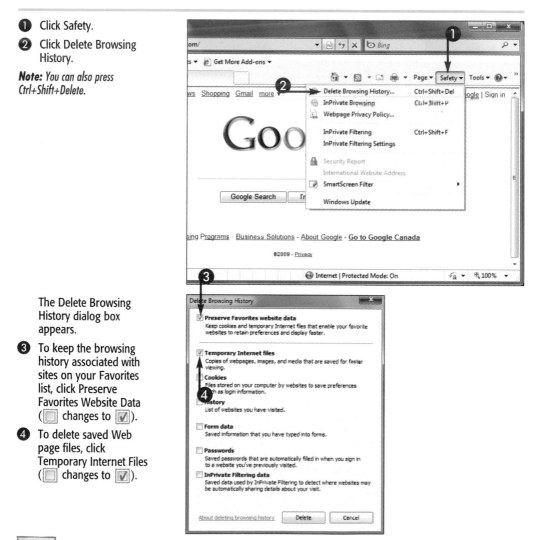

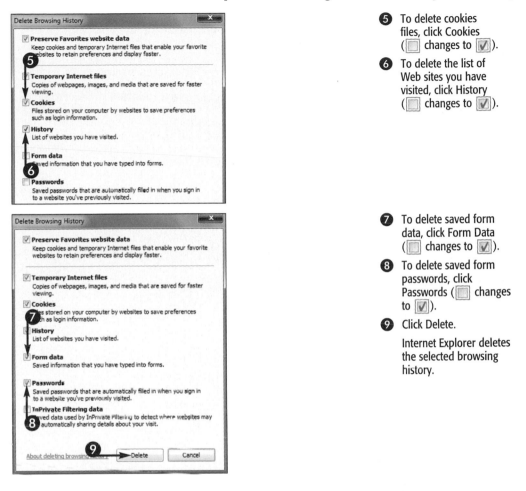

⑤ To delete cookies files, click Cookies (☐ changes to ☑).

⑥ To delete the list of Web sites you have visited, click History (☐ changes to ☑).

⑦ To delete saved form data, click Form Data (☐ changes to ☑).

⑧ To delete saved form passwords, click Passwords (☐ changes to ☑).

⑨ Click Delete.

Internet Explorer deletes the selected browsing history.

Try This!

If you visit sensitive or private Web sites, you can tell Internet Explorer not to save any browsing history for those sites. When you use the InPrivate Browsing feature, Internet Explorer stops saving browsing history when you visit Web sites. To activate this feature, click Safety and then click InPrivate Browsing (you can also press Ctrl+Shift+P).

More Options!

If you regularly delete all your browsing history, constantly running the Delete Browsing History command can get tiresome. Fortunately, you can configure Internet Explorer to make this chore automatic. Click Tools and then click Internet Options to display the Internet Options dialog box. Click the General tab, and then click the Delete Browsing History on Exit check box (☐ changes to ☑). Click OK.

You can keep your Internet passwords safe by configuring Internet Explorer not to save them on your computer.

Many World Wide Web sites require registration to access certain pages and content. In almost all cases, before you can navigate to any of these restricted pages you must first enter a password, along with your user name or e-mail address. When you fill in this information and log on to the site, Internet Explorer displays the AutoComplete dialog box and offers to remember the password so that you do not have to type it

again when you visit the same page in the future. If you click Yes and then access the site's login page at a later date, Internet Explorer fills in the password for you automatically.

This is convenient, to be sure, but it has a downside: Anyone who uses your computer can also access the password-protected content. If you do not want this to happen, one solution is to click No when Internet Explorer asks to remember the password. Alternatively, you can tell Internet Explorer not to remember any passwords, as described in this task.

① In Internet Explorer, click Tools.

② Click Internet Options.

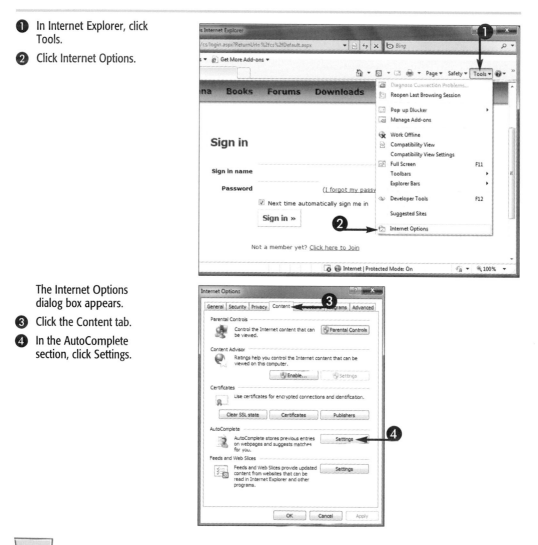

The Internet Options dialog box appears.

③ Click the Content tab.

④ In the AutoComplete section, click Settings.

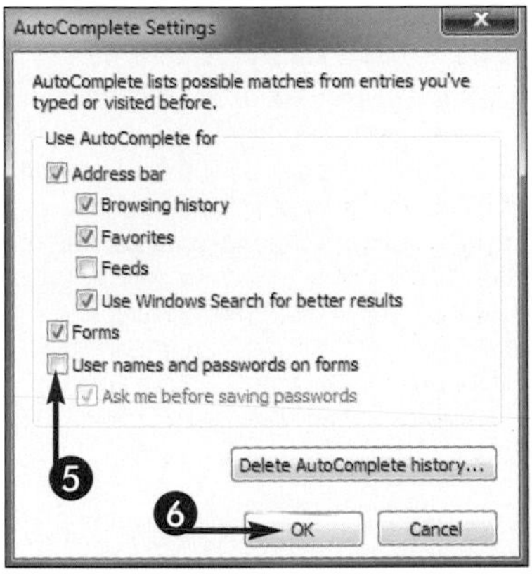

The AutoComplete
Settings dialog box
appears.

5 Click User Names and
Passwords on Forms
(☑ changes to ☐).

6 Click OK.

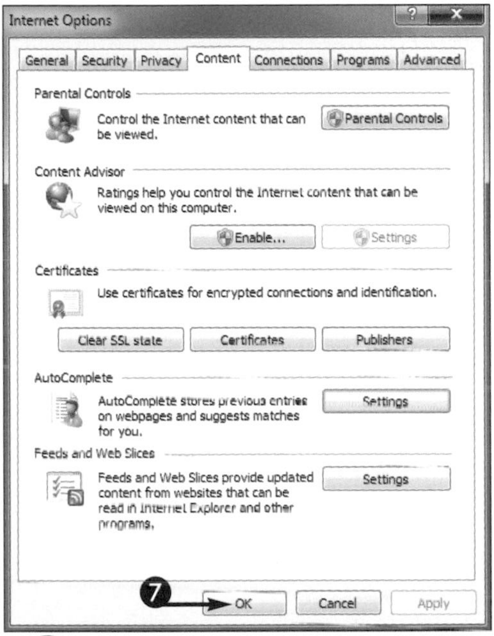

7 Click OK.

Internet Explorer no
longer prompts you to
save form passwords.

TIPS

Important!

Many Web sites offer to "remember" your
login information. They do this by placing
your user name and password in a small
file called a *cookie* that gets stored on your
computer. Although safe, it may lead to a
problem: Other people who use your
computer can access the password-
protected content. To avoid this, be sure to
click the check box that asks if you want to
save your login data (☑ changes to ☐).

Did You Know?

If you already have some login passwords
or cookies stored on your computer, you
may want to delete them. To do this,
follow the steps shown earlier in the
"Delete Your Browsing History to Ensure
Privacy" task, and be sure to click the
Cookies and Passwords check boxes
(☐ changes to ☑).

You can set options in Windows Media Player that ensure media downloaded from or played on an Internet site is safe and that enhance the privacy of the Internet media you play.

You can play Internet media either by downloading the music or video to your computer and playing it in Windows Media Player or by using a version of Windows Media Player that resides inside a Web page. Either way, the person who created the media may have included extra commands in a script designed to control the playback.

Unfortunately, scripts can also contain commands that can harm your computer, so preventing these scripts from running is the best option.

Also, Windows Media Player stores the names of media files that you play and the addresses of Web sites that you visit to access content. If other people use or have access to your computer, you may want to enhance your privacy by not allowing Windows Media Player to store this history.

---

① In Windows Media Player, click Organize.

② Click Options.

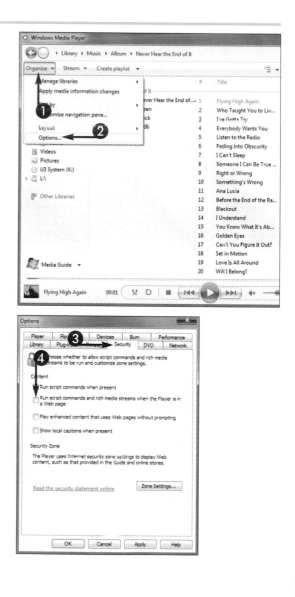

The Options dialog box appears.

③ Click the Security tab.

④ Click the Run Script Commands and Rich Media Streams When the Player Is in a Web Page check box (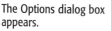 changes to).

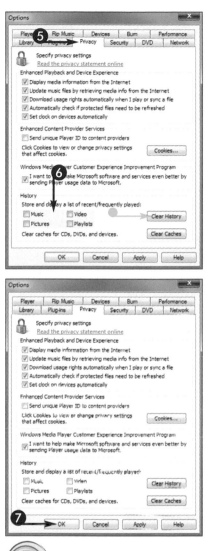

⑤ Click the Privacy tab.

⑥ In the History section, click the check box for each type of media you do not want to appear in Media Player's history list (☑ changes to ☐).

● If you want to clear the existing history list, click Clear History.

⑦ Click OK.

Windows Media Player puts the new security and privacy options into effect.

TIPS

More Options!

Some media sites display *enhanced content,* or Web pages that give you information related to the media. Because these pages can contain malicious content, Media Player asks if you want to see the enhanced content. If you trust your sites, bypass this prompt by displaying the Security tab and clicking the Play Enhanced Content That Uses Web Pages Without Prompting check box (☐ changes to ☑).

Important!

Some content sites require a Player ID before you can play any media. For example, a site may request the ID for billing purposes. In that case, enable Media Player to send the ID by displaying the Privacy tab and clicking the Send Unique Player ID to Content Providers check box (☐ changes to ☑).

Thwart E-mail Viruses by Reading Messages in Text

You can reduce the danger of accidentally unleashing a virus on your computer by reading all your e-mail messages in text format.

E-mail messages come in two formats: plain text and HTML. The HTML format utilizes the same codes used to create Web pages. Therefore, just as some Web pages are unsafe, so are some e-mail messages. Specifically, messages can contain scripts that run automatically when you open or even just preview a message. You can prevent these scripts from running by viewing all your messages in the plain text format.

When you are viewing a message as plain text, you may realize that the message is innocuous and that it is okay to view the HTML version. To switch quickly to HTML, press Alt, click View, and then click Message in HTML. You can also press Alt+Shift+H.

---

① In Windows Live Mail, click Menus.

② Click Options.

The Options dialog box appears.

③ Click the Read tab.

④ Click Read All Messages in Plain Text (changes to ✓).

⑤ Click OK.

E-mail messages now appear only in plain text.

You can make your e-mail address more private by thwarting the Web bugs inserted into some e-mail messages.

A *Web bug* is a small and usually invisible image, the code for which is inserted into an e-mail message. That code specifies a remote address from which to download the Web bug image when you open or preview the message.

However, the code also includes a reference to your e-mail address. The remote server makes note of the fact that you received the message, which means your address is a working one and is therefore a good target for further spam messages. By blocking Web bugs, you undermine this confirmation and so receive less spam.

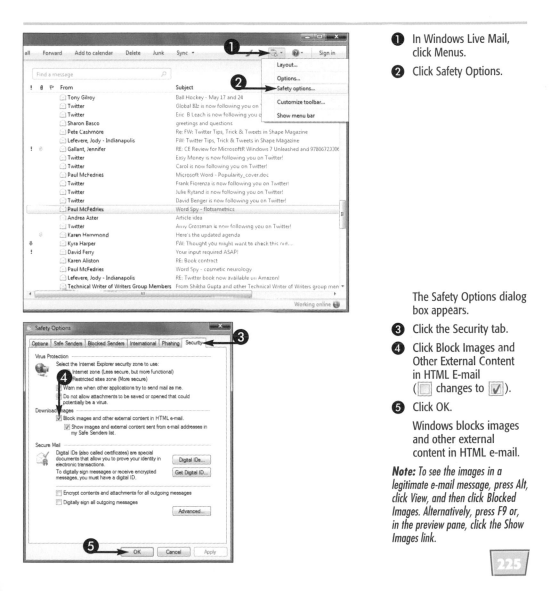

❶ In Windows Live Mail, click Menus.

❷ Click Safety Options.

The Safety Options dialog box appears.

❸ Click the Security tab.

❹ Click Block Images and Other External Content in HTML E-mail (☐ changes to ☑).

❺ Click OK.

Windows blocks images and other external content in HTML e-mail.

Note: *To see the images in a legitimate e-mail message, press Alt, click View, and then click Blocked Images. Alternatively, press F9 or, in the preview pane, click the Show Images link.*

If you receive a great deal of junk mail, you can raise the Windows Live Mail Junk E-mail protection level so that the junk e-mail filter catches more spam.

For most people, the default protection level — Low — is ideal because it flags only messages with obvious spam content. This is the level to use if you get only a few junk e-mails each day.

However, as junk e-mail becomes a larger problem, you might find that the default protection level no longer catches all or even most of the junk e-mail that you receive.

In that case, you should bump up the protection to the High level, which handles spam aggressively, so it almost never misses a junk e-mail. On the downside, the High level also generates regular false positives, so you may need to tell Windows Live Mail that some messages are not junk.

If your spam problem is particularly bad, you can take things up to an even higher level of protection. See "Eliminate Spam by Using the Safe Senders List," later in this chapter.

SET THE JUNK E-MAIL PROTECTION LEVEL

 In Windows Live Mail, click Menus.

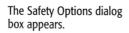 Click Safety Options.

The Safety Options dialog box appears.

 Click the Options tab.

④ Click High (⊙ changes to ⦿).

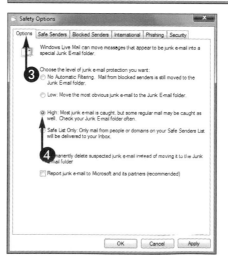

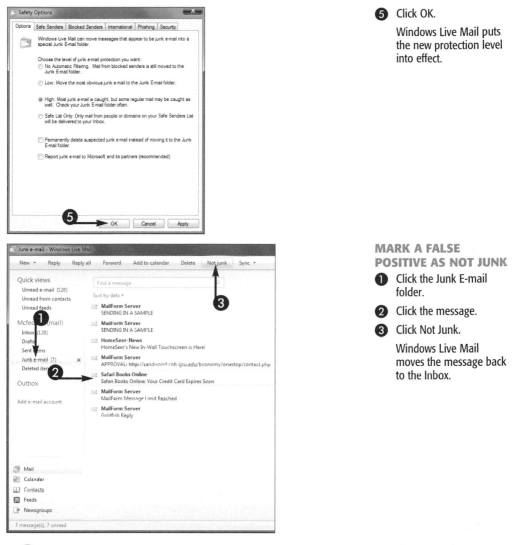

⑤ Click OK.

Windows Live Mail puts the new protection level into effect.

MARK A FALSE POSITIVE AS NOT JUNK

① Click the Junk E-mail folder.

② Click the message.

③ Click Not Junk.

Windows Live Mail moves the message back to the Inbox.

Caution!

A false positive is a legitimate message that Windows Live Mail has mistakenly marked as spam and moved to the Junk E-mail folder. If you select the High protection level, you run a greater risk of false positives, so you should check your Junk E-mail folder more often to look for legitimate messages.

Try This!

When you use the High protection level, Windows Live Mail should miss junk e-mail messages only rarely. However, if the program does miss a spam message, click the message in the Inbox, and then click Junk. Windows Live Mail moves the message to the Junk E-mail folder.

If you have a junk e-mail problem that feels out of control, you can eliminate all spam from your Inbox by using Windows Live Mail's Safe Senders list.

Windows Live Mail normally marks a message as junk if it detects spam characteristics within the message. A different approach is to set up a *whitelist* of allowable addresses. Windows Live Mail offers such a whitelist: the Safe Senders list. If a person's address (such as someone@somewhere.com) or an organization's domain (such as somewhere.com) is on the Safe

Senders list, then Windows Live Mail never treats messages from that person or domain as spam.

If you add all your contacts to the Safe Senders list, then you can configure the Windows Live Mail junk e-mail protection level to accept messages only from people or domains in the Safe Senders list. All other messages are marked as spam.

Note, too, that by default Windows Live Mail also trusts e-mail from people in your Windows Live Contacts list.

① In Windows Live Mail, click Menus.

② Click Safety Options.

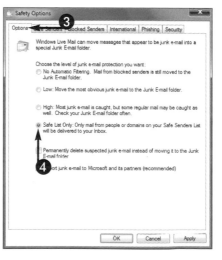

The Safety Options dialog box appears.

③ Click the Options tab.

④ Click Safe List Only (◎ changes to ◉).

⑤ Click Safe Senders.

⑥ Click Add.

The Add Address or Domain dialog box appears.

⑦ Type an address or domain that you want to include in your Safe Senders list.

⑧ Click OK.

● Windows Live Mail adds the address to the list.

⑨ Repeat steps 6 to 8 as necessary.

● Leave this check box activated (☑) so that Windows Live Mail also trusts your Contacts.

⑩ Click OK.

Windows Live Mail now only delivers messages from your safe senders to your Inbox, and it marks all other messages as spam.

Note: If you find a legitimate message in your Junk E-mail folder, click it and then click Not Junk.

TIPS

Try This!

If you have messages from some or all of the people or domains you want to include in your Safe Senders list, Windows Live Mail gives you an easier way to add them. Right-click a message, click Junk E-mail, and then click Add Sender to Safe Senders List. For the domain name, click Add Sender's Domain (@example.com) to Safe Senders List, instead.

More Options!

You can configure Windows Live Mail to automatically add to your Safe Senders list anyone to whom you send a reply or an original message. Follow steps 1, 2, and 5 to display the Safe Senders tab, and then click Automatically Add People I E-mail to the Safe Senders List (☐ changes to ☑). Click OK.

Add a Person to Your Blocked Senders List

If you receive spam or other unwanted messages from a particular person, you can configure Windows Live Mail to block that person's address so that you do not have to see or deal with messages from that person again.

Spam messages are most often sent with fake return addresses that change with each message. However, it often happens that a particular person sends junk messages using a legitimate return e-mail address. In this case, you can add that address to the Windows Live Mail Blocked Senders list. Any future messages

from that person — as well as any messages from that person currently in your Inbox folder — are automatically rerouted to the Junk E-mail folder.

However, the Blocked Senders list is not just for spam. If you have a person who is sending you annoying, insulting, or offensive messages, you can add that person's address to the Blocked Senders list. Again, Windows Live Mail automatically moves that person's messages to the Junk E-mail folder so you do not have to deal with them.

---

① In Windows Live Mail, click Menus.

② Click Safety Options.

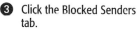

The Safety Options dialog box appears.

③ Click the Blocked Senders tab.

④ Click Add.

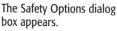

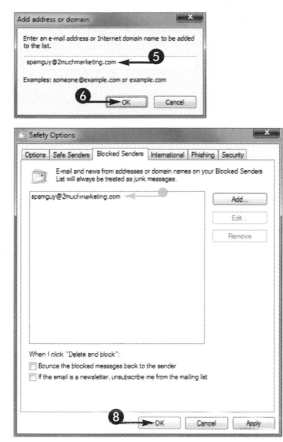

The Add Address or Domain dialog box appears.

⑤ Type the address of the person you want to block.

⑥ Click OK.

● Windows Live Mail adds the address to the Blocked Senders list.

⑦ Repeat steps 4 to 6 to add more addresses to your Blocked Senders list.

⑧ Click OK.

When you receive messages from any of the people you added to the Blocked Senders list, Windows Live Mail moves those messages to the Junk E-mail folder.

TIPS

Try This!

Some spammers use varying addresses that change the user name but keep the same domain name — for example, sales@spammer.com, offers@spammer. com, and so on. To block all messages from this type of spammer, add just the domain name — @spammer.com in this example — to the Blocked Senders list.

More Options!

If you have a message from a person you want to block, right-click the message and then click Junk E-mail. In the menu that appears, click either Add Sender to Blocked Senders List or Add Sender's Domain (@example.com) to Blocked Senders List.

Block Messages from a Country to Reduce Spam

If you receive a great deal of spam from e-mail addresses that originate in a particular country, you can avoid dealing with those messages by telling Windows Live Mail to block messages that come from that country.

On the Internet, a *domain name* is a name that specifies an Internet location. The main domain name takes the form mydomain.com, and most domains also have subdomains such as a Web site — usually www.mydomain.com — or a mail server — usually mail.mydomain.com.

The part of the domain name after the last dot is called the top-level domain, and some, such as com, edu, and org that are not

country-specific. However, many top-level domains do use country or region codes. For example, ca is the top-level domain for Canada, uk is for Great Britain, de is for Germany, and us is for the United States.

If you find that you are getting many spam messages from addresses that use a top-level domain for a particular country, you can configure Windows Live Mail to block messages from such domains. Any future messages from that country — as well as any messages from that country currently in your Inbox folder — are automatically moved to the Junk E-mail folder.

---

① In Windows Live Mail, click Menus.

② Click Safety Options.

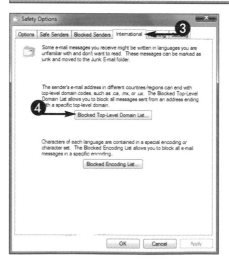

The Safety Options dialog box appears.

③ Click the International tab.

④ Click Blocked Top-Level Domain List.

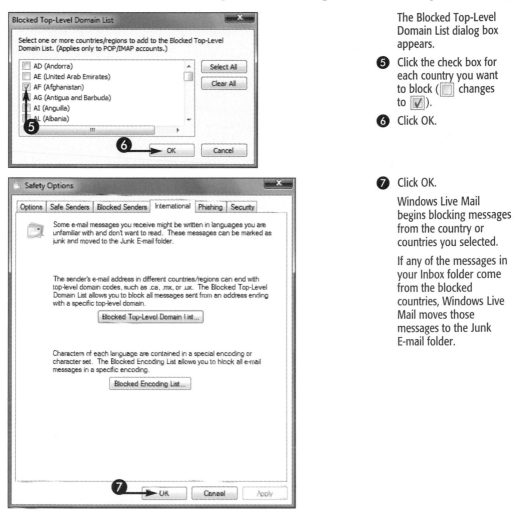

The Blocked Top-Level Domain List dialog box appears.

⑤ Click the check box for each country you want to block (changes to).

⑥ Click OK.

⑦ Click OK.

Windows Live Mail begins blocking messages from the country or countries you selected.

If any of the messages in your Inbox folder come from the blocked countries, Windows Live Mail moves those messages to the Junk E-mail folder.

More Options!
If you want to block messages from all foreign countries with just a few exceptions, activating most of the check boxes in the Blocked Top-Level Domain List dialog box can be time-consuming. An easier method is to click Select All to activate every check box and then click to uncheck the countries you do not want blocked (changes to).

Try This!
If you regularly get messages written in a different language that you do not understand, you should treat such messages as junk e-mail. To configure Windows Live Mail to block such messages, follow steps 1 to 3 and then click Blocked Encoding List. In the Blocked Encodings List dialog box, click the check box for each language you want to block (changes to), and then click OK.

You can avoid dealing with phishing messages by configuring Windows Live Mail to automatically move all phishing messages to the Junk E-mail folder.

Phishing refers to creating a replica of an existing Web page to fool a user into submitting personal, financial, or password data. The term comes from the fact that Internet scammers are using increasingly sophisticated lures as they "fish" for users' financial information and password data. The most common ploy is to copy the Web page

code from a major site — such as AOL or eBay — and use it to set up a replica page that appears to be part of the company's site. (This is why another name for phishing is *spoofing*.)

However, phishing usually begins by a scammer sending out a fake e-mail message with a link to this page, which solicits the user's credit card data or password. Windows Live Mail looks for phishing messages and automatically blocks links and other content in those messages, but it does not automatically move those messages to the Junk E-mail folder.

① **In Windows Live Mail, click Menus.**

② **Click Safety Options.**

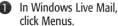

The Safety Options dialog box appears.

③ **Click the Phishing tab.**

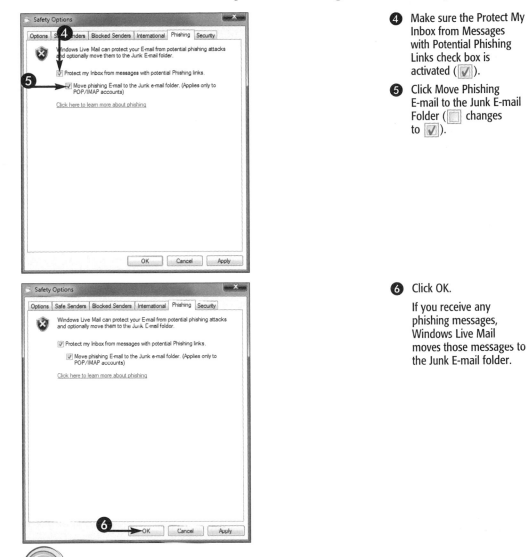

④ Make sure the Protect My Inbox from Messages with Potential Phishing Links check box is activated (☑).

⑤ Click Move Phishing E-mail to the Junk E-mail Folder (☐ changes to ☑).

⑥ Click OK.

If you receive any phishing messages, Windows Live Mail moves those messages to the Junk E-mail folder.

Caution!
Although Windows Live Mail does a decent job of recognizing phishing messages, it sometimes creates false positives: legitimate messages that Windows Live Mail has mistakenly marked as phishing messages and moved to the Junk E-mail folder. Therefore, you should check your Junk E-mail folder more often to look for legitimate messages.

Did You Know?
To help you avoid phishing Web sites, Internet Explorer 8 comes with a tool called the SmartScreen Filter. This filter alerts you to potential phishing scams by analyzing the site content for known phishing techniques, and by checking a global database of known phishing sites. In Internet Explorer 8, click Safety, click SmartScreen Filter, and then click Turn On SmartScreen Filter.

You can block Windows Live Mail from sending a message that confirms you have opened a message.

The Internet e-mail system occasionally breaks down and some e-mail messages never arrive at their destination. Often you get no indication that there was a problem, so you assume the message got through.

A person sending an important message may want to know whether you have read the message because then at least they know the message was delivered safely. A *read receipt* is a short message that Windows Live Mail

automatically fires back to the sender when you open or preview a message from that person. The read receipt — which must be requested by the sender — ensures the sender that you have viewed the message. However, many people consider this an invasion of privacy, so they block Windows Live Mail from sending read receipts.

By default, Windows Live Mail displays a dialog box that tells you the sender has requested a read receipt. You can block read receipts either by declining to send one each time Windows Live Mail asks or by blocking read receipts entirely.

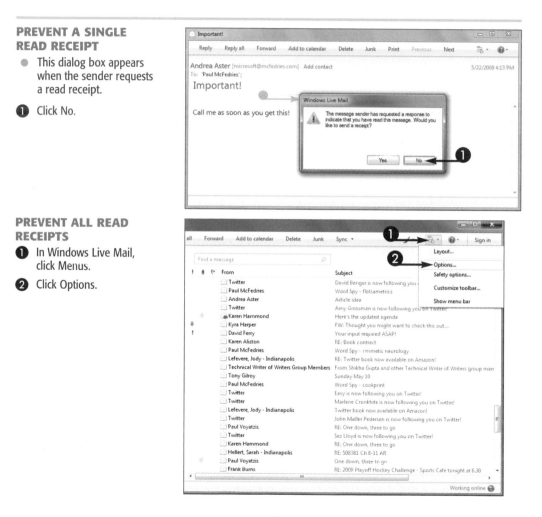

PREVENT A SINGLE READ RECEIPT

- This dialog box appears when the sender requests a read receipt.

① Click No.

PREVENT ALL READ RECEIPTS

① In Windows Live Mail, click Menus.

② Click Options.

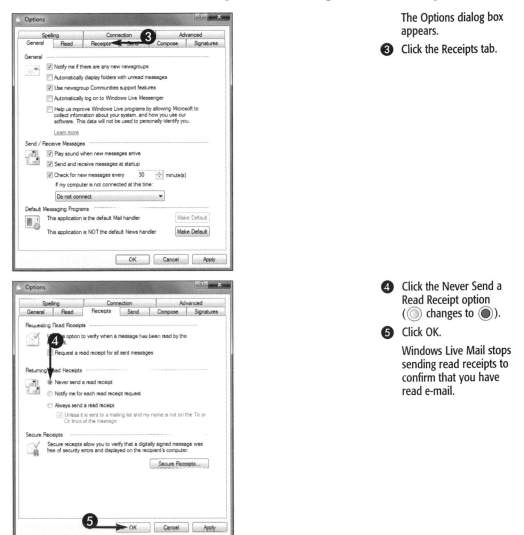

The Options dialog box appears.

③ Click the Receipts tab.

④ Click the Never Send a Read Receipt option (◯ changes to ◉).

⑤ Click OK.

Windows Live Mail stops sending read receipts to confirm that you have read e-mail.

TIPS

More Options!
You may find that read receipts are useful in business. For example, if someone sends you an important message, it is easier to confirm that you have received the message by having Windows Live Mail send a read receipt than sending a response yourself. In that case, click the Notify Me for Each Read Receipt Request option (◯ changes to ◉). This enables you to control when you send a read receipt.

More Options!
If you do not mind that other people know when you read a message, you may not want to be bothered with the read receipt dialog box each time a request comes in. In that case, click the Always Send a Read Receipt option (◯ changes to ◉).

237

Maximizing Windows 7 Networking

Most computers today do not operate in isolation. Instead, they are usually connected by one method or another to form a network. If you use your computer in a corporate or small business setting, then your network probably consists of computers wired together through devices such as hubs, switches, and routers. If you use your computer at home, then your network probably consists of computers connected wirelessly through a wireless access point.

Whatever the configuration of your network, it usually takes a bit of extra effort to get the network working smoothly and to ensure that users can access network resources. The tasks in this chapter can help you get the most out of your network. You learn how to view the current network status; repair network problems; customize your network name and icon; change the homegroup password; share folders with other network users and protect those folders with advanced permissions; connect to a wireless network; and change the order of your wireless connections.

Quick Tips

You can make sure your network is operating at its most efficient by checking its current status from time to time.

These days, networks are generally quite reliable and you can often go for long periods without any problem. Of course, networks are not perfect, so slowdowns, outages, glitches, and other problems are bound to arise occasionally.

You can anticipate potential problems and gather network information in the event of a

problem by viewing the network status. The status first tells you the most basic piece of information you require: whether the computer has a connection to the network. Beyond that, the status also tells you how long the computer has been connected to the network, how fast the network connection is and, for a wireless network, the strength of the wireless signal.

① Click the Network icon.

② Click Open Network and Sharing Center.

The Network and Sharing Center window appears.

③ Click Change Adapter Settings.

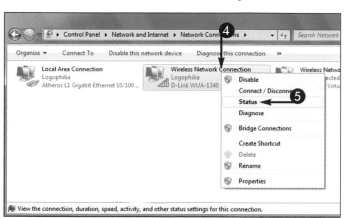

The Network Connections window appears.

④ Right-click the connection you want to check.

⑤ Click Status.

The network connection's Status dialog box appears.

● The Duration tells you how long this computer has been connected to the network.

● The Speed tells you the current network connection speed.

● The Signal Quality tells you the strength of the wireless signal (the more green bars you see, the stronger the connection).

⑥ Click Close.

TIPS

Did You Know?

It is not unusual these days for a computer to have multiple network connections. For example, you may have a wired connection with a couple of other computers at home, while also having a wireless connection to a gateway device that is connected to the Internet. In such cases, the Network Connections window shows both connections: These are usually called Local Area Connection (wired) and Wireless Network Connection (wireless).

More Options!

On occasion you may need to know your computer's current IP (Internet Protocol) address, which is a unique value that identifies your computer on the network. To see your computer's current IP address, follow steps 1 to 5 to display the network connection's Status dialog box. Click Details to display the Network Connection Details dialog box, and then read the IPv4 Address value. Click Close.

Run the Network Diagnostics Tool to Repair Problems

If you have trouble connecting to or accessing your network, Windows 7 comes with a diagnostics tool that can examine your network and then offer solutions.

Networking in Windows 7 usually works quite well right out of the box. That is, you connect your computer to a wired or wireless network, and you can usually see other computers and work with their shared resources right away without the need for a complex configuration procedure.

However, despite the simple networking interface that Windows 7 presents to you, networks are complex structures with many different hardware and software components

working together. If just one of those components stops working or becomes unstable, you may encounter network problems. For example, you may no longer be able to log on to a network, you might not see other network computers, or you might not be able to access shared network resources.

When network problems occur, tracking down and solving them is often quite difficult. Fortunately, Windows 7 comes with a tool called Windows Network Diagnostics that automates the process. It analyzes many different aspects of your network setup, and then offers solutions you can try.

① Right-click the Network icon.

② Click Troubleshoot Problems.

The Windows Network Diagnostics dialog box appears.

③ Implement the solution suggested by Network Diagnostics.

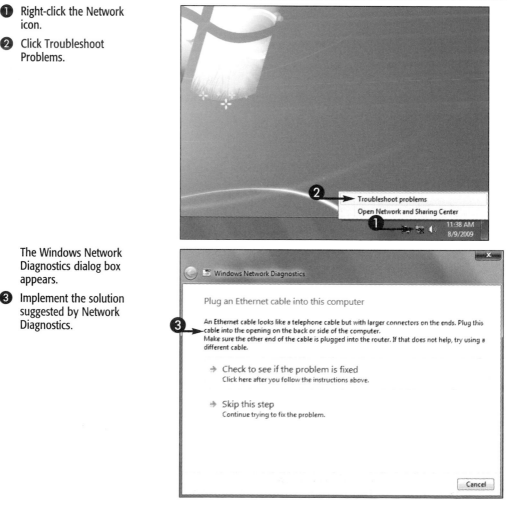

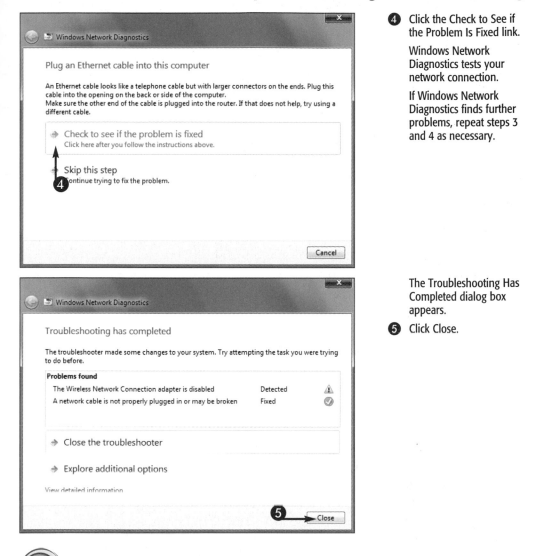

Windows Network Diagnostics

Plug an Ethernet cable into this computer

An Ethernet cable looks like a telephone cable but with larger connectors on the ends. Plug this cable into the opening on the back or side of the computer.
Make sure the other end of the cable is plugged into the router. If that does not help, try using a different cable.

→ Check to see if the problem is fixed
   Click here after you follow the instructions above.

Skip this step
Continue trying to fix the problem.

Cancel

Windows Network Diagnostics

Troubleshooting has completed

The troubleshooter made some changes to your system. Try attempting the task you were trying to do before.

Problems found

The Wireless Network Connection adapter is disabled	Detected	⚠
A network cable is not properly plugged in or may be broken	Fixed	✓

→ Close the troubleshooter

→ Explore additional options

View detailed information

Close

④ Click the Check to See if the Problem Is Fixed link.

Windows Network Diagnostics tests your network connection.

If Windows Network Diagnostics finds further problems, repeat steps 3 and 4 as necessary.

The Troubleshooting Has Completed dialog box appears.

⑤ Click Close.

TIPS

More Options!
If you have multiple network adapters in your computer, you may need to test your network connections separately. Click Start, type **connections**, and then click View Network Connections. Right-click the connection you want to test, and then click Diagnose to start Windows Network Diagnostics on that connection.

Try This!
If you have multiple network adapters in your computer, you can often solve a networking problem by disabling all but one of the connections. Click Start, type **connections**, and then click View Network Connections. For each connection you want to disable, right-click the connection and then click Disable.

Personalize Your Network Name and Icon

You can make the Network and Sharing Center easier to navigate and you can help to differentiate between multiple networks by personalizing the network names and icons.

When you set up a network, Windows 7 gives the network a default name and icon that appear in the Network and Sharing Center. The name is either a generic name such as Network or the default name that the network administrator has set up in a router or gateway device.

If you find yourself working in the Network and Sharing Center window frequently, you may find the window easier to navigate if you assign more meaningful names to each network. This can also help you differentiate between networks.

---

① Click the Network icon.

② Click Open Network and Sharing Center.

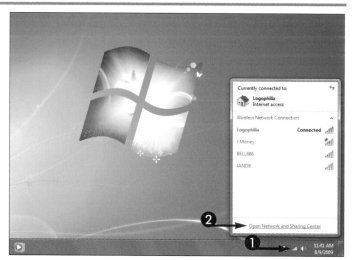

The Network and Sharing Center window appears.

③ Click the network icon.

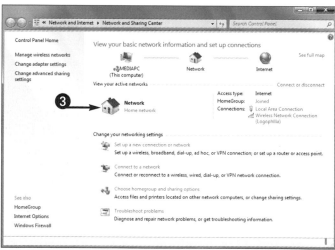

The Set Network Properties dialog box appears.

④ Use the Network Name text box to type the new network name.

⑤ Click Change.

The Change Network Icon dialog box appears.

⑥ Click the icon you want to use.

⑦ Click OK.

⑧ Click OK to close the Set Network Properties dialog box.

TIPS

More Options!
To give yourself more choices when selecting a network icon, follow steps 1 to 5 to display the Change Network Icon dialog box. In the Look for Icon in This File text box, type the following addresses (one at a time):

%SystemRoot%\system32\imageres.dll
%SystemRoot%\system32\shell32.dll

Important!
The Network and Sharing window also displays the current category of the network. There are three categories: Home (used by home and small business networks), Public (used with networks available in public places such as coffee shops and airports), and Work (used by corporate networks). Make sure your home or small business network is *not* set as Public. If it is, follow steps 1 to 3, click Public Network, click Home Network, and then click Close.

Display a Network Folder as a Disk Drive

You can gain easier access to a shared network folder by displaying the folder as though it were a disk drive on your computer.

You can use the Network window (click Start, click Computer, and then click Network) to view the computers that are part of your network workgroup. If you want to work with a shared folder on one of these computers, you must open the computer that contains the folder, and then open the folder. If you want to work with a subfolder, you must also drill down through the subfolders until you get the one you want.

This is not a big problem if you access network shares only rarely. However, navigating a number of folders every time you want to work with a shared resource is inefficient and time-consuming. To save time, Windows 7 enables you to display any shared network folder as though it were a disk drive on your computer. This is called *mapping* the network folder. The advantage of mapping is that an icon for the mapped folder appears in the Computer window (click Start and then Computer), so you can double-click the icon to access the folder.

---

① Click Start.

② Right-click Computer.

③ Click Map Network Drive.

The Map Network Drive dialog box appears.

④ Use the Drive list to click the drive letter you want to use for the mapped network folder.

⑤ Type the address of the shared network folder.

● If you are not sure of the address, click Browse, use the Browse For Folder dialog box to click the network folder, and then click OK.

⑥ Click Finish.

● Windows 7 opens a new window to display the contents of the mapped folder.

⑦ Click Computer.

● An icon for the mapped folder appears in the Network Location section of the Computer window.

⑧ Click the Close button.

TIPS

Caution!

If you use a removable drive such as a USB flash drive or memory card, Windows 7 automatically assigns a drive letter to such a drive. This often causes a conflict if you have a mapped network folder that uses a lower drive letter (such as D, E, or F). Therefore, using higher drive letters (such as X, Y, and Z) for your mapped network folders is good practice.

Remove It!

To speed up the Windows 7 startup and reduce clutter in the Computer window, you can disconnect mapped network folders that you no longer use. To disconnect a mapped folder, click Start, right-click Computer, and then click Disconnect Network Drive. In the Disconnect Network Drives dialog box, click the network drive you want to disconnect, and then click OK.

Change the Homegroup Password

You can make your Windows 7 homegroup more secure by regularly changing the password.

In a traditional network, file sharing is accomplished via user accounts. If you have just a single user account on a computer, you configure that account's permissions for each shared resource, and you then provide other network users with the user name and password. A more likely scenario is to add a user account for each network user, and then configure permissions on shared resources for

each of those accounts. This type of file sharing is time-consuming at best and, for new users, dauntingly complex, at worst.

With Windows 7's homegroup feature, access to shared resources is governed by a single password. You set up the homegroup using one Windows 7 computer, and you then share the password among the other Windows 7 computers on the network.

This is much easier, but the password is crucial for network security. To ensure the network remains secure, you should change the homegroup password regularly.

① On the computer where you originally created the homegroup, click Windows Explorer.

② Right-click Homegroup.

③ Click Change Homegroup Settings.

The Homegroup window appears.

④ Click Change the Password.

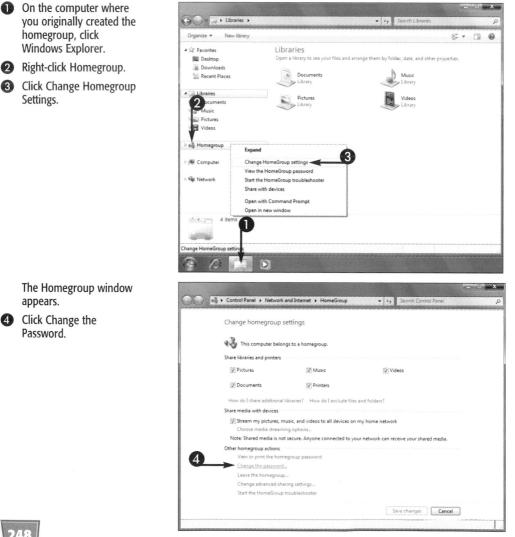

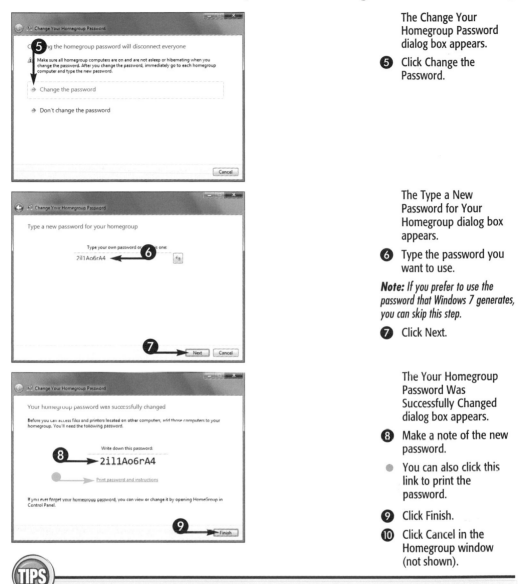

The Change Your
Homegroup Password
dialog box appears.

5 Click Change the
Password.

The Type a New
Password for Your
Homegroup dialog box
appears.

6 Type the password you
want to use.

Note: *If you prefer to use the
password that Windows 7 generates,
you can skip this step.*

7 Click Next.

The Your Homegroup
Password Was
Successfully Changed
dialog box appears.

8 Make a note of the new
password.

● You can also click this
link to print the
password.

9 Click Finish.

10 Click Cancel in the
Homegroup window
(not shown).

TIPS

Apply It!
To enter the new password in another
homegroup computer, log on to that
computer and then follow steps 1 to 3 to
open the Homegroup window. Click Type
New Password to open the Update Your
Homegroup Password dialog box. Type
the new password, click Next, and then
click Finish.

View It!
If you forget the homegroup password,
follow steps 1 to 3 to open the
Homegroup window. On the PC where
you created the homegroup, click View or
Print the Homegroup Password; on any
other PC, click the Choose What You Want
to Share and View the Homegroup
Password link, and then click Next.

You can configure Windows 7 to use user accounts for network connections instead of the homegroup password, which enables you to customize security for each account.

Windows 7's new homegroup feature is designed to make it radically easier to share data over a network connection because all shared data is accessible through a single password. However, what a homegroup makes up for in simplicity, it loses in flexibility. For example, although you can block anyone from viewing a file or folder, and you can apply read

or write permissions to a file or folder, those permissions apply to anyone who knows the homegroup password.

You might prefer more flexibility when it comes to network security. For example, for a single shared resource you might prefer to assign read-only permissions to some people, and write permission to other people.

To do this, you must configure Windows 7 to use advanced sharing (as described in Chapter 3) and user accounts for managing network connections.

1 Click the Network icon.

2 Click Open Network and Sharing Center.

The Network and Sharing Center window appears.

3 Click Change Advanced Sharing Settings.

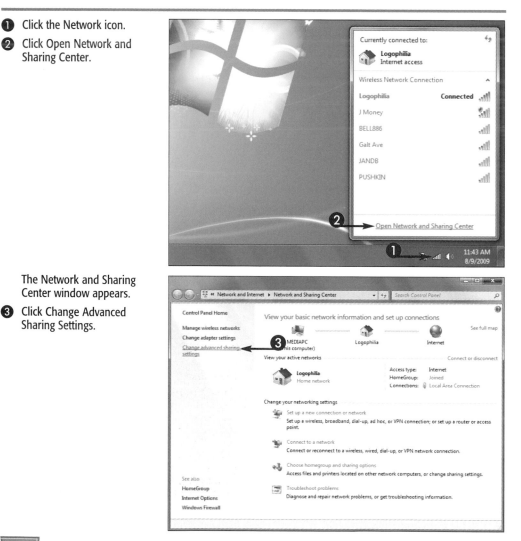

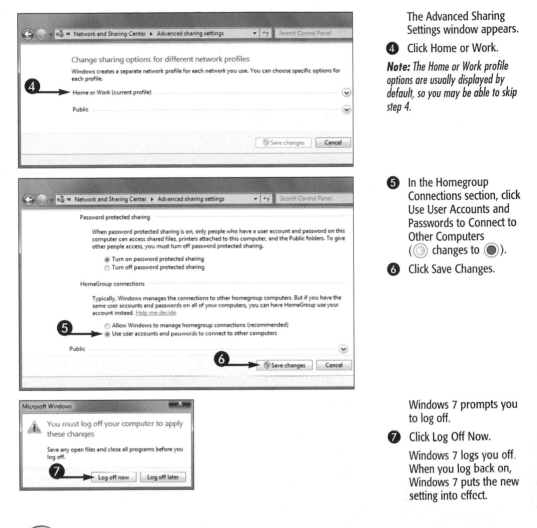

The Advanced Sharing Settings window appears.

④ Click Home or Work.

Note: The Home or Work profile options are usually displayed by default, so you may be able to skip step 4.

⑤ In the Homegroup Connections section, click Use User Accounts and Passwords to Connect to Other Computers (○ changes to ◉).

⑥ Click Save Changes.

Windows 7 prompts you to log off.

⑦ Click Log Off Now.

Windows 7 logs you off. When you log back on, Windows 7 puts the new setting into effect.

TIPS

Important!

To fully implement user account-based file sharing, you must deactivate Windows 7's default Sharing Wizard and switch to advanced sharing permissions. You learned how to do this in Chapter 3, in the task titled "Switch to Advanced Sharing to Improve Security."

Important!

To ensure successful resource sharing, you should also ensure that you have Windows 7's file and printer sharing feature turned on. Follow steps 1 to 4 to open the Advanced Sharing Settings window and display the Home and Work profile options. In the File and Printer Sharing section, click Turn On File and Printer Sharing (○ changes to ◉).

You can collaborate with other people on your network and allow users to work with some of your documents by sharing a folder with the network.

The purpose of most networks is to share resources between the computers connected to the network. For example, the users on a network can share a single printer or an Internet connection.

This resource sharing also applies to documents. It might be a presentation that you want other people to comment on, a database with information that you want others

to use, or a worksheet that you want people to modify. In all these cases, the easiest way to give other people access to your documents is to share the document folder with the network. This task shows you how to set up basic folder sharing. See the next task to learn how to protect your shared folders with permissions.

To follow the steps in this task, you need to deactivate the Windows 7 Sharing Wizard. See Chapter 3 to learn how to deactivate this wizard.

---

① Open the folder that contains the folder you want to share.

② Click the folder you want to share.

③ Click Share With.

④ Click Advanced Sharing.

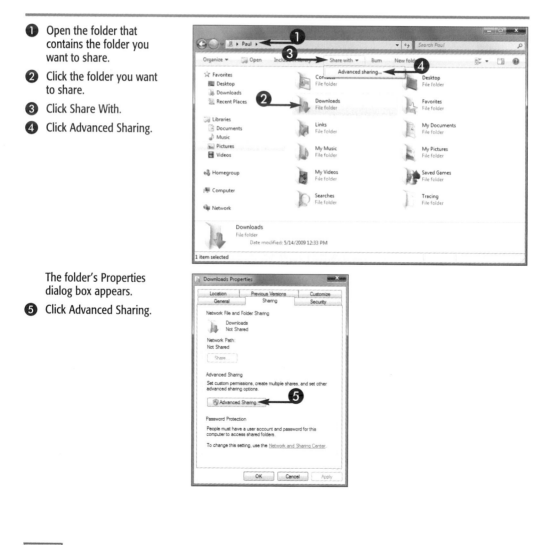

The folder's Properties dialog box appears.

⑤ Click Advanced Sharing.

The Advanced Sharing dialog box appears.

6 Click the Share This Folder check box (☐ changes to ☑).

7 Edit the Share Name, if desired.

8 Click OK.

---

9 Click Close.

Windows 7 begins sharing the folder.

Advanced Sharing

☑ Share this folder

Settings

Share name:

Downloads

Add   Remove

Limit the number of simultaneous users to: 20

Comments:

Permissions   Caching

OK   Cancel   Apply

Downloads Properties

Location   Previous Versions   Customize
General   Sharing   Security

Network File and Folder Sharing

Downloads
Shared

Network Path:
\\MEDIAPC\Downloads

Share...

Advanced Sharing

Set custom permissions, create multiple shares, and set other advanced sharing options.

Advanced Sharing...

Password Protection

People must have a user account and password for this computer to access shared folders.

To change this setting, use the Network and Sharing Center.

Close   Cancel   Apply

TIPS

More Options!

If you want to change the share name of your folder, first follow steps 1 to 5 to display the Advanced Sharing dialog box. Click Add to display the New Share dialog box, type the new share name you want to use, and then click OK. Use the Share Name list to click the old share name and then click Remove. Click OK and then click Close.

Reverse It!

If you no longer want network users to access a folder, you can stop sharing it. Follow steps 1 to 5 to open the Advanced Sharing dialog box. Click the Share This Folder check box (☑ changes to ☐). Click OK and then click Close.

Protect Your Shared Files with Advanced File Permissions

You can use file permissions to specify which network users can access which folders, and what exactly those users can do with the files in those folders.

Chapter 3 discussed using file permissions to control what other users on your computer can do with your files. Windows 7 offers a similar set of permissions for folders that you have shared with the network. Permissions designate exactly what specified users can do with the contents of the protected network folder. In this case, there are three types of permissions.

With **Full Control** permission, network users can view and modify the shared resource, as well as change permissions on the resource. With **Change** permission, network users can view the folder contents, open files, edit files, create new files and subfolders, delete files, and run programs. With **Read** permission, network users can open files but cannot edit them.

In each case, you can either allow the permission or deny it.

① Follow steps 1 to 5 in the previous task to open the Advanced Sharing dialog box.

② Click Permissions.

The folder's Permissions dialog box appears.

③ Click Add.

The Select Users or Groups dialog box appears.

④ Type the name of the user you want to work with.

⑤ Click OK.

● The user appears in this list.

⑥ Click the new user to select it.

⑦ In the Allow column, click each permission that you want to allow (☐ changes to ☑).

⑧ Click OK.

⑨ Click OK in the Advanced Sharing dialog box (not shown).

⑩ Click Close in the folder's Properties dialog box (not shown).

Windows protects the folder with the permissions you selected.

TIPS

Caution!

By default, Windows 7 assigns Read permission to the Everyone group. This group represents every user or group not otherwise specified in the Permissions dialog box. For extra security, make sure you do not give the Everyone group Full Control or Change permission. If you want only your specified users and groups to access your shared folder, follow steps 1 and 2, click Everyone, and then click Remove.

More Options!

You can save time when setting up shared folder security by assigning permissions to groups instead of individual users. For example, if you know that some of the network users have administrator accounts, you could add the Administrators group; similarly, all standard Windows 7 users are part of the Users group. Follow the same steps, but when you get to step 4, type the name of the group instead of the name of a user.

Create a Computer-to-Computer Wireless Network

If you do not have a wireless access point, Windows 7 enables you to set up a temporary network between two or more computers.

To set up a wireless network, you need two types of devices: a wireless network card in each computer that you want on the network, and a wireless access point, which is a device that receives and transmits signals from wireless computers to form a wireless network. This is called an *infrastructure wireless network*.

However, you can also create a wireless network directly between two or more computers, without using a wireless access point. This is called an *ad hoc wireless network*, and it is useful if you need to share folders, devices, or an Internet connection if you do not have a wireless access point, or if your access point is broken.

Note that the computers must be within 30 feet of each other for this type of connection to work.

① Click Start.

② In the Search box, type **ad hoc**.

③ Click Set Up an Ad Hoc (Computer-to-Computer) Network.

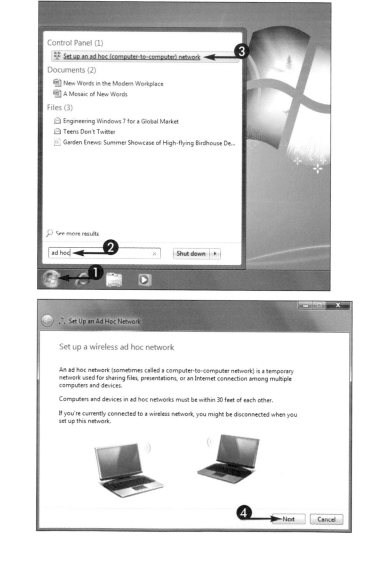

The Set Up an Ad Hoc Network Wizard appears.

④ Click Next.

The Give Your Network a Name and Choose Security Options dialog box appears.

⑤ Type a name for your network.

⑥ In the Security Type list, click WPA2-Personal.

⑦ Type a security key that users must enter to access the network.

Note: *The security key must be at least eight characters long.*

⑧ Click Next.

Set Up an Ad Hoc Network

Give your network a name and choose security options

Network name: My Ad Hoc Network ◀ ⑤

Security type: WPA2-Personal ▾ ⑥

Security key: adhocnetpass ◀ ⑦   ☐ Hide characters

☐ Save this network

⑧ ▶ Next Cancel

Windows 7 sets up your network.

● If your computer is connected to the Internet and you want to share that connection, click Turn On Internet Connection Sharing.

⑨ Click Close.

Set Up an Ad Hoc Network

The My Ad Hoc Network network is ready to use

This network will appear in the list of wireless networks and will stay active until everyone disconnects from it. Give the network name and security key (if any) to people you want to connect to this network.

Wireless network name: My Ad Hoc Network

Network security key: ●●●●●●

To share files, open Network and Sharing Center in Control Panel and turn on file sharing.

Recommended options:

⚡ Turn on Internet connection sharing

Share an Internet connection on an ad hoc network

⑨ ▶ Close

TIPS

Reverse It!
If you no longer want to share your Internet connection with your ad hoc network, open the Network and Sharing Center, click Change Adapter Settings, right-click the network connection that you use for Internet access, and then click Properties. Click the Sharing tab, click Allow Other Network Users to Connect through This Computer's Internet Connection (☑ changes to ☐), and then click OK.

Remove It!
When you are done with your ad hoc network, you can remove it to reduce clutter in your list of available wireless networks. First, ensure that every other user has disconnected from the network. Then click the taskbar's Network icon to display the list of wireless networks, click your ad hoc network, and then click Disconnect.

If a nearby wireless network is not broadcasting its identity, you can still connect to that network by entering the connection settings manually.

Each wireless network has a network name — often called the Service Set Identifier, or SSID — that identifies the network to wireless devices and computers with wireless network cards. By default, most wireless networks broadcast the network name so that you can see the network and connect to it. However, some wireless networks disable network name broadcasting as a security precaution. The idea

behind this is that if an unauthorized user cannot see the network, he or she cannot attempt to connect to it. (However, some devices can pick up the network name when authorized computers connect to the network, so this is not a foolproof security measure.)

You can still connect to a hidden wireless network by entering the connection settings by hand. You need to know the network name, the network's security type and encryption type, and the network's security key or passphrase.

 Click the Network icon.

② Click Open Network and Sharing Center.

The Network and Sharing Center window appears.

③ Click Set Up a New Connection or Network.

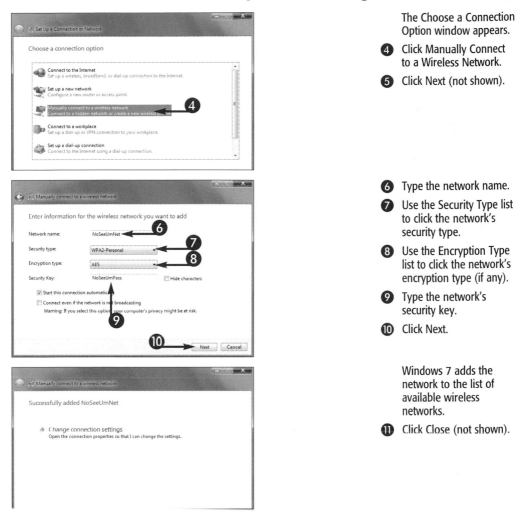

The Choose a Connection Option window appears.

④ Click Manually Connect to a Wireless Network.

⑤ Click Next (not shown).

⑥ Type the network name.

⑦ Use the Security Type list to click the network's security type.

⑧ Use the Encryption Type list to click the network's encryption type (if any).

⑨ Type the network's security key.

⑩ Click Next.

Windows 7 adds the network to the list of available wireless networks.

⑪ Click Close (not shown).

Apply It!

Windows 7 does not connect you to the hidden wireless network automatically. The steps you followed in this task only added the network to the list of available wireless networks. To make the connection, click the taskbar's Network icon, click the wireless network, and then click Connect. If Windows 7 prompts you for the security key, type the key and click OK.

More Options!

By default, Windows 7 activates the Start This Connection Automatically check box. This saves you from having to repeat the steps in this task each time you want to connect to the network. However, Windows 7 may not connect automatically if the network is not broadcasting. To work around this, click the Connect Even if the Network Is Not Broadcasting check box (☐ changes to ☑) after step 9 above.

You can change the order in which Windows 7 connects automatically to your wireless networks to ensure that you always connect first to the network you want.

It is not unusual to have multiple wireless networks configured on your computer. For example, you may have two or more wireless gateways in your home or office. Windows 7 also enables you to set up computer-to-computer wireless connections to share files or an Internet connection without going through a wireless access point. See "Create a Computer-to-Computer Wireless Network," earlier in this chapter.

By default, Windows 7 configures a wireless network with an automatic connection, so you get on the network as soon as Windows 7 detects it. If you have multiple wireless networks, Windows 7 maintains a priority list, and a network higher in that list gets connected before a network lower in that list. If you are not getting connected to the wireless network you want, it may be that the network is lower on the network priority list. To work around this problem, you can move the network higher in the list.

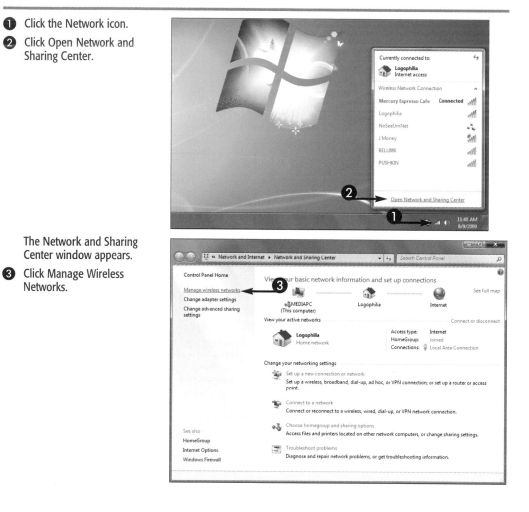

1 Click the Network icon.

2 Click Open Network and Sharing Center.

The Network and Sharing Center window appears.

3 Click Manage Wireless Networks.

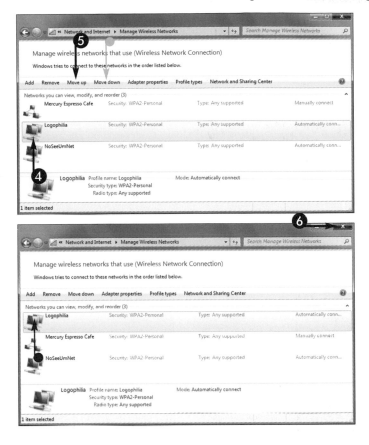

The Manage Wireless Networks window appears.

④ Click the network you want to work with.

⑤ Click Move Up until the network is in the position you want.

● If you want to move a network down in the list, click Move Down, instead.

Note: You can also reorder the networks by clicking and dragging the network icons and dropping them in the position you want.

● Windows 7 reorders the networks.

⑥ Click the Close button.

More Options!
You can also use the Manage Wireless Networks window to remove any wireless networks that you no longer use. Follow steps 1 to 3 to open the window. Click the network you want to delete and then click Remove. When Windows 7 asks you to confirm, click OK.

Try This!
When you connect to a wireless network, Windows 7 makes that connection available to every user account on your computer. If you prefer that each user have his or her own set of wireless network, follow steps 1 to 3 to open the Manage Wireless Networks window, and then click Profile Types. Click Use All-User and Per-User Profiles (⊙ changes to ⊚), and then click Save.

Work with Network Files Offline

You can work with network files and folders even when you are not connected to the network.

The benefit of using shared network folders is lost when you disconnect from the network. For example, suppose you have a notebook computer that you use to connect to the network while you are at the office. When you take the notebook on the road, you must disconnect from the network.

Fortunately, you can still get network access of a sort when you are disconnected from the network, or *offline*. Windows 7 has an offline files feature that enables you to preserve copies of network files on your computer. You can then view and work with these files as though you were connected to the network.

When you reconnect to the network, Windows 7 automatically *synchronizes* the files. This means that Windows 7 does two things: First, it updates your offline files by creating copies of any new or changed files in the shared network folder. Second, it updates the shared network folder with the files you changed while you were offline. This synchronization occurs automatically when you log on to the network and when you log off the network.

---

① In Windows Explorer, click Network.

● If the network computer is part of a Windows 7 homegroup, click Homegroup, instead.

② Double-click the network computer you want to work with.

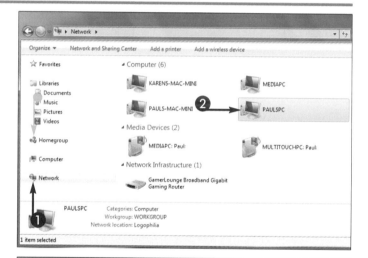

The network computer's shared resources appear.

③ If the files you want to use offline are in a subfolder, open the folders until you see the subfolder you want.

④ Right-click the folder you want to use offline.

⑤ Click Always Available Offline.

Windows 7 makes local copies of the folder's files.

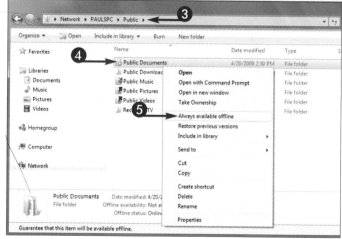

The Always Available Offline dialog box appears.

6 Click Close.

Note: *The Always Available Offline dialog box closes itself automatically after a few seconds.*

● Windows 7 adds the Sync icon to the folder's regular icon.

● The Offline Availability property changes to Always Available.

You can now use the folder's files even when you are disconnected from the network.

TIPS

Did You Know?

You can also synchronize the offline files yourself. Follow steps 1 to 3 to display the shared network folder, open the folder, click the Sync button in the taskbar, and then click Sync Offline Files in This Folder. If you have many offline folders to synchronize, click Start, type **sync**, click Sync Center, and then click Sync All.

Important!

When Windows 7 synchronizes your offline files, it may find that a file has been changed both on the network share and on your offline computer. In that case, the Sync Center displays a "conflict" link. Click that link, click the conflict, and then click Resolve. The Resolve Conflict dialog box gives you three options: keep the offline version of the file (you lose the network changes); keep the network version of the file (you lose your offline changes); or keep both versions (the offline version is saved under a modified file name).

Getting More Out of Your Notebook PC

Windows 7 comes with many new features for notebook PCs and has support for Tablet PCs built into the operating system (except for the Starter and Home Basic editions of Windows 7). If you use a notebook PC regularly, then you will appreciate Windows 7 features such as using an alarm to warn you when your battery power gets low, improving battery life with a custom power plan, and defining what action Windows 7 performs when you press the notebook's power buttons. You also learn about advanced notebook features such allowing wake timers, controlling the processor speed, and GPS settings.

Windows 7 also enables you to set up your notebook with a special configuration whenever you use your notebook to give a presentation. For example, you can turn off your screen saver, mute the volume, and pick out a special desktop background.

For Tablet PCs, Windows 7 has many useful features, including the following: support for the latest touch displays; support for flicks, which enable you to navigate documents and perform everyday chores with your digital pen or your finder on a touch display; and a program that lets you capture parts of the screen using your digital pen or finger.

Quick Tips

Set Battery Alarms to Avoid Running Out of Power

You can configure Windows 7 to warn you when your notebook PC battery level is running low so that your computer does not shut down on you unexpectedly.

If you are on a plane or in some other location where no AC outlet is available, you have no choice but to run your notebook PC on batteries. The ability to run on battery power is why notebooks are so convenient, but it has a downside: If your notebook battery runs out, you can lose your work.

To prevent this, you can configure Windows 7 to display a notification when the battery is low. This warning gives you enough time to save your work and possibly shut down the computer until you can recharge it.

Windows 7 enables you to set the *low battery level*, which is the percentage of remaining battery life that triggers the alarm. The default low battery level is ten percent. If you opt for a lower value, you can also configure Windows 7 to automatically go to sleep or shut down when the low battery level is reached.

---

① Click the Power icon in the notification area.

② Click More Power Options.

Note: You can also right-click the Power icon and then click Power Options.

The Power Options window appears.

③ Click Change Plan Settings.

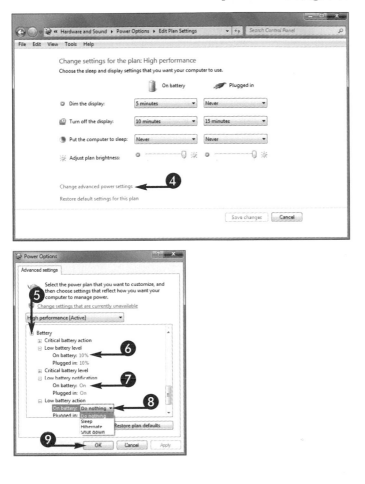

The Edit Plan Settings window appears.

④ Click Change Advanced Power Settings.

The Power Options dialog box appears.

⑤ Open the Battery branch.

⑥ Open Low Battery Level, click On Battery, and type the percentage at which the low battery alarm triggers.

⑦ Open Low Battery Notification, click On Battery, and click On.

⑧ Open Low Battery Action, click On Battery, and click the action you want Windows 7 to take at the low battery level.

⑨ Click OK.

TIPS

More Options!

Windows 7 offers three different power plans: Balanced, High Performance, and Power Saver. You can set a low battery level and low battery action for each power plan. Follow steps 1 and 2 to display the Power Options window, click the Change Plan Settings link beside the power plan you want to customize, and then follow steps 4 to 9.

More Options!

Windows 7 also supports a *critical battery level*, which triggers when your battery power reaches five percent. Windows 7 immediately puts the computer into hibernate mode. To change this, follow steps 1 to 5, open the Critical Battery Action branch, click On Battery, and click the action you want. You can also open the Critical Battery Level branch to specify the critical level.

You can improve your notebook PC's battery life or increase your productivity by creating a custom power plan that suits the way you work.

When you use a notebook PC on battery power, you always have to choose between increased battery life and computer performance. For example, to increase battery life, Windows 7 shuts down components such as the display and the hard disk after a short time. This reduces the performance of the notebook because you have to wait for these components to come back on again before you

can return to work. Conversely, to increase notebook performance, Windows 7 waits longer to shut down components, which uses up more battery power. These two extremes are controlled by two of Windows 7's predefined power plans: Power Saver and High Performance. The third power plan, Balanced, offers options that strike a balance between battery life and performance.

You may find that none of the predefined power plans is exactly right for you. If so, you can create a custom plan that suits your needs.

---

① Click the Power icon in the notification area.

② Click More Power Options.

Note: *You can also right-click the Power icon and then click Power Options.*

The Power Options window appears.

③ Click Create a Power Plan.

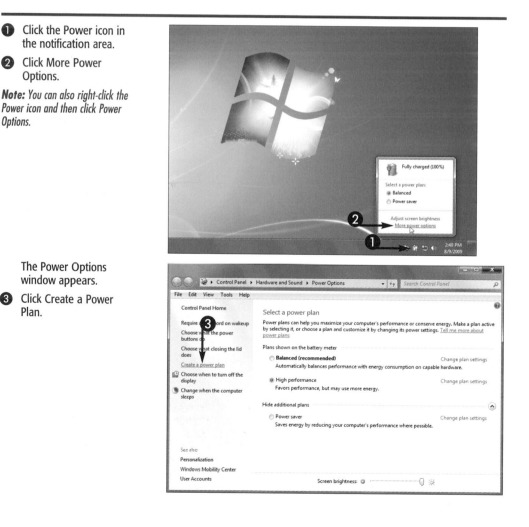

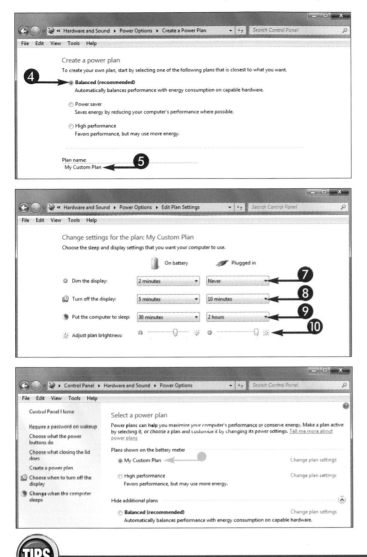

The Create a Power Plan window appears.

④ Click the predefined power plan to use as a starting point option (⊙ changes to ⊙).

⑤ Use the Plan Name text box to type a name for your plan.

⑥ Click Next (not shown).

The Edit Plan Settings window appears.

⑦ Use these lists to choose when Windows 7 dims your display.

⑧ Use these lists to choose when Windows 7 turns off the display.

⑨ Use these lists to choose when Windows 7 puts your notebook PC to sleep.

⑩ Use these sliders to set the screen brightness.

⑪ Click Create (not shown).

● The Power Options window appears with your custom plan displayed.

TIPS

More Options!

To configure more-advanced power options, such as when your hard disk powers down, open the Power Options window and click the Change Plan Settings link beside your custom plan, and then click the Change Advanced Power Settings link. In the Power Options dialog box, use branches, such as Hard Disk, Sleep, and Processor Power Management to set the idle intervals. Click OK and then click Save Changes.

Delete It!

To remove the custom plan, first change to a different plan by clicking the Power icon and then clicking another plan. Click the Power icon and then click More Power Options to open the Power Options window. Beside your custom plan, click Change Plan Settings, and then click Delete This Plan. When Windows 7 asks you to confirm, click OK.

Define Actions for Notebook Power Buttons

You can get easy access to the Windows 7 notebook power-down modes — shut down, sleep, and hibernate — by configuring your notebook's power buttons.

In shut down mode, Windows 7 closes your open programs and shuts off every computer component. The notebook uses no power while shut down.

In sleep mode, Windows 7 saves all open programs and documents to memory, and turns off everything but the memory chips. The notebook uses a bit of power (for the memory chips) while off. When you restart,

Windows 7 restores your desktop as it was in just a few seconds.

In hibernate mode, Windows 7 saves your open programs and documents to a file and then shuts down. The notebook uses no power while it is off. When you restart, Windows 7 restores your desktop from the file. This takes longer than in sleep mode, but less time than in shut down mode.

Most notebooks enable you to configure three "power buttons": the on/off button, the sleep button, and closing the lid. When you activate these buttons, they put your system into shut down, sleep, or hibernate mode.

1 Click the Power icon in the notification area.

2 Click More Power Options.

Note: You can also right-click the Power icon and then click Power Options.

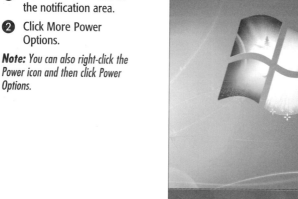

The Power Options page appears.

3 Click Choose What the Power Buttons Do.

The System Settings window appears.

4 Under On Battery, use the When I Press the Power Button list to click Do Nothing, Sleep, Hibernate, or Shut Down.

5 Under On Battery, use the When I Press the Sleep Button list to click Do Nothing, Sleep, or Hibernate.

6 Under On Battery, use the When I Close the Lid list to click Do Nothing, Sleep, Hibernate, or Shut Down.

7 Repeat steps 4 to 6 for the lists in the Plugged In column.

8 Click Save Changes.

Windows 7 puts the new power button settings into effect.

TIPS

More Options!

When you wake your notebook from sleep mode, Windows 7 displays the logon screen. This is desirable behavior because it prevents other people from getting access to your desktop when your computer wakes up. If you prefer to go straight to the desktop when your computer wakes from sleep mode, follow steps 1 to 3, click Change Settings that Are Currently Unavailable, click Don't Require a Password (○ changes to ◉), and then click Save Changes.

Did You Know?

Many notebook computers do not come with a separate sleep button. On these computers, you usually simulate the sleep button by quickly tapping the machine's on/off button. Some keyboards come with a sleep key — it usually has an icon of a crescent moon — so if you have such a keyboard attached to your notebook you can enter sleep mode by pressing that key.

You can configure your notebook PC to respond to wakeup calls from software programs and devices.

Some software programs respond to external events. For example, if you have Windows Fax and Scan configured to automatically receive incoming faxes on your computer, then Windows Fax and Scan runs its fax reception feature when it detects an incoming call.

Similarly, you may have devices on your network that require periodic access to your computer. For example, if you have a Windows Home Server machine on your network, Windows Home Server attempts to back up your computer each night.

If your computer is in sleep mode when an action is required, the program or device attempts to wake up your computer. This is called a *wake timer*, and it means that the program or device wakes up your computer, performs its task, and then returns your computer to sleep mode.

However, on notebook PCs, Windows 7 disallows wake timers because the notebook might be running on battery power. If you need your notebook to respond to wake timers, you must configure Windows 7 to allow them.

① Click the Power icon in the notification area.

② Click More Power Options.

Note: *You can also right-click the Power icon and then click Power Options.*

The Power Options window appears.

③ Click Change Plan Settings.

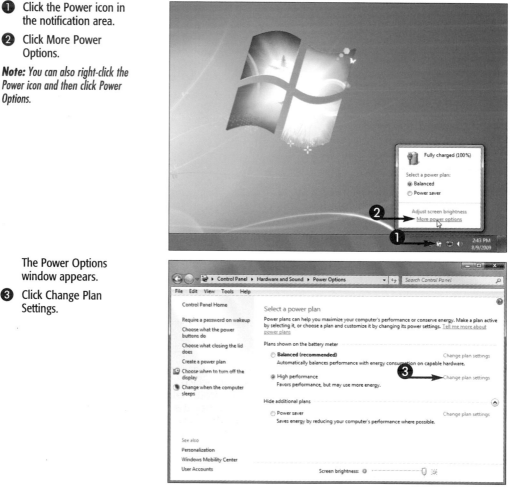

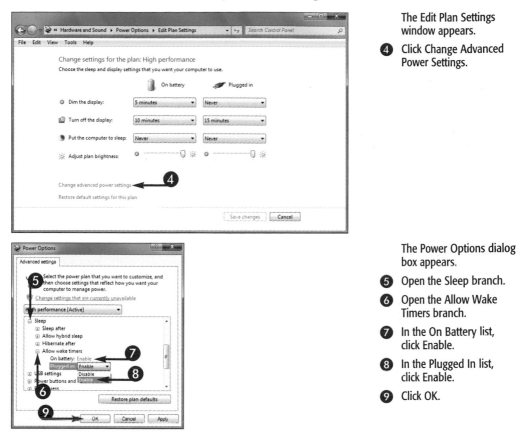

The Edit Plan Settings window appears.

④ Click Change Advanced Power Settings.

The Power Options dialog box appears.

⑤ Open the Sleep branch.

⑥ Open the Allow Wake Timers branch.

⑦ In the On Battery list, click Enable.

⑧ In the Plugged In list, click Enable.

⑨ Click OK.

More Options!

If you use your notebook PC to share media with other computers on your network, Windows 7 is configured to not enter sleep mode, which makes sense. However, Windows 7 does offer an alternative called away mode, which is a low-power state that still allows media streaming. Follow steps 1 to 4, open the Multimedia Settings branch, open When Sharing Media, and then click Allow the Computer to Enter Away Mode in the On Battery list and the Plugged In list. Click OK to put the new settings into effect.

If you need to strictly control your notebook PC's battery power consumption, you can set a maximum processor speed to conserve power.

If you are using your notebook PC on battery power and you are working on a crucial task, your goal should be to use as little power as possible. One way you can achieve that goal is to reduce the use of the notebook's processor (also known as the central processing unit, or CPU). In particular, Windows 7 enables you to set a maximum processor speed as a

percentage — where 0 percent means the processor is not in use, and 100 percent means the processor is running at full speed. By setting a maximum state of, say, 50 percent, your notebook may run slower on occasion, but you can still get your work done.

This not only saves the power that the processor itself uses, but it also saves on the power used by the notebook's cooling fan, because less processor usage means the system runs cooler.

① Click the Power icon in the notification area.

② Click More Power Options.

Note: You can also right-click the Power icon and then click Power Options.

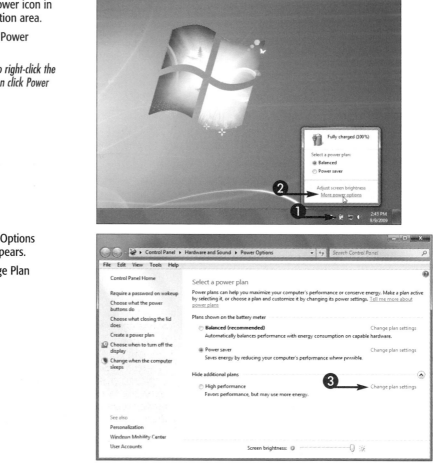

The Power Options window appears.

③ Click Change Plan Settings.

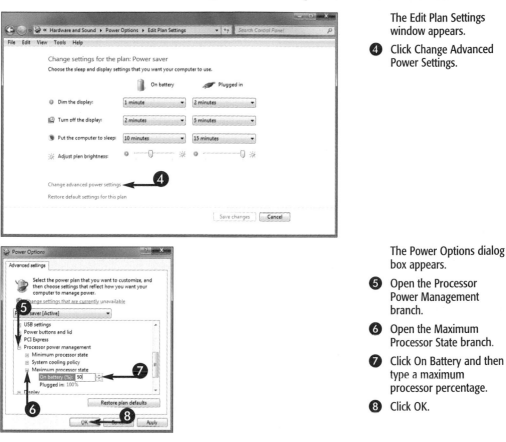

The Edit Plan Settings window appears.

④ Click Change Advanced Power Settings.

The Power Options dialog box appears.

⑤ Open the Processor Power Management branch.

⑥ Open the Maximum Processor State branch.

⑦ Click On Battery and then type a maximum processor percentage.

⑧ Click OK.

TIPS

More Options!

Windows 7 also includes a system cooling policy: *active cooling* increases the fan speed to cool the system; *passive cooling* reduces the processor speed to cool the system. Use passive cooling when you need to conserve your battery. Follow steps 1 to 5, open the System Cooling Policy branch, and then use the On Battery list to click Passive.

More Options!

If wireless connectivity is not important, you can configure your notebook's wireless network adapter to use as little power as possible. Follow steps 1 to 4, open the Wireless Adapter Settings branch, open Power Saving Mode, and then use the On Battery list to click Maximum Power Saving. Click OK to put the new setting into effect.

If you use your notebook computer to make presentations, you can configure Windows 7 to use settings that ensure Windows 7 does not interfere with your presentation.

When you give a presentation, your goal should be to have the audience focus on you and the material you are presenting. Unfortunately, if you use a notebook computer to show the presentation, it may interfere with that goal. For example, if your presentation is delayed while a discussion takes place, the computer might go to sleep or your screen

saver might activate. Similarly, your computer may display a notification that you have received a new e-mail message, or you may have a distracting desktop background image.

You can solve all of these problems by activating an option that tells Windows 7 you are currently giving a presentation. Windows 7 automatically keeps the computer awake and turns off system notifications. You can also configure Windows 7 to disable the screen saver and the desktop background while you are presenting.

 Click **Start**.

 Click **Control Panel**.

The Control Panel window appears.

 Click **Hardware and Sound**.

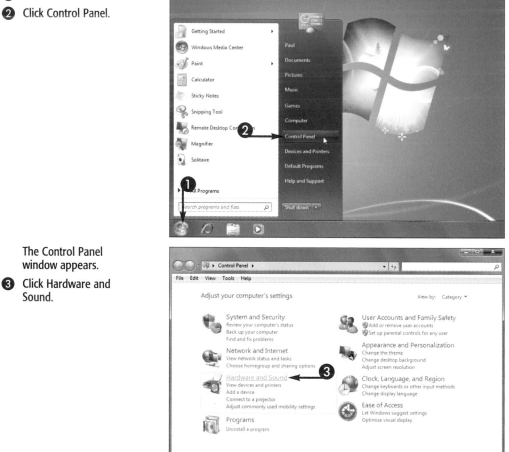

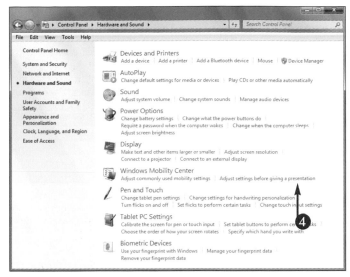

The Hardware and Sound window appears.

④ Click Adjust Settings Before Giving a Presentation.

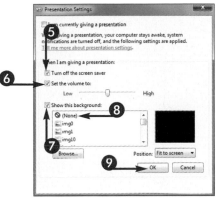

The Presentation Settings dialog box appears.

⑤ Click the Turn Off the Screen Saver check box (☐ changes to ✓).

⑥ If you want to set the presentation volume, click the Set the Volume To check box (☐ changes to ✓) and click and drag the slider.

⑦ Click the Show This Background check box (☐ changes to ✓).

⑧ Click None.

⑨ Click OK.

TIPS

More Options!

Instead of disabling the desktop background, you may prefer to display a company logo or a photo of the product you are discussing. To display a background, follow steps 1 to 7, click Browse, use the Browse dialog box to click the image you want to use, and then click Open. In the Position list, click Center, Tile, or Fit to Screen.

Important!

When you are ready to give your presentation, you must turn on the presentation settings that you configured in this task. One method is to follow steps 1 to 4 and then click the I Am Currently Giving a Presentation check box (☐ changes to ✓). Alternatively, click Start, type **mobility**, click Windows Mobility Center, and then click Turn On in the Presentation Settings section.

If you use location-aware programs, but you do not have a location sensor installed on your notebook PC, you can configure Windows 7 with your default location.

Many software programs can work with location data to tailor their data and services. For example, a mapping program might use your current location to provide directions to a destination or to show you restaurants and coffee shops that are nearby.

Most location-aware programs can work with the data provided by a location sensor, such as a global positioning system (GPS) receiver. However, what if you do not have such a device installed on your notebook PC? In that case, you can enter your current location by hand to specify what Windows 7 calls your *default location*. You can enter either your current ZIP or postal code along with your country, or you can enter a specific street address.

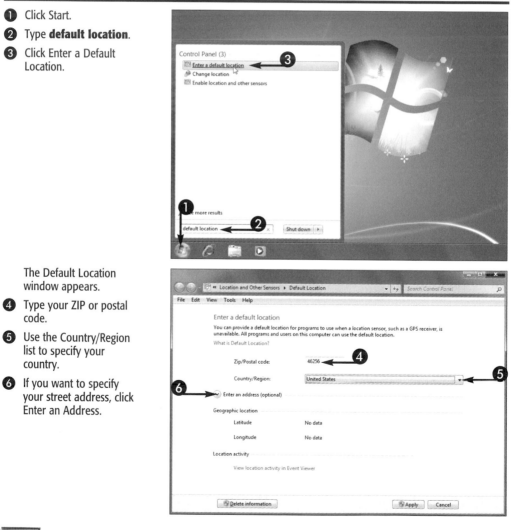

① Click Start.

② Type **default location**.

③ Click Enter a Default Location.

The Default Location window appears.

④ Type your ZIP or postal code.

⑤ Use the Country/Region list to specify your country.

⑥ If you want to specify your street address, click Enter an Address.

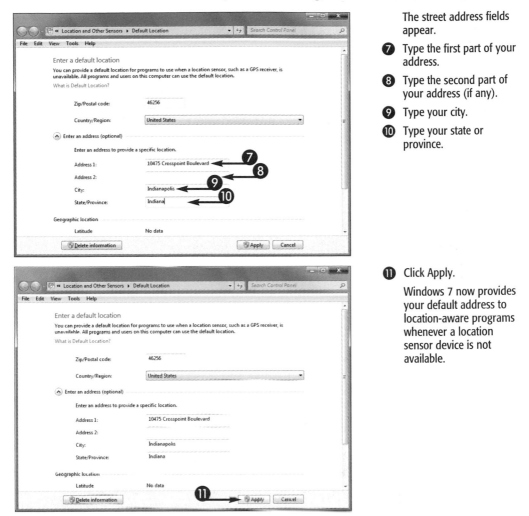

The street address fields appear.

7 Type the first part of your address.

8 Type the second part of your address (if any).

9 Type your city.

10 Type your state or province.

11 Click Apply.

Windows 7 now provides your default address to location-aware programs whenever a location sensor device is not available.

Remove It!

If you no longer want programs to access your default location, you can remove the data from your PC. Follow steps 1 to 3 to open the Default Location window. At the bottom of the window, click the Delete Information button. Windows 7 removes all your data from the Default Location window.

Did You Know?

Windows 7 keeps track of when programs use either your default location or location data supplied by a GPS device. To see which programs are accessing your location, follow steps 1 to 3 to open the Default Location window, and then click the View Location Activity in Event Viewer link. Windows 7 launches Event Viewer and displays the Location Activity log.

If your notebook PC comes with a touch screen, you can configure Windows 7 to use touch input.

On a notebook that comes with a touch display, touch input refers to using your finger to interact with the objects on the screen in much the same way that you would use your mouse. That is, you can use your finger to tap an object to select it; double-tap an object to activate it; and tap-and-drag an object to move it. To use these gestures, the flicks discussed in the next task (see "Use Flicks to Scroll Documents"), and the Snipping Tool (see

"Capture Part of the Screen with the Snipping Tool"), you must configure touch input in Windows 7.

Note, too, that another way to interact with the screen via touch is to tap-and-hold an object to display its shortcut menu, which is the touch equivalent of right-clicking the object. However, you can make this easier by enabling the touch pointer, a large mouse icon that enables you to perform the equivalent of a right-click by tapping the icon's right mouse button.

---

① Click Start.

② Click Control Panel.

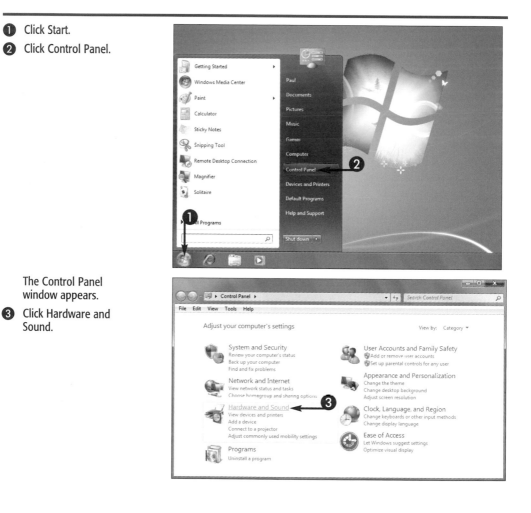

The Control Panel window appears.

③ Click Hardware and Sound.

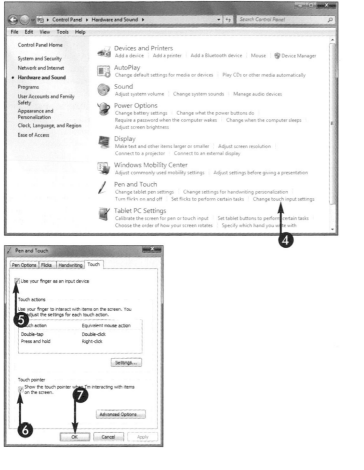

The Hardware and Sound window appears.

④ Click Change Touch Input Settings.

The Pen and Touch dialog box appears with the Touch tab displayed.

⑤ Click Use Your Finger as an Input Device (changes to ✓).

⑥ If you want to see the touch pointer when you use touch input, click this check box (☐ changes to ✓).

⑦ Click OK.

You can now use your finger for touch input in Windows 7.

TIPS

More Options!
If you find that the touch pointer is too intrusive, you can make it both smaller and more transparent. Follow steps 1 to 4 to display the Touch tab, and then click Advanced Options. In the Advanced Options dialog box, drag the Transparency slider to the left to increase the transparency of the touch pointer. Drag the Size slider to the left to make the touch pointer smaller.

Important!
The usefulness of touch gestures declines if touch input is not calibrated to your screen. For example, this can cause taps and double-taps to occur in places that are slightly off where you intended them to occur. To calibrate touch input, follow steps 1 to 3 and then click Calibrate the Screen for Pen or Touch Input.

If you are using your Tablet PC's digital pen or a multi-touch display, you can make it easier to navigate and edit documents by activating the Windows 7 flicks option.

With a Tablet PC or multi-touch display, you can navigate a document either by using the Input Panel's on-screen keyboard or by using the program itself — for example, tap-and-dragging the vertical or horizontal scroll box or tapping the program's built-in navigation features.

Windows 7 gives you a third choice for navigating a document: flicks. These are gestures that you can use in any application to scroll or navigate. To scroll up, gesture — that is, move the pen or move your finger on a multi-touch display — straight up; to scroll down, gesture straight down; to navigate backward in Internet Explorer or Windows Explorer, gesture straight left; and to navigate forward, gesture straight right.

The flicks feature also supports the following editing gestures: Copy (gesture up and to the left); Paste (up and to the right); Delete (down and to the right); and Undo (down and to the left).

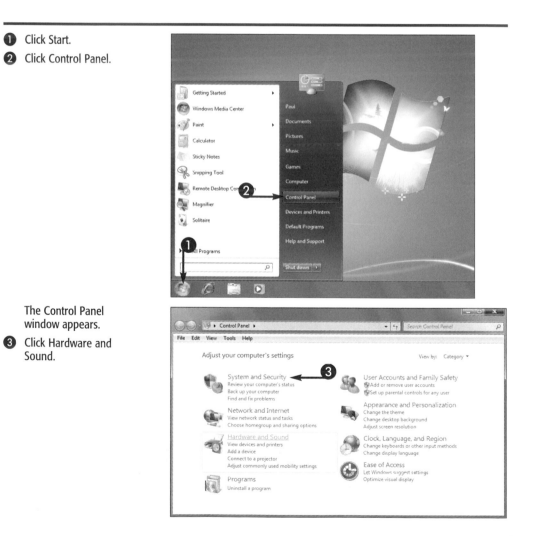

① Click Start.

② Click Control Panel.

The Control Panel window appears.

③ Click Hardware and Sound.

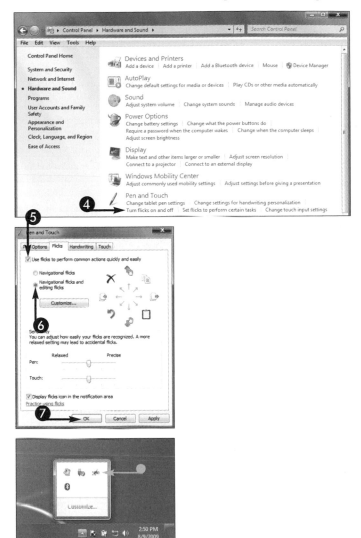

The Hardware and Sound window appears.

④ Click Turn Flicks On and Off.

The Pen and Touch dialog box appears with the Flicks tab displayed.

⑤ Make sure the Use Flicks to Perform Common Actions Quickly and Easily check box is activated (☑).

⑥ Click the Navigational Flicks and Editing Flicks option (◯ changes to ◉).

⑦ Click OK.

● After you perform your first flick, the Flicks icon appears within the notification area's hidden icons. Click the icon to see a summary of the flicks gestures.

TIPS

More Options!

After you click the Navigational Flicks and Editing Flicks option, the Customize button becomes active. Click Customize to display the Customize Flicks dialog box, which enables you to specify custom actions for the flick gestures. For each flick gesture, click its associated drop-down list and then click the action you want the gesture to perform. Click OK when you are done.

Important!

For a flick to work, you need to follow these techniques when performing the gesture: Move your pen or finger across the screen for about half an inch (at least 10mm); move your pen or finger very quickly; move your pen or finger in a straight line; and lift your pen or finger off the screen quickly at the end of the flick.

Capture Part of the Screen with the Snipping Tool

You can use the Snipping Tool to capture part of the screen with your digital pen or your finger on a touch display and save the result to an image file or Web page.

You can capture the current screen image by pressing the Print Screen key, opening Paint (or some other graphics program), and then running the Paste command to copy the screen image. An alternative is to press Alt+Print Screen to capture just the currently active window.

What if you want to capture just part of the screen? For example, you may want to show someone part of a Web site or a dialog box.

One solution would be use Print Screen to capture and paste the screen and then use your graphics program to crop the image to the section you want.

Windows 7 offers Tablet PC and touch display users (and also regular screen users) an easier method. It is called the Snipping Tool and it enables you to use your digital pen or finger (or your mouse) to "draw" the area of the screen that you want to capture. You can then save the resulting "snip" as an image or an HTML file (Web page).

① Display the image on screen that you want to capture.

② Click Start.

③ Click All Programs.

④ Click Accessories.

⑤ Click Snipping Tool.

The Snipping Tool window appears.

⑥ Use your digital pen or finger to draw the area of the screen that you want to capture.

A red line shows you the boundaries of the snip.

Note: *The Snipping Tool window disappears temporarily from the screen as you draw the clip.*

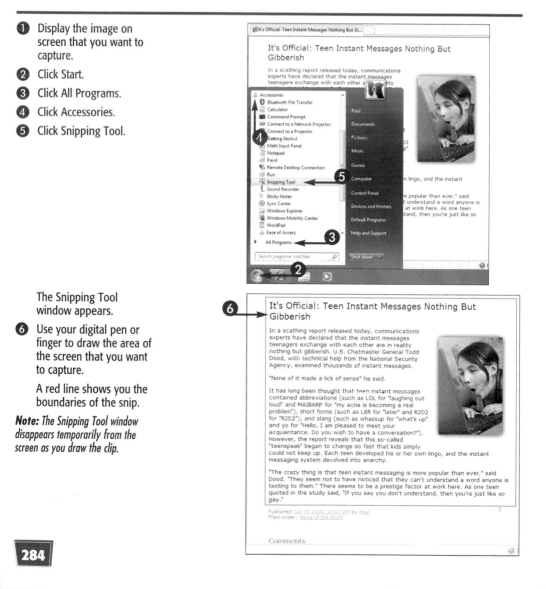

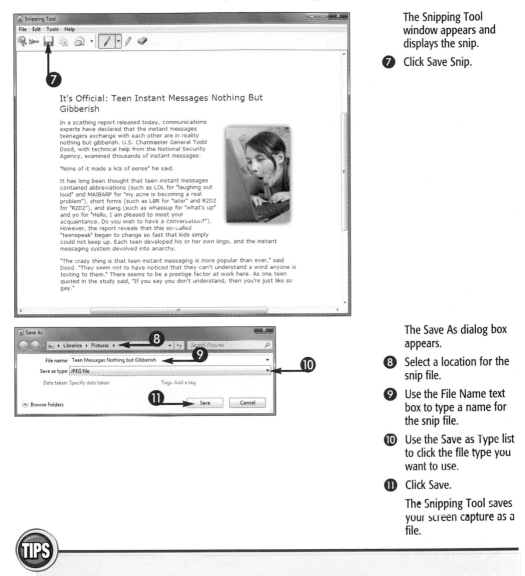

The Snipping Tool window appears and displays the snip.

⑦ Click Save Snip.

The Save As dialog box appears.

⑧ Select a location for the snip file.

⑨ Use the File Name text box to type a name for the snip file.

⑩ Use the Save as Type list to click the file type you want to use.

⑪ Click Save.

The Snipping Tool saves your screen capture as a file.

TIPS

More Options!

If you want to share your snip with another person, you can send it via e-mail, which means you do not need to save it first. After you capture your snip, click File, click Send To, and then click E-mail Recipient. In the message window that appears, type the recipient's address in the To text box, type a Subject, and then click Send.

More Options!

You can annotate the snip before you save it or send it. To write text on the snip, click Tools, click Pen, and then click a pen color. Use your digital pen to write your text on the snip. If you want to highlight snip text, click Tools, click Highlighter, and then drag the digital pen across the text. You can also click Tools and then Eraser to erase any annotations that you added.

Index

Index

Index